D1201072

NATURAL RESOURCE ECONOMICS

Natural Resource Economics

Notes and Problems

JON M. CONRAD

Cornell University

and

COLIN W. CLARK

University of British Columbia

The right of the
University of Cambridge
to print and sell
all manner of books
was granted by
Henry VIII in 1534.
The University has printed
and published continuously
since 1584.

CAMBRIDGE UNIVERSITY PRESS

Cambridge

New York   New Rochelle   Melbourne   Sydney

Published by the Press Syndicate of the University of Cambridge
The Pitt Building, Trumpington Street, Cambridge CB2 1RP
32 East 57th Street, New York, NY 10022, USA
10 Stamford Road, Oakleigh, Melbourne 3166, Australia

First published 1987

Printed in the United States of America

Library of Congress Cataloging in Publication Data
Conrad, Jon M.
Natural resource economics.
Bibliography: p.
Includes index.
1. Natural resources. 2. Environmental policy.
I. Clark, Colin Whitcomb, 1931-   II. Title.
HC59.C693   1987   333.7   87-11582
ISBN 0-521-33188-9 hard cover
ISBN 0-521-33769-0 paperback

British Library Cataloging-in-Publication applied for.

Contents

Preface

This book was undertaken to bridge what we regard as a gap between the theory of resource economics and the application of the theory, which typically involves the use of statistical and numerical methods. While the dearth of empirical studies in resource economics is largely the result of limited or nonexistent data, another impediment is the incomplete or disjointed way in which students are exposed to theory and the methods of applied analysis. One way of narrowing the gap between theory and practice is through the solving of numerical problems. In the process, the student is forced to make the theory operational (to see how it works) and must often apply numerical techniques to solve the equations which define a potential solution.

The numerical problems in this volume do *not* involve the application of econometric or other statistical techniques to estimate the parameters of a model. Instead, parameter values will be given (sometimes they are based on previous empirical research) and the exercise is to structure and solve a well-posed resource allocation problem. Thus the theory (and artistry) of measurement, data manipulation, and the selection of appropriate techniques for estimation of parameters within a resource or environmental system are not covered in this book. While the student is spared this dimension of applied research, we hope that he or she will find the remaining tasks of problem formulation and solution challenging, instructive, and enjoyable.

The notes in this volume pertain to a now vast literature dealing with the optimal use of renewable, exhaustible, and environmental resources. The major theme in most of the recent literature is the optimal harvest, extraction, or search for such resources over time. Thus, dynamic optimization and more specifically optimal control via the maximum principle is a cornerstone to much of the theory. With this underlying theme in mind, we have organized the book into five chapters. The first chapter reviews the methods of static and dynamic optimization and some of the techniques for actually solving optimization problems. The second chapter presents some of the basic theory and models dealing with renewable resources. These models attempt to synthesize the relevant biological and economic attributes and have been referred to as bioeconomic models. The third chapter examines the central theory of exhaustible resources and looks at the issues of optimal extraction and exploration. The fourth chapter looks at the static and dynamic use of environmental resources, principally air and water, to determine the optimal location and timing of effluent (waste) discharge. Chapter five treats stochastic resource models, in which random fluctuations and uncertainty are involved. In all chapters, problems are presented and solved to illustrate the theory and solution techniques. At the end of each chapter a set of numerical problems and answers is given. The challenge is to verify our answers and to contemplate new wrinkles or variations that might be introduced to create alternative, perhaps more interesting or realistic models.

This book was not meant to be a "stand-alone" text in resource economics. Rather, it was designed to complement the more detailed, but often purely theoretical texts in resource economics. Alternatively, it might be used in a graduate course in resource economics when supplemented by a reading list which draws from the large and growing literature in the field. While not exhaustive, we feel the notes in this volume cover much of the important theory on renewable, exhaustible, and environmental resources.

Jon M. Conrad
Colin W. Clark

Chapter 1

Resource allocation and optimization

Economics has been defined as the science of allocating scarce resources among competing ends. Much of the microeconomic theory encountered in a first semester graduate course is concerned with the *static* allocation problem faced by firms and consumers. Techniques of constrained optimization, in particular the method of Lagrange multipliers, are employed in developing the theory of the firm and the consumer.

The optimal harvest of renewable resources or extraction of exhaustible resources is inherently a *dynamic* allocation problem; that is, the firm or resource manager is concerned with the best harvest or extraction rate through time. It turns out that the method of Lagrange multipliers can be extended to intertemporal or dynamic allocation problems in a relatively straightforward fashion. This "discrete-time" extension of the method of Lagrange multipliers serves as a useful springboard to the "continuous-time" solution of dynamic allocation problems via the maximum principle. The method of Lagrange multipliers and its various extensions reduce the original optimization problem to a system of equations to be solved. Solving this system of equations, unfortunately, can often be exceedingly difficult, especially for dynamic problems. There are also technical problems concerning sufficiency conditions for the solutions so obtained (and also pertaining to the existence of a solution to the given problem). In these notes we will normally consider problems which are simple enough that these difficulties are minimized.

Before presenting the dynamic techniques we will briefly review the method of Lagrange multipliers within the context of allocating scarce resources among competing ends at a single point in time.

1.1 Constrained optimization and the method of Lagrange multipliers

In resource economics as in other fields of economics, we often encounter constrained optimization problems. The general form of such problems is

$$\text{maximize} \quad V(x_1, \ldots, x_n)$$
$$\text{subject to} \quad (x_1, \ldots, x_n) \in A \tag{1.1}$$

where $V(\cdot)$ is a given *objective* (or *value*) *function* of n decision variables $x_1, \ldots, x_n$ which are required to be in some given *constraint set* A.

In the case of a *static* optimization problem, the decision variables x_i are real numbers and the constraint set A is a subset of $I\!\!R^n$–Euclidean n-space. For *dynamic* optimization problems, on the other hand, some (or all) of the decision variables are functions of time t (usually separated into so-called *state* variables and *control* variables). The constraint condition then typically involves the system's *dynamics*, expressed as a system of differential or difference equations. Other constraints may also be present. As before, $V(\cdot)$ is real-valued, frequently involving integration (or summation) over time. Dynamic optimization problems will be considered in Section 1.2.

1.1.1 Static optimization: no constraints

The simplest optimization problem is

$$\text{maximize} \quad V(x_1, \ldots, x_n) \tag{1.2}$$

where the decision variables are unconstrained.[1] The reader is assumed to be familiar with the first order necessary conditions

$$\frac{\partial V(\cdot)}{\partial x_i} = 0 \qquad\qquad i = 1, \ldots, n \tag{1.3}$$

By "necessary" conditions we mean that equations (1.3) must be satisfied by the maximizing values of $x_1, \ldots, x_n$. The conditions (1.3) are not sufficient conditions for a maximum, however (they also pertain to minimal solutions and to values x_i which are neither maxima nor minima). We will not attempt to delineate sufficient conditions in these notes [see Intriligator (1971, p 26)], since such conditions often are complicated and of very limited practical use (but popular with economics professors). If the objective function $V(\cdot)$ is known to be concave, the necessary conditions (1.3) are also sufficient.[2] Note that (1.3) constitutes a system of n possibly nonlin-

---

[1] We shall assume throughout that $V(\cdot)$ is a smooth function; that is, all required partial derivatives exist.

[2] The function $V(X)$ is said to be concave if

$$V(\alpha \bar{X} + (1 - \alpha)\tilde{X}) \geq \alpha V(\bar{X}) + (1 - \alpha)V(\tilde{X})$$

for all $\bar{X} = (\bar{x}_1, \ldots, \bar{x}_n)$, $\tilde{X} = (\tilde{x}_1, \ldots, \tilde{x}_n)$ and $0 \leq \alpha \leq 1$.

ear equations in n unknowns $x_1, \ldots, x_n$. Thus the optimization problem has been "reduced" to the solution of n equations. Unfortunately, solving the system in practice may be almost as difficult as the original optimization problem. Numerical algorithms for the solution of such systems are available in computing centers, but do not always work (see Section 1.6.2 for an example). Frequently a direct optimization algorithm (based on a direct "search" of the feasible set) will outperform any method based on the first order necessary conditions.

Nevertheless, insight into economics is often obtained from the necessary conditions without actually solving them explicitly. For example, if $V(\cdot)$ is a net benefit function, the statement "marginal net benefit of each input x_i must equal zero" is equivalent to (1.3) and carries economic significance.

1.1.2 Static optimization: equality constraints

Consider next the constrained problem

$$\begin{aligned} \text{maximize} \quad & V(x, y, z) \\ \text{subject to} \quad & G(x, y, z) = c \end{aligned} \tag{1.4}$$

where for simplicity we have only three decision variables x, y, and z. The equation $G(\cdot) = c$, where c is a known constant, determines a constraint set in x, y, z space, which is in fact a surface, which we will denote by S_G. The problem, then, is to determine the largest value of the function $V(x, y, z)$ for points (x, y, z) on the surface S_G.

One approach to this problem is first to solve the constraint equation $G(\cdot) = c$ for one of the variables, say $z = h(x, y)$. The constrained problem in three variables may be replaced by the unconstrained two variable problem

$$\text{maximize} \quad V(x, y, h(x, y)) \tag{1.5}$$

with first order necessary conditions

$$\left. \begin{aligned} \frac{\partial V}{\partial x} + \frac{\partial V}{\partial z} \frac{\partial h}{\partial x} &= 0 \\ \frac{\partial V}{\partial y} + \frac{\partial V}{\partial z} \frac{\partial h}{\partial y} &= 0 \end{aligned} \right\} \tag{1.6}$$

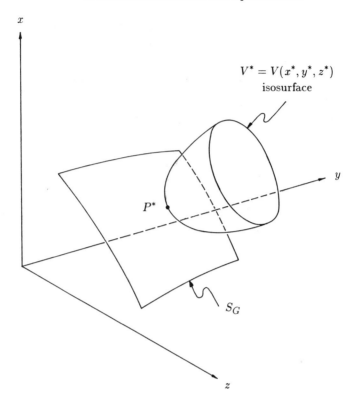

$$V^* = V(x^*, y^*, z^*)$$
isosurface

Figure 1.1   The tangency criterion: if $V(\cdot)$ is maximized on S_G at P^* then the V^* isosurface through P^* is tangent to S_G.

Differentiating the constraint equation implicitly implies

$$\left.\begin{aligned}\frac{\partial G}{\partial x} + \frac{\partial G}{\partial z}\frac{\partial h}{\partial x} = 0 \\[2mm] \frac{\partial G}{\partial y} + \frac{\partial G}{\partial z}\frac{\partial h}{\partial y} = 0\end{aligned}\right\} \tag{1.7}$$

and Equations (1.6) can therefore be written in the form

$$\left.\begin{aligned}V_x G_z - V_z G_x = 0 \\[1mm] V_y G_z - V_z G_y = 0\end{aligned}\right\} \tag{1.8}$$

where V_x is shorthand for $\partial V / \partial x$, etc.

Equations (1.8) can be obtained from an alternative geometrical derivation which gives important mathematical and economic insight. Figure 1.1 shows the solution to (1.4) as it would appear in x, y, z space. The constraint surface is shown as S_G. Suppose $P^* = (x^*, y^*, z^*)$ is the point on S_G for which $V(x, y, z)$ attains its maximum. Consider also the isosurface of $V(\cdot)$ passing through P^*; this is the surface

$$V(x, y, z) = V(x^*, y^*, z^*) \tag{1.9}$$

After a moment's reflection, one would conclude that $V(x^*, y^*, z^*)$ must be tangent to the constraint surface S_G. If it were not, it would either cut through S_G or not touch it at all. In the latter case the constraint is not satisfied. In the former case there would be a projection of the isosurface on S_G and there would be points on S_G lying inside and outside the projection.[3] Since $V = V^*$ on the projection we must have $V > V^*$ on one side (say inside) of the projection and $V < V^*$ on the other side (outside) of the projection. But V^* was by assumption the maximum of $V(\cdot)$ on S_G. Therefore no points of S_G can have a value $V > V^*$, which would be a contradiction. The conclusion: The maximizing isosurface must be tangent to S_G at P^*.

Recall now from calculus that the *gradient vector*

$$\overrightarrow{\nabla} V = (V_x, V_y, V_z) \tag{1.10}$$

is always perpendicular (normal) to the isosurface $V(\cdot) = $ constant at any given point. Two isosurfaces passing through a point P^* are therefore tangent at P^* if and only if their gradient vectors have the same direction. This means that $\overrightarrow{\nabla} V = \lambda \overrightarrow{\nabla} G$ for some $\lambda \neq 0$. This vector equation means, in turn, that

$$\left. \begin{array}{l} V_x = \lambda G_x \\ V_y = \lambda G_y \\ V_z = \lambda G_z \end{array} \right\} \tag{1.11}$$

at point P^*.

Note that, by dividing pairs of equations, (1.11) reduces to the necessary conditions (1.8). Conversely (1.8) implies (1.11).[4] Equations (1.11), however, have an appealing symmetry lacking in (1.8). They also generalize in a nice way, as we shall see.

---

[3] The projection on an isosurface which cuts through S_G might appear as a bent circle or ellipse in Figure 1.1. Think of the "nose" of some other isosurface lying on the "other side" of S_G and the projection as a closed contour on S_G.

[4] From (1.8) we have $V_x/G_x = V_y/G_y = V_z/G_z$. Call the common value $\lambda = V_z/G_z$.

1.1.3 Lagrange multipliers

It is customary to rewrite Equations (1.11) in the form

$$\left.\begin{array}{l} V_x - \lambda G_x = 0 \\ V_y - \lambda G_y = 0 \\ V_z - \lambda G_z = 0 \end{array}\right\} \qquad (1.12)$$

If we define the expression

$$L = V(x, y, z) - \lambda[G(x, y, z) - c] \qquad (1.13)$$

then Equations (1.12) are also obtained as

$$L_x = L_y = L_z = 0 \qquad (1.14)$$

The expression L is called the *Lagrangian* associated with the original constrained optimization problem (1.4). The number λ is referred to as a *Lagrange multiplier*. Thus, the critical observation in the development of the *method of Lagrange multipliers* was that differentiation of the Lagrangian expression would lead to the same first order necessary conditions as obtained in the simple "constraint substitution" technique used to transform an equality constrained problem into an unconstrained problem [i.e., going from problem (1.4) to problem (1.5)].

Consider now the general optimization problem with multiple equality constraints

$$\text{maximize} \quad V(x_1 \ldots, x_n)$$
$$\text{subject to} \quad G_j(x_1, \ldots, x_n) = c_j, \quad j = 1, \ldots, m \qquad (1.15)$$

The associated Lagrangian is

$$L = V(\cdot) - \sum_{j=1}^{m} \lambda_j [G_j(\cdot) - c_j] \qquad (1.16)$$

Note that each of the m constraints gives rise to a Lagrange multiplier, λ_j. By the same sort of tangency argument as before it can be shown that the following equations are necessary conditions for $x_1, \ldots, x_n$ to be a solution to the above optimization problem

$$\frac{\partial L}{\partial x_i} = 0 \qquad\qquad i = 1, \ldots, n \qquad (1.17)$$

Explicitly, these equations are

$$\frac{\partial V}{\partial x_i} - \sum_{j=1}^{m} \lambda_j \frac{\partial G_j}{\partial x_i} = 0 \qquad\qquad i = 1, \ldots, n \qquad (1.18)$$

We might also note that

$$\frac{\partial L}{\partial \lambda_j} = -G_j(\cdot) + c_j = 0 \qquad\qquad j = 1, \ldots, m \qquad (1.19)$$

and that when taken together, Equations (1.18) and (1.19) constitute a system of $n+m$ equations in $n+m$ unknowns: $x_1, \ldots, x_n$; $\lambda_1, \ldots, \lambda_m$. In principle this system should have at most a finite number of solutions, one of which will be the solution to our original optimization problem. In practice, as we noted earlier, solving this system of equations may be difficult indeed.

Consider the following example

$$\text{maximize} \quad 2x - 3y + z$$

$$\text{subject to} \quad x^2 + y^2 + z^2 = 9$$

The Lagrangian for this problem is

$$L = 2x - 3y + z - \lambda(x^2 + y^2 + z^2 - 9)$$

with the first order necessary conditions

$$\frac{\partial L}{\partial x} = 2 - 2\lambda x = 0$$

$$\frac{\partial L}{\partial y} = -3 - 2\lambda y = 0$$

$$\frac{\partial L}{\partial z} = 1 - 2\lambda z = 0$$

$$\frac{\partial L}{\partial \lambda} = -x^2 - y^2 - z^2 + 9 = 0$$

The first and second and first and third equations imply $y = -3x/2$ and $z = x/2$; which upon substitution into the constraint equation yields

$$x^2 + \left(\frac{-3x}{2}\right)^2 + \left(\frac{x}{2}\right)^2 = 0$$

which may be solved for $x = \pm 3\sqrt{2/7}$ leading to two solutions

$$x_1 = 3\sqrt{2/7} = 1.60 \qquad y_1 = -9/\sqrt{14} = -2.41 \qquad z_1 = 3/\sqrt{14} = 0.80$$

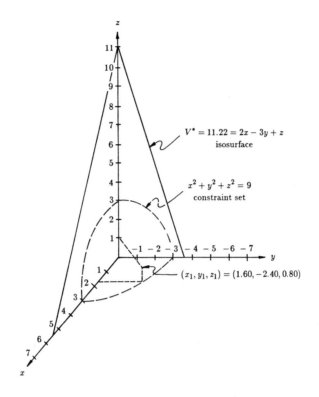

Figure 1.2   Depiction of the problem: maximize $2x - 3y + z$, subject to $x^2 + y^2 + z^2 = 9$, which has a solution at $(x_1, y_1, z_1) = (1.60, -2.41, 0.80)$.

and

$$x_2 = -3/\sqrt{2/7} = -1.60 \quad y_2 = 9/\sqrt{14} = 2.41 \quad z_2 = -3/\sqrt{14} = -0.80$$

We note, however, that

$$V(x_1, y_1, z_1) = 42/\sqrt{14} = 11.22$$

$$V(x_2, y_2, z_2) = -42/\sqrt{14} = -11.22$$

Thus, the maximizing point is (x_1, y_1, z_1), while (x_2, y_2, z_2) is a minimizing point. The problem and solution are depicted in Figure 1.2.

1.1.4 Economic interpretation

The Lagrange multipliers λ_j were not part of the original optimization problem. In the above example, for instance, we eliminated λ and then forgot about it. But Lagrange multipliers do have an important economic interpretation.

Clearly the solution to the general problem (1.15) will depend upon the values of the parameters $c_1, \ldots, c_m$ in the constraint equations $G_j(\cdot) = c_j$, $j = 1, \ldots, m$. In fact we may explicitly state this dependence as

$$x_i^* = x_i(c_1, \ldots, c_m) \qquad (1.20)$$

If the optimal values for the decision variables depend on the parameters then so does the value of the objective function. Consider

$$\frac{\partial V}{\partial c_k} = \sum_{i=1}^{n} \frac{\partial V}{\partial x_i} \frac{\partial x_i}{\partial c_k} \qquad k = 1, \ldots, m \qquad (1.21)$$

From Equations (1.18) we know

$$\frac{\partial V}{\partial x_i} = \sum_{j=1}^{m} \lambda_j \frac{\partial G_j}{\partial x_i} \qquad (1.22)$$

and thus

$$\frac{\partial V}{\partial c_k} = \sum_{i=1}^{n} \left(\sum_{j=1}^{m} \lambda_j \frac{\partial G_j}{\partial x_i} \right) \frac{\partial x_i}{\partial c_k} \qquad k = 1, \ldots, m \qquad (1.23)$$

Finally, differentiating the constraint equation $G_j(\cdot) = c_j$ with respect to c_k, we have

$$\sum_{i=1}^{n} \frac{\partial G_j}{\partial x_i} \frac{\partial x_i}{\partial c_k} = \delta_{j,k} = \begin{cases} 1 & \text{if } k = j \\ 0 & \text{if } k \neq j \end{cases} \qquad (1.24)$$

Hence we find that

$$\frac{\partial V}{\partial c_k} = \sum_{j=1}^{m} \lambda_j \delta_{j,k} = \lambda_k \qquad (1.25)$$

The Lagrange multiplier λ_k thus equals the incremental change in value from an incremental change in the constraint parameter c_k. In other words, λ_k represents the marginal value of relaxing the kth constraint. If c_k represents the available supply of some input or resource, then λ_k represents the "price" (or value) of the input in terms of V; hence λ_k is often called the *shadow price* of the input c_k.

Consider a resource-based economy which can allocate labor (L) to harvest timber (T) or fish (F). Assume that the economy exports both timber and fish, facing constant world prices denoted P_T and P_F, respectively. The transformation curve, relating technically efficient combinations of timber, fish, and labor, is given by

$$G(T, F; L) = T^2 + F^2/4 - L = 0$$

Suppose $P_T = \$500$/metric ton, $P_F = \$1,000$/metric ton and $L = 1700$ is the number of available hours of labor to be allocated between harvesting timber or fish. The static optimization problem seeks to maximize the value of harvest subject to the transformation function; that is

$$\text{maximize} \quad V = 500T + 1,000F$$
$$\text{subject to} \quad T^2 + F^2/4 - 1700 = 0$$

The Lagrangian expression may be written as

$$L = 500T + 1,000F - \lambda(T^2 + F^2/4 - 1700)$$

and has first order necessary conditions which require

$$\frac{\partial L}{\partial T} = 500 - 2\lambda T = 0$$
$$\frac{\partial L}{\partial F} = 1,000 - 0.5\lambda F = 0$$

and

$$\frac{\partial L}{\partial \lambda} = -T^2 - F^2/4 + 1700 = 0$$

Taking the ratio of the first two equations to eliminate λ implies $F = 8T$. Substituting this expression for F into the transformation function yields

$$T^2 + 64T^2/4 = 1700$$
$$T^2 = 100$$

and

$$T = 10 \qquad F = 80 \qquad \lambda = 25$$

Thus, the economy should allocate the available labor so as to produce 10 metric tons of timber and 80 metric tons of fish. The marginal value (shadow price) of an additional unit of labor is $\$25$/hour.[5]

---

[5] A check of the appropriate second order conditions would reveal $T = 10$, $F = 80$, $\lambda = 25$ to be a maximum. Note: L is concave in T and F.

1.1.5 Static optimization with inequality constraints

Next let us consider the problem

$$\text{maximize} \quad V(x, y, z)$$
$$\text{subject to} \quad G(x, y, z) \leq c \qquad (1.26)$$

The constraint set A now consists of all points lying either on the surface S_G or one particular side of S_G. There are just two possibilities: (a) the optimizing point (x, y, z) lies on one side of S_G satisfying the strict inequality $G(x, y, z) < c$ and $\partial V / \partial x = \partial V / \partial y = \partial V / \partial z = 0$, or (b) the optimizing point (x, y, z) lies on S_G, satisfying the equality $G(x, y, z) = c$ in which case the Lagrangian conditions apply and $\partial L / \partial x = \partial L / \partial y = \partial L / \partial z = 0$, where $L = V(\cdot) - \lambda[G(\cdot) - c]$.

The two cases can be combined into a single condition called the *Kuhn–Tucker condition*, which is a necessary condition, and may be written as

$$\frac{\partial L}{\partial x} = \frac{\partial L}{\partial y} = \frac{\partial L}{\partial z} = 0$$
$$\lambda \begin{cases} = 0 & \text{if } G(\cdot) < c \\ \geq 0 & \text{if } G(\cdot) = c \end{cases} \qquad (1.27)$$

The student should check that this indeed covers cases (a) and (b) above. A frequently encountered form, equivalent to (1.27) is

$$\frac{\partial L}{\partial x} = \frac{\partial L}{\partial y} = \frac{\partial L}{\partial z} = 0$$
$$\lambda[G(\cdot) - c] = 0 \qquad (1.28)$$
$$\lambda \geq 0$$

In many applications of constrained optimization in economics the decision variables are required to be *nonnegative*; i.e., $x \geq 0$, $y \geq 0$, $z \geq 0$. If problem (1.26) is amended to include nonnegativity constraints then the Kuhn–Tucker conditions become

$$x \left(\frac{\partial L}{\partial x} \right) = y \left(\frac{\partial L}{\partial y} \right) = z \left(\frac{\partial L}{\partial z} \right) = 0$$
$$x \geq 0 \qquad y \geq 0 \qquad z \geq 0 \qquad (1.29)$$
$$\lambda[G(\cdot) - c] = 0 \qquad \lambda \geq 0$$

The Kuhn–Tucker conditions are readily generalized to the case of x_1, ..., x_n decision variables (which may be unrestricted or nonnegative in value) plus inequality constraints $G_j(x_1, \ldots, x_n) \leq c_j, j = 1, \ldots, m$. The

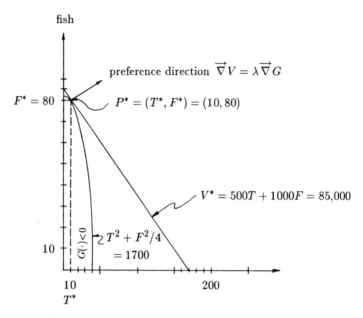

Figure 1.3   Optimal production in the timber/fish economy.

student could write out the general Kuhn–Tucker conditions as an exercise [and compare his or her version with that found in Intriligator (1971), p. 52)].

To see why $\lambda \geq 0$ let us reconsider our timber-fish economy. Suppose the transformation function were expressed as an inequality constraint; $G(T, F; L) = T^2 + F^2/4 - L \leq 0$. This constraint and the isorevenue line $V^* = 500T + 1,000F = 85,000$ are drawn in Figure 1.3. The point $P^* = (T^*, F^*) = (10, 80)$ gives the maximum revenue for $P_T = 500$, $P_F = 1,000$ on the constraint surface. Higher isorevenue lines would be parallel but lie to the right of V^* and thus unattainable given harvest technology and available labor.

Recall from calculus that the gradient vector, here $\vec{\nabla} V = (V_T, V_F)$, which is perpendicular to the contour $V = V^*$ also points in the direction of increasing values of V. Hence both $\vec{\nabla} V$ and $\vec{\nabla} G$ point in the same direction from P^* (namely outwards from $G(\cdot) < 0$ or inwards to $V > V^*$). Thus

$$\vec{\nabla} V = \lambda \vec{\nabla} G \qquad (1.30)$$

with $\lambda > 0$.

With reference to problem (1.26) and the Kuhn–Tucker conditions as expressed in (1.27), it is possible for $\lambda = 0$ if the maximum of $V(\cdot)$ on S_G is also a *local* or *global maximum* of $V(\cdot)$ in this case $\overrightarrow{\nabla} V = 0$ so that $\lambda = 0$ in (1.30). This explains why $\lambda \geq 0$ in (1.27)–(1.29).

1.2 An extension of the method of Lagrange multipliers to dynamic allocation problems

The method of Lagrange multipliers can be employed in solving dynamic or intertemporal allocation problems and the discrete-time formulation provides a convenient introduction to control theory and the maximum principle, often presented in a continuous-time context. Let

$t = 0, 1, \ldots, T$ be the set of time periods of relevance for the dynamic allocation problem, where $t = 0$ is the present and $t = T$ is the terminal (last) period,

x_t represent a state variable, describing the system in period t,

y_t represent a control or instrument variable in period t,

$V = V(x_t, y_t, t)$ represent net economic return in period t,

$F(x_T)$ represent a final function indicating the value of alternative levels of the state variable at terminal time T, and

$x_{t+1} - x_t = f(x_t, y_t)$ be a difference equation defining the change in the state variable from period t to $(t+1)$, $t = 0, \ldots, T - 1$.

The reader should note that time has been partitioned into a finite number of discrete periods, $(T+1)$ to be exact, although we can allow for an infinite horizon by letting $T \to \infty$. We will restrict ourselves to the single state, single control variable case for simplicity. The problem may be readily generalized to I state variables and J control variables. The objective function $V(\cdot)$ may have the period index t as a variable while the difference equation does not, thus $f(\cdot)$ is said to be *autonomous*.

An example of a dynamic allocation problem would be one which seeks to

$$\begin{aligned}
\underset{\{y_t\}}{\text{maximize}} \quad & \sum_{t=0}^{T-1} V(x_t, y_t, t) + F(x_T) \\
\text{subject to} \quad & x_{t+1} - x_t = f(x_t, y_t) \\
& x_0 = a \quad \text{given}
\end{aligned} \qquad (1.31)$$

The objective in (1.31) is to maximize the sum of intermediate values plus the net value associated with the terminal state x_T. This must be done subject to the difference equation describing the change in the state variable over the horizon, assuming $x_0 = a$; that is, the initial condition is given. The problem becomes one of determining the optimal values for y_t, $t = 0, 1, \ldots, T - 1$ which will, via the difference equation, imply values for x_t, $t = 1, \ldots, T$.

We can use the method of Lagrange multipliers by noting that the difference equation is a constraint equation which serves to define x_{t+1}. The Lagrangian expression may be written

$$L = \sum_{t=0}^{T-1} \{V(\cdot) + \lambda_{t+1}(x_t + f(\cdot) - x_{t+1})\} + F(\cdot) \qquad (1.32)$$

where λ_{t+1} is a multiplier associated with x_{t+1}. Because there are T such constraint equations $(t = 0, \ldots, T - 1)$ it is appropriate to include them within the summation operation.

With no nonnegativity constraints the first order necessary conditions require:

$$\frac{\partial L}{\partial y_t} = \frac{\partial V(\cdot)}{\partial y_t} + \lambda_{t+1}\frac{\partial f(\cdot)}{\partial y_t} = 0 \qquad\qquad t = 0, \ldots, T - 1 \quad (1.33)$$

$$\frac{\partial L}{\partial x_t} = \frac{\partial V(\cdot)}{\partial x_t} + \lambda_{t+1}\left(1 + \frac{\partial f(\cdot)}{\partial x_t}\right) - \lambda_t = 0 \qquad t = 1, \ldots, T - 1 \quad (1.34)$$

$$\frac{\partial L}{\partial x_T} = -\lambda_T + F'(\cdot) = 0 \qquad\qquad\qquad\qquad (1.35)$$

$$\frac{\partial L}{\partial \lambda_{t+1}} = x_t + f(\cdot) - x_{t+1} = 0 \qquad\qquad t = 0, \ldots, T - 1 \quad (1.36)$$

Most of the partials are straightforward with the exception of (1.34) which warrants some discussion. In taking the partial of L with respect to x_t one looks at where x_t appears in the tth term of the summation. This accounts for the first two expressions on the RHS of (1.34). If, however, one were to back up to the $(t-1)$ term one would also find a $-x_t$ premultiplied by λ_t, hence the third expression $-\lambda_t$ in (1.34).

Rewriting the first order conditions will facilitate their interpretation and put them in a form more useful when making comparisons to their continuous time counterparts. They are rewritten as

$$\frac{\partial V(\cdot)}{\partial y_t} + \lambda_{t+1}\frac{\partial f(\cdot)}{\partial y_t} = 0 \qquad t = 0, 1, \ldots, T-1 \qquad (1.37)$$

$$\lambda_{t+1} - \lambda_t = -\left(\frac{\partial V(\cdot)}{\partial x_t} + \lambda_{t+1}\frac{\partial f(\cdot)}{\partial x_t}\right) \qquad t = 1, \ldots, T-1 \qquad (1.38)$$

$$x_{t+1} - x_t = f(\cdot) \qquad (1.39)$$

$$\lambda_T = F'(\cdot) \qquad (1.40)$$

$$x_0 = a \qquad (1.41)$$

Equations (1.37) will typically define a marginal condition that y_t must satisfy. However, in the dynamic allocation problem there is a term not found in static problems. In many problems in resource economics $\partial V(\cdot)/\partial y_t$ will have the interpretation of being a net marginal benefit *in period* t. This is consistent with our earlier interpretation. In the dynamic context there is a second term to be accounted for in determining the optimal y_t. This term, $\lambda_{t+1}(\partial f(\cdot)/\partial y_t)$ explicitly reflects the influence of y_t on the change in the state variable. If an increase in y_t reduces the amount of *variable* x_{t+1} then this second term reflects an inter-temporal cost, often referred to as *user cost*. Less obvious, but perhaps more important, is that in the optimal solution of the problem λ_{t+1}^* can be shown to reflect the effect that an increment in x_{t+1} would have over the *remainder* of the horizon $(t+1, \ldots, T)$. Thus there is a second cost which must be considered when undertaking an incremental action today; that is, the marginal losses that might be incurred over the remaining future.

Equation (1.38) is a difference equation which must hold through time and relates the change in the Lagrange multiplier to terms involving partials of x_t. This expression can be given a nice, intuitive interpretation within the context of harvesting a renewable resource and we postpone its discussion till then. For now it is to be regarded as an equation defining how the multiplier must optimally change through time.

Equation (1.39) is simply a restatement of the difference equation for the state variable and Equations (1.40) and (1.41) are referred to as *boundary conditions* defining the terminal value of the multiplier sequence (λ_T) and the initial condition on the state variable. Because one condition is an initial condition and the other is a terminal condition, the boundary conditions are described as "split." [6]

Collectively, Equations (1.37)–(1.41) form a system of $(3T+1)$ equations in $(3T+1)$ unknowns: y_t for $t = 0, 1, \ldots, T-1$; x_t for $t = 0, 1, \ldots, T$; and λ_t for $t = 1, \ldots, T$. It may be possible to solve the system simultaneously for y_t, x_t, and λ_t although the structure for a particular problem may suggest a more efficient solution algorithm than treating it as a fully simultaneous system. If x_t, y_t, and λ_t are restricted to being nonnegative one must formulate the appropriate Kuhn–Tucker conditions and a solution might be obtained via a nonlinear programming, gradient-based algorithm.

One way of classifying dynamic problems is on the basis of whether terminal time and terminal state are given (fixed) or free to be chosen. From this perspective problem (1.31) would be classified as a "fixed-time, free-state" problem because the horizon was specified but the terminal state was not. In a free-time problem the decision-maker must determine the optimal horizon (i.e., solve for the optimal T). [7] A "restricted free-time" problem may impose a constraint on the length of horizon (e.g., $\underline{t} \leq T^* \leq \overline{t}$ where $\underline{t}$ and $\overline{t}$ are given). An *infinite* horizon problem, where $T \to \infty$, begs the question of whether or not the solution variables might converge to a set of values and remain unchanged thereafter. Such a solution is referred to as a *steady* or *stationary* state. If in an infinite horizon problem a steady state is attained in period τ then

$$y_t = y^*, \quad x_t = x^*, \quad \text{and} \quad \lambda_t = \lambda^* \text{ for all } t \geq \tau \qquad (1.42)$$

The solution to finite (fixed) horizon problems may also lead to a stationary state. For example, it may be optimal for the manager of a mine to deplete his reserves before the end of a given planning horizon. Finally, a "terminal surface" might be specified giving the decision-maker some freedom in the selection of T and x_T, in that he must choose from permissible combinations given by $\phi(T, x_T) = 0$.

---

[6] It may seem to be a minor technicality that, whereas the state variable x_t is specified *initially* by Eq. (1.41), the multiplier λ_t is specified *terminally* by Eq. (1.40). However, this observation is a basic feature of dynamic optimization problems. If λ_t could also be specified initially, the system (1.39)–(1.41) could be completely solved by numerical iteration starting at $t = 0$. The fact that this cannot be done is what makes dynamic optimization difficult—and interesting!

[7] In continuous-time the optimal horizon might be determined by a differential condition $\partial L / \partial T = 0$. In discrete-time there would be no differential relationship and the decision-maker would have to explore horizons of different length, determine the optimal behavior for each horizon (T), and then compare the sum of net economic returns.

Space precludes an exhaustive discussion of the nuances of these terminal conditions. The reader is referred to Kamien and Schwartz (1981) for additional detail.

Because of its importance in many resource management situations we would like to examine more closely the infinite horizon problem and the concept of steady state. Consider the problem

$$\begin{aligned}
\text{maximize} \quad & \sum_{t=0}^{\infty} V(x_t, y_t) \\
\{y_t\} \quad & \\
\text{subject to} \quad & x_{t+1} - x_t = f(x_t, y_t) \\
& x_0 = a \quad \text{given}
\end{aligned} \tag{1.43}$$

In contrast to problem (1.31) the above presumes that the objective function has no explicit time dependence (t is not an argument of $V(\cdot)$) and since $T \to \infty$ there is no final function.

The Lagrangian becomes

$$L = \sum_{t=0}^{\infty} \left\{ V(\cdot) + \lambda_{t+1}(x_t + f(\cdot) - x_{t+1}) \right\} \tag{1.44}$$

with first order necessary conditions including:

$$\frac{\partial V(\cdot)}{\partial y_t} + \lambda_{t+1} \frac{\partial f(\cdot)}{\partial y_t} = 0 \tag{1.45}$$

$$\lambda_{t+1} - \lambda_t = -\left(\frac{\partial V(\cdot)}{\partial x_t} + \lambda_{t+1} \frac{\partial f(\cdot)}{\partial x_t} \right) \tag{1.46}$$

$$x_{t+1} - x_t = f(\cdot) \tag{1.47}$$

which must hold for $t = 0, 1, \ldots$. In steady state, with unchanging values for y_t, x_t, and λ_t, Equations (1.45)–(1.47) become a three equation system

$$\frac{\partial V(\cdot)}{\partial y} + \lambda \frac{\partial f(\cdot)}{\partial y} = 0 \tag{1.48}$$

$$\frac{\partial V(\cdot)}{\partial x} + \lambda \frac{\partial f(\cdot)}{\partial x} = 0 \tag{1.49}$$

$$f(\cdot) = 0 \tag{1.50}$$

which might be solved for the steady-state optimum y^*, x^*, and λ^*. By eliminating λ from Equations (1.48) and (1.49) and solving (1.50) for y as a function of x it is often possible to obtain a single equation in the variable x^*.

If a steady-state optimum exists for an infinite horizon problem, if it is unique, and can be found from (1.48)–(1.50), then one might ask: "If we are currently not at the steady-state optimum (i.e., $x_0 \neq x^*$), what is the best way to get there?" There are essentially two types of optimal approach paths from x_0 to x^*, assuming x^* is *reachable* from x_0. The first type is an asymptotic approach in which $x_t \to x^*$ as $t \to \infty$. The second type is called the most rapid approach path (MRAP) in which case x_t is driven to x^* as rapidly as possible, usually reaching x^* in finite time. To drive x_t to x^* as rapidly as possible will often involve a "bang-bang" control where y_t, during the MRAP assumes some maximum or minimum value.

Spence and Starrett (1975) have identified the conditions under which MRAP is optimal. The conditions for problem (1.43) are that (a) via constraint-substitution $V(x_t, y_t)$ must be expressed as an additively separable function in x_t and x_{t+1} and (b) via proper indexing, the problem may be made equivalent to optimization of $\sum_{t=1}^{\infty} w(x_t)$, where $w(\cdot)$ is quasi-concave. Interestingly enough, there are many intuitive specifications for dynamic problems which satisfy the necessary and sufficiency conditions for MRAP to be optimal. If these conditions are met, the solution of the "bang-bang" approach is a relatively trivial matter. We will give an example of such a case, shortly. Before doing so it is appropriate to introduce a more modern control theory concept: the Hamiltonian.

Look closely at conditions (1.37) to (1.39). These conditions define the dynamics between the boundary points. The *Hamiltonian* is defined as

$$\mathcal{H}(x_t, y_t, \lambda_{t+1}, t) = V(x_t, y_t, t) + \lambda_{t+1} f(x_t, y_t) \tag{1.51}$$

and it is possible to write the first order necessary conditions directly as partials of the Hamiltonian. First, note that the Lagrangian expression (1.32) may be written in terms of the Hamiltonian:

$$L = \sum_{t=0}^{T-1} \{ \mathcal{H}(\cdot) + \lambda_{t+1}[x_t - x_{t+1}] \} + F(\cdot) \tag{1.52}$$

Then the first order conditions become

$$\frac{\partial L}{\partial y_t} = \frac{\partial \mathcal{H}(\cdot)}{\partial y_t} = 0 \qquad\qquad t = 0, \ldots, T-1 \tag{1.53}$$

$$\frac{\partial L}{\partial x_t} = \frac{\partial \mathcal{H}(\cdot)}{\partial x_t} + \lambda_{t+1} - \lambda_t = 0 \qquad t = 1, \ldots, T-1 \tag{1.54}$$

$$\frac{\partial L}{\partial x_T} = -\lambda_T + F'(\cdot) = 0 \tag{1.55}$$

$$\frac{\partial L}{\partial \lambda_{t+1}} = \frac{\partial \mathcal{H}(\cdot)}{\partial \lambda_{t+1}} + x_t - x_{t+1} = 0 \qquad t = 0, \dots, T-1 \tag{1.56}$$

In their most familiar form these conditions are written as the set

$$\frac{\partial \mathcal{H}(\cdot)}{\partial y_t} = 0 \qquad \lambda_{t+1} - \lambda_t = -\frac{\partial \mathcal{H}(\cdot)}{\partial x_t} \qquad x_{t+1} - x_t = \frac{\partial \mathcal{H}(\cdot)}{\partial \lambda_{t+1}}$$

$$\lambda_T = F'(\cdot) \qquad x_0 = a \tag{1.57}$$

The original problem, stated in (1.31), is an example of a subclass of control problems called *open-loop problems*. The solution of such a problem is a control trajectory $\{y_t^*\}$ determined as a function of time, or in our discrete-time problem, in tabular form. Knowing $\{y_t^*\}$ and x_0 one can use the difference equation $x_{t+1} = x_t + f(\cdot)$ to solve forward for the optimal trajectory x_t, denoted $\{x_t^*\}$.

Consider the following problem. As manager of a mine, you are asked to determine the optimal production schedule $\{y_t^*\}$ for $t = 0, \dots, 9$. The mine is to be shut down and abandoned at $t = 10$. The price per unit of ore is given as $p = 1$ and the cost of extracting y_t is $c_t = y_t^2/x_t$, where x_t is *remaining reserves* at the beginning of period t.

Net revenue may be written as $\pi_t = py_t - y_t^2/x_t = [1 - y_t/x_t]y_t$ and the difference equation describing the change in remaining reserves is $x_{t+1} - x_t = -y_t$, where initial reserves are assumed given with $x_0 = 1,000$. Maximization of the sum of net revenues subject to reserve dynamics leads to the Hamiltonian:

$$\mathcal{H}(\cdot) = [1 - y_t/x_t]\, y_t - \lambda_{t+1} y_t$$

with the first order necessary conditions requiring:

$$\frac{\partial \mathcal{H}(\cdot)}{\partial y_t} = 1 - 2y_t/x_t - \lambda_{t+1} = 0 \qquad t = 0, \dots, 9$$

$$\lambda_{t+1} - \lambda_t = -\frac{\partial \mathcal{H}(\cdot)}{\partial x_t} = -y_t^2/x_t^2 \qquad t = 1, \dots, 9$$

$$x_{t+1} - x_t = -y_t \qquad t = 0, \dots, 9$$

$$x_0 = 1,000, \quad \lambda_{10} = F'(\cdot) = 0$$

In this problem there is no final function and any units of x remaining in period 10 must be worthless. Note that this is a fixed-time free-state prob-

```
10 REM PROGRAM 1.1: MINE PROBLEM
20 DIM X(11),Y(11),Z(11),L(11)
30 L(10) = 0
40 FOR T = 9 TO 0 STEP -1
50    Z(T) = (1 - L(T+1)) / 2
60    L(T) = L(T+1) + Z(T)^2
70 NEXT T
80 X(0) = 1000
90 FOR T = 0 TO 9
100   Y(T) = X(T) * Z(T)
110   X(T+1) = X(T) - Y(T)
120 NEXT T
130 LPRINT " T          X(T)          Y(T)          L(T)"
140 LPRINT "------------------------------------------------------"
150 LPRINT 0,X(0),Y(0)
160 FOR T = 1 TO 10
170   LPRINT T,X(T),Y(T),L(T)
180 NEXT T
190 END
```

T	X(T)	Y(T)	L(T)
0	1000	138.9018	
1	861.0982	129.3185	.7221965
2	731.7798	119.6851	.6996428
3	612.0947	109.993	.6728931
4	502.1016	100.2317	.6406012
5	401.8699	90.38798	.6007513
6	311.482	80.44653	.550163
7	231.0354	70.39361	.4834595
8	160.6418	60.24068	.390625
9	100.4011	50.20057	.25
10	50.20057	0	0

Program 1.1 Solution and algorithm to the mine manager's problem.

lem and that the first order conditions represent a system of 31 equations in 31 unknowns: y_t for $t = 0, 1, \ldots, 9$, x_t for $t = 0, 1, \ldots, 10$, and λ_t for $t = 1, 2, \ldots, 10$. Solution of this problem is most easily accomplished by defining $z_t = y_t/x_t$. Evaluating the $\partial \mathcal{H}(\cdot)/\partial y_t$ at $t = 9$ implies $z_9 = 0.5$ (since $\lambda_{10} = 0$). Evaluating the expression for $\lambda_{t+1} - \lambda_t$ at $t = 9$ implies $\lambda_9 = (z_9)^2 = 0.25$. Knowing λ_9 we can return to $\partial \mathcal{H}(\cdot)/\partial y_t$ to solve for z_8, then back down to the second equation for λ_8, and so forth. The last step in the recursion gives us $z_0 = 0.1389$ and $\lambda_0 = 0.7415$. Knowing that $x_0 = 1000$ we can solve for $y_0 = x_0 z_0 = 138.90$ and $x_1 = x_0 - y_0 = 861.10$. Knowing x_1 we can solve for $y_1 = x_1 z_1 = 129.32$, $x_2 = x_1 - y_1 = 731.78$, and so forth. A solution algorithm (programmed in BASIC) and the complete results are given in Program 1.1.

The optimal time paths $\{y_t^*\}$ and $\{x_t^*\}$ are plotted in Figure 1.4(a), while a plot of the point (x_t^*, λ_t^*) is shown in Figure 1.4(b). The latter

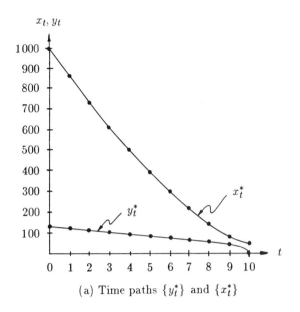

(a) Time paths $\{y_t^*\}$ and $\{x_t^*\}$

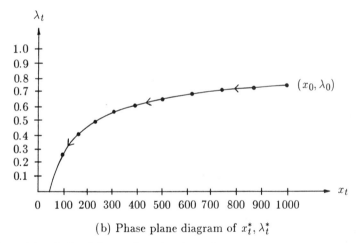

(b) Phase plane diagram of x_t^*, λ_t^*

Figure 1.4   Optimal time paths and a phase plane diagram for the mine manager's problem.

graph is referred to as a *phase plane diagram*. Arrows indicate the movement of (x_t^*, λ_t^*) over time. This simple problem can be used to illustrate other aspects of dynamic optimization problems in general and exhaustible resources in particular. We will return to this problem once more in this chapter and again in Chapter 3. We now turn to another important technique for solving dynamic optimization problems.

1.3 Dynamic programming

Consider the following problem:

$$\text{maximize } \sum_{t=0}^{T} V(x_t, y_t, t)$$
$$\{y_t\}$$

$$\text{subject to } x_{t+1} = f(x_t, y_t, t), \quad t = 0, 1, \ldots, T-1 \qquad (1.58)$$

$$y_t \in Y, \quad t = 0, 1, \ldots, T$$

$$x_0 = a \text{ given}$$

In comparison to Problem (1.31) the final function has been incorporated as $V(x_T, y_T, T)$, all x_t terms have been collected on the right hand side of the difference equation, and y_t must come from the set Y, for $t = 0, \ldots, T$ (as opposed to $t = 0, \ldots, T-1$). However, these changes are mainly for notational convenience only.

Define $J_n(x)$ as the maximum total value when only n periods remain, and the state variable at the outset of these n periods is x. Thus

$$J_n(x) = \max \sum_{t=T-(n-1)}^{T} V(x_t, y_t, t), \quad \text{given } x_{T-(n-1)} = x \qquad (1.59)$$

subject to the same constraints as in the original problem for $t \geq T-(n-1)$.

For $n = 1$ we have simply

$$J_1(x) = \max_{y_T \in Y} V(x_T, y_T, T), \quad x_T = x \qquad (1.60)$$

that is, a single constrained static optimization problem. Suppose this problem to have been solved for every value of x in a range of interest. Next consider $n = 2$ and

$$J_2(x) = \max_{Y_{T-1} \in Y} [V(x_{T-1}, y_{T-1}, T-1)$$
$$+ J_1(f(x_{T-1}, y_{T-1}, T-1))] \qquad (1.61)$$
$$x_{T-1} = x$$

This equation is easily explained: Let some decision on y be adopted in period $T-1$. The first term on the right of (1.61) is the immediate payoff. After this decision is made, only one period remains and the state of the system will be $x_T = f(x_{T-1}, y_{T-1}, T-1)$ as per our difference equation in

Problem (1.58). If the entire policy is optimal *this final decision must also be taken optimally*. But the optimal terminal period value is

$$J_1(x_T) = J_1(f(x_{T-1}, y_{T-1}, T-1)) \tag{1.62}$$

Finally, y_{T-1} itself must be chosen optimally so that (1.61) is valid.

Now observe that if $J_1(x)$ is assumed known for all x, (1.61) is again a static optimization problem. Having solved this problem we can continue:

$$J_3(x) = \max_{Y_{T-2} \in Y} [V(x_{T-2}, y_{T-2}, T-2)$$

$$+ J_2(f(x_{T-2}, y_{T-2}, T-2))] \tag{1.63}$$

$$x_{T-2} = x$$

and so on, until $n = T + 1$ and the original problem has been solved. This is the famous method of *dynamic programming* (Bellman 1957), sometimes called "backwards induction"—for obvious reasons. The general expression for n "periods to go" is

$$J_n(x) = \max_{Y_{T-(n-1)}} [V(x_{T-(n-1)}, y_{T-(n-1)}, T-(n-1))$$

$$+ J_{n-1}(f(x_{T-(n-1)}, y_{T-(n-1)}, T-(n-1)))] \tag{1.64}$$

$$x_{T-(n-1)} = x$$

and is called "Bellman's equation." The argument giving rise to it is the "principle of optimality" which states:

> An optimal policy has the property that whatever the initial state and decision are, the remaining decisions must constitute an optimal policy with regard to the state resulting from the first decision. (Bellman, 1957)

What practical difficulties might arise in using dynamic programming? Each of the static optimization problems must be solved for all the relevant values of the initial variable x. In cases where x is multidimensional this problem may be highly nontrivial—Bellman called this the "curse of dimensionality." Nevertheless, dynamic programming has found wide application.

As an example, suppose we sought to

$$\underset{\{y_t\}}{\text{maximize}} \quad V = \sum_{t=0}^{4} [10x_t - 0.1y_t^2]$$

$$\text{subject to} \quad x_{t+1} = x_t + y_t$$
$$x_0 = 0, \quad y_t \geq 0$$

We begin by noting that the value function with one period to go is

$$J_1 = \max_{y_4 \geq 0} [10x_4 - 0.1y_4^2]$$

Since a positive level for y_4 will only reduce J_1 we quickly determine $y_4^* = 0$ and $J_1 = 10x_4$. Proceeding backwards

$$J_2 = \max_{y_3 \geq 0} [10x_3 - 0.1y_3^2 + J_1]$$
$$= \max_{y_3 \geq 0} [10x_3 - 0.1y_3^2 + 10x_4]$$
$$= \max_{y_3 \geq 0} [10x_3 - 0.1y_3^2 + 10(x_3 + y_3)]$$

Taking the partial derivative of the last bracketed expression with respect to y_3 requires $-0.2y_3 + 10 = 0$, or $y_3 = 50$. Substituting this value back into the bracketed expression produces $J_2 = 20x_3 + 250$.

Continuing backwards

$$J_3 = \max_{y_2 \geq 0} [10x_2 - 0.1y_2^2 + J_2]$$
$$= \max_{y_2 \geq 0} [10x_2 - 0.1y_2^2 + 20x_3 + 250]$$
$$= \max_{y_2 \geq 0} [10x_2 - 0.1y_2^2 + 20(x_2 + y_2) + 250]$$

Taking the partial of $[\cdot]$ with respect to y_2 requires $-0.2y_2 + 20 = 0$ or $y_2 = 100$ and thus $J_3 = 30x_2 + 1,250$.

Proceeding in a similar fashion back to $J_5 = -0.1y_0^2 + 40y_0 + 3500$ the following solution obtains:

t	y_t	x_t
0	200	0
1	150	200
2	100	350
3	50	450
4	0	500

$$V = J_5 = 7,500$$

1.4 Continuous-time problems and the maximum principle

When time is taken as continuous the optimization interval becomes $0 \leq t \leq T$ and the difference equation describing the change in the state variable is replaced by the differential equation $dx(t)/dt = \dot{x} = f(\cdot)$. The continuous-time analogue to problem (1.31) is

$$\text{maximize} \quad \int_0^T V\left(x(t), y(t), t\right) dt + F(x(T))$$

$$\text{subject to} \quad \dot{x} = f(x(t), y(t)) \tag{1.65}$$

$$x(0) = a \quad \text{given}$$

Note that the integration operator has replaced the discrete-time summation operator and that, by convention, the continuous-time variables parenthesize t as opposed to subscripting. In the continuous-time problem it is necessary to assume $x(t)$ is continuous and $y(t)$ piecewise continuous. In the following development, note the close analogy with the discrete-time problem discussed above.

Proceeding as before we may form a Lagrangian expression

$$L = \int_0^T \left[V(\cdot) + \lambda(t)(f(\cdot) - \dot{x})\right] dt + F(\cdot) \tag{1.66}$$

The term $-\lambda(t)\dot{x}$ may be integrated by parts to yield $\int_0^T \dot{\lambda}x(t) \, dt - [\lambda(T)x(T) - \lambda(0)x(0)]$ which upon substitution into (1.66) gives

$$L = \int_0^T \left[V(\cdot) + \lambda(t)f(\cdot) + \dot{\lambda}x(t)\right] dt + F(\cdot) - [\lambda(T)x(T) - \lambda(0)x(0)] \tag{1.67}$$

Defining the continuous-time Hamiltonian as

$$\mathcal{H}(x(t), y(t), \lambda(t), t) = V(x(t), y(t), t) + \lambda(t)f(x(t), y(t)) \tag{1.68}$$

we may rewrite the Langrangian expression yet again as

$$L = \int_0^T \left[\mathcal{H}(\cdot) + \dot{\lambda}x(t)\right] dt + F(\cdot) - [\lambda(T)x(T) - \lambda(0)x(0)] \tag{1.69}$$

The first order necessary condition may be derived in the following heuristic manner. Consider a change in the control trajectory from $y(t)$ to $y(t) + \Delta y(t)$ which causes a change in the state trajectory from $x(t)$ to

$x(t) + \Delta x(t)$. The change in the Lagrangian is:

$$\Delta L = \int_0^T \left[\frac{\partial \mathcal{H}(\cdot)}{\partial y(t)} \Delta y(t) + \frac{\partial \mathcal{H}(\cdot)}{\partial x(t)} \Delta x(t) + \dot{\lambda} \Delta x(t) \right] dt + \left[F'(\cdot) - \lambda(T) \right] \Delta x(T)$$

(1.70)

For a maximum it is necessary that the change in the Lagrangian vanish for any $\{\Delta y(t)\}$, thus

$$\frac{\partial \mathcal{H}(\cdot)}{\partial y(t)} = 0$$

$$\dot{\lambda} = -\frac{\partial \mathcal{H}(\cdot)}{\partial x(t)}$$

(1.71)

$$\lambda(T) = F'(\cdot)$$

From the definition of $\mathcal{H}(\cdot)$, and taking into account the initial condition, we may write the necessary conditions in their entirety as

$$\frac{\partial \mathcal{H}(\cdot)}{\partial y(t)} = 0 \qquad \dot{\lambda} = -\frac{\partial \mathcal{H}(\cdot)}{\partial x(t)} \qquad \dot{x} = \frac{\partial \mathcal{H}(\cdot)}{\partial \lambda(t)}$$

$$\lambda(T) = F'(\cdot) \qquad\qquad x(0) = a$$

(1.72)

The reader should compare conditions (1.72) with their discrete-time analogues given in (1.57). In both discrete- and continuous-time we might summarize as follows:

(a) $x_t, x(t)$ is the state variable.
(b) $y_t, y(t)$ is the control variable.
(c) $\lambda_t, \lambda(t)$ is the adjoint or costate variable.
(d) $x_{t+1} - x_t = f(\cdot)$, $\dot{x} = f(\cdot)$ is the state equation or equation of motion.
(e) $\partial \mathcal{H}(\cdot)/\partial y_t = 0$, $\partial \mathcal{H}(\cdot)/\partial y(t) = 0$ is the maximum condition.
(f) $\lambda_{t+1} - \lambda_t = -\partial \mathcal{H}(\cdot)/\partial x_t$, $\dot{\lambda} = -\partial \mathcal{H}(\cdot)/\partial x(t)$ is the adjoint equation.

As before, alternative terminal conditions may be considered. For example, suppose $x(T) = b$ is specified. Then the last term in (1.70) disappears (because $\Delta x(T) = 0$) so that the last equation in (1.71) is no longer valid. (The total number of terminal conditions on $x(T)$ and $\lambda(T)$ always remains the same.) If terminal time is free we must have $\partial L/\partial T = 0$. From (1.69) we obtain

$$\frac{\partial L}{\partial T} = \mathcal{H}(T) + \dot{\lambda}(T)x(T) + F'(\cdot)\dot{x}(T) - \dot{\lambda}(T)x(T) - \lambda(T)\dot{x}(T) = \mathcal{H}(T) = 0$$

from the last condition in (1.71). Thus, the free terminal-time condition is simply

$$\mathcal{H}(T) = \mathcal{H}(x(T), y(T), \lambda(T), T) = 0 \tag{1.73}$$

which along with $\lambda(T) = F'(\cdot)$, when it applies, are referred to as the *transversality conditions*.

Finally, the conditions

$$\frac{\partial \mathcal{H}(\cdot)}{\partial y(t)} = 0$$

$$\dot{\lambda} = -\frac{\partial \mathcal{H}(\cdot)}{\partial x(t)} \qquad \lambda(T) = F'(\cdot) \tag{1.74}$$

$$\mathcal{H}(x(T), y(T), \lambda(T), T) = 0$$

are collectively referred to as the *maximum principle*. The above form of the maximum principle, which was part of the calculus of variations, does not pertain to the case where control constraints, such as $y(t) \in Y$, exist. In this case, it has been proved (Pontryagin et al. 1962) that the maximum condition, $\partial \mathcal{H}(\cdot)/\partial y(t) = 0$, takes the more general (and more incisive) form:

$$y(t) \quad \text{maximizes} \quad \mathcal{H}(x(t), y, \lambda(t), t)$$

$$\text{over} \quad y(t) \in Y \quad \text{for} \quad 0 \le t \le T \tag{1.75}$$

If $y(t)$ is an interior point of the control set Y then (1.75) reduces to $\partial \mathcal{H}(\cdot)/\partial y(t) = 0$. This apparently minor generalization has had a profound effect for the theory and applications of dynamic optimization. Nowadays, the phrase "maximum principle" is usually taken to imply the more general maximum condition (1.75).[8]

The economic interpretation of $\lambda(t)$ is facilitated by defining the value function

$$J(x, t) = \max_{\{y(t)\}} \int_t^T V(x(t), y(t), t) \, dt \tag{1.76}$$

for $\dot{x} = f(\cdot)$, $y(t) \in Y$, and $x(t) = x$ (given). In analogy to the discrete-time case it can be shown that, for the optimal solution

$$\lambda(t) = \partial J/\partial x \tag{1.77}$$

that is, the shadow price $\lambda(t)$ equals the marginal value of the state variable at time t.

---

[8] This condition has been proven to hold for discrete-time problems; see Cannon, Cullum, and Polak (1970).

The Hamiltonian

$$\mathcal{H}(t) = \mathcal{H}(x(t), \lambda(t), t) = V(\cdot) + \lambda(t)f(\cdot) \tag{1.78}$$

can now be interpreted as the total rate of increase in the value of assets: The first term, $V(\cdot)$, is the flow of net returns at instant t while the second term, $\lambda(t)f(\cdot)$, is the increase in the value of the stock, x. With this interpretation, the maximum condition (1.75) makes eminent sense—the optimal control maximizes the total rate of increase of assets.

As an example, suppose a renewable resource may be costlessly harvested and sold at the price $p(t)$. Let $h(t)$ denote the rate of harvest and assume that capital or other fixed factors limit harvest so that $0 \le h(t) \le \bar{h}$. If $x(t)$ is the stock or biomass of the renewable resource, assume that $\dot{x} = F(x) - h(t)$ is the change in the stock where $F(x)$ is a function defining the net natural growth rate and $x(0)$ is given.[9] The problem for a resource manager or owner may be to

$$\text{maximize} \quad \int_0^T p(t)h(t)\, dt$$

$$\text{subject to} \quad \dot{x} = F(x) - h(t)$$

$$0 \le h(t) \le \bar{h}, \qquad x(0) \quad \text{given}$$

The Hamiltonian for this problem is

$$\mathcal{H}(x(t), y(t), \lambda(t), t) = p(t)h(t) + \lambda(t)[F(x) - h(t)]$$

$$= h(t)[p(t) - \lambda(t)] + \lambda(t)F(x)$$

The maximum condition says that $h(t)$ must maximize this expression, and since $\mathcal{H}(\cdot)$ is linear in harvest this implies

$$h(t) = \begin{cases} 0 & \text{if } p(t) < \lambda(t) \\ \bar{h} & \text{if } p(t) > \lambda(t) \end{cases}$$

The most important case, however, is when $p(t) = \lambda(t)$. In this case we know $\dot{p} = \dot{\lambda}$. But from the adjoint equation we also know

$$\dot{\lambda} = -\frac{\partial \mathcal{H}(\cdot)}{\partial x(t)} = -\lambda(t)F'(\cdot)$$

or

$$F'(\cdot) = -\dot{p}/p(t)$$

---

[9] The function $F(x)$ will be discussed in greater detail in Chapter 2.

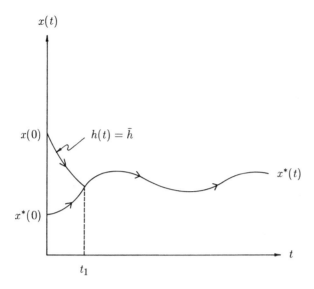

Figure 1.5 Optimal time path for $x(t)$ obtained from the solution of $F'(\cdot) = -\dot{p}/p(t)$.

This equation implies that the biomass of the resource should be maintained so that the change in the net natural growth rate equals the negative of the percentage rate of change in price.[10] With $p(t)$ known and continuous this equation will imply an optimal time path $x^*(t)$ (assuming $F(\cdot) = -\dot{p}/p(t)$ can be solved for $x^*(t)$). Such a path is drawn in Figure 1.5.

From the maximum principle we have learned that either the optimal solution must coincide with $x^*(t)$, or else $h(t) = 0$ or $\bar{h}$. Clearly the complete solution must be given by

$$h(t) = \begin{cases} 0 & \text{if } x(t) < x^*(t) \\ h^*(t) = F(x^*(t)) - \dot{x}^*(t) & \text{if } x(t) = x^*(t) \\ \bar{h} & \text{if } x(t) > x^*(t) \end{cases}$$

This is an example of the Most Rapid Approach Path (MRAP) or a "bang-bang" control, where, in this case, harvest takes place at its lower or upper bound to return stock to its optimal level as rapidly as possible.[11] In Figure 1.5 if the initial stock $x(0) > x^*(0)$, then $h(t) = \bar{h}$ until $x(t) = x^*(t)$ at $t = t_1$. The solution $x^*(t)$ is called a *singular* solution. Such solutions arise in control problems in which the Hamiltonian expression is *linear* in

---

[10] If revenues were discounted at rate δ the rule would be $F'(\cdot) = \delta - \dot{p}/p(t)$. Discounting will be discussed more fully in the next section.

[11] There could also be a "bang-bang" adjustment to the terminal value $x(T)$ if $T < \infty$.

the control variable. The coefficient of $h(t)$ in the Hamiltonian, in this case,

$$\sigma(t) = p(t) - \lambda(t)$$

is called a *switching function* because it determines whether $h(t)$ should switch from $h = \bar{h}$ to $h = 0$ or $h = h^*(t)$; the latter case occurring when $\sigma(t) \equiv 0$.

In economics and operations research, singular solutions are often called *myopic* solutions. Why? In determining the optimal resource stock at a particular point in time we only needed to know the current price $p(t)$ and the rate of change in price $\dot{p}(t)$. Future price changes (i.e., the complete time path $p(t)$) need not be known to formulate the optimal policy! While this is an encouraging result for planners it must be realized that it will hold only under special assumptions. Namely, that there must be zero adjustment costs and the price must not fluctuate so rapidly that the myopic path $x^*(t)$ becomes infeasible (see Clark 1976, Chapter 2).

As a second example, consider the following nonlinear, free-time, free-state problem [12]

$$\text{maximize} \quad V = \int_0^T \frac{a}{b}(1 - e^{-by(t)})\gamma(t)\,dt$$

$$\text{subject to} \quad \dot{x}(t) = -y(t)$$

$$x(0) \quad \text{given} \qquad x(t) \geq 0$$

where $a > 0$, $b > 0$, $\gamma(t) > 0$ and to set the stage for discounting suppose $\dot{\gamma}/\gamma(t) = -\delta < 0$, where $\delta > 0$. The Hamiltonian for this problem may be written as

$$\mathcal{H}(\cdot) = \frac{a}{b}\left(1 - e^{-by(t)}\right)\gamma(t) - \lambda(t)y(t)$$

and the maximum principle requires

$$\frac{\partial \mathcal{H}(\cdot)}{\partial y(t)} = ae^{-by(t)}\gamma(t) - \lambda(t) = 0$$

$$\dot{\lambda} = -\frac{\partial \mathcal{H}(\cdot)}{\partial x(t)} = 0$$

The adjoint equation implies $\lambda(t) = \lambda$, a constant. Taking the time derivative of the maximum condition, we obtain

$$-abe^{-by(t)}\dot{y}\gamma(t) + ae^{-by(t)}\dot{\gamma} = \dot{\lambda} = 0$$

---

[12] This can be thought of as a simplistic exhaustible resource model.

which simplifies to

$$\dot{y} = \frac{\dot{\gamma}}{b\gamma(t)} = -\frac{\delta}{b} \quad (\text{recall } \dot{\gamma}/\gamma = -\delta)$$

This last expression may be integrated directly to imply

$$y(t) = -\frac{\delta}{b}t + c_0$$

where c_0 is a constant of integration. The *transversality condition* takes the form:

$$\mathcal{H}(T) = \frac{a}{b}(1 - e^{-by(T)})\gamma(t) - \lambda y(T) = 0$$

which will only hold for $y(T) = 0$. Evaluating $y(t)$ at $t = T$ gives

$$y(T) = -\frac{\delta T}{b} + c_0 = 0, \quad \text{or} \quad c_0 = \frac{\delta T}{b}$$

Thus,

$$y(t) = \frac{\delta}{b}(T - t)$$

If $x(T) > 0$ it would be possible to increase $y(t)$ which would increase V so in this case it is also optimal for $x(T) = 0$, which in turn implies

$$x(0) = \int_0^T y(t)\, dt = \int_0^T \frac{\delta}{b}(T - t)\, dt$$

$$= \frac{\delta}{b}\left(Tt - \frac{t^2}{2}\right)\Big|_0^T = \frac{\delta T^2}{2b}$$

Solving for T yields

$$T = \sqrt{2bx(0)/\delta}$$

Given specific values for b, $x(0)$, and δ one can calculate T^*, $y^*(t)$, and $x^*(t)$.

1.5 Discounting

Discounting is a technique for calculating the *present value* of a future stream of net income. In discrete-time models we could calculate the present value of future net incomes N_t, $t = 0, 1, 2, \ldots, T$ according to

$$N = \sum_{t=0}^{T} N_t/(1 + \delta)^t = \sum_{t=0}^{T} \rho^t N_t \tag{1.79}$$

where $\rho = 1/(1+\delta)$ is the discount *factor* and δ is the periodic *discount rate*. In searching for the "best" dynamic allocation one frequently encounters objective functions that represent a present value.

In continuous time the present value of net incomes $N(t)$, $0 \leq t \leq T$ may be calculated according to

$$N = \int_0^T N(t)e^{-rt}\,dt \tag{1.80}$$

In Equation (1.80) the term e^{-rt} is the continuous (or instantaneous) discount factor and r is the instantaneous rate of discount. Assuming that the time units are the same in (1.79) and (1.80), we see that

$$e^{-r} = \frac{1}{1+\delta}, \qquad \text{i.e.,} \qquad r = \ln(1+\delta)$$

For example, a 10% discount rate compounded annually is equivalent to a continuous rate of 9.53%. Other compounding periods may be treated by a similar calculation.

For varying discount rates we have the following formulas for the discount factor:

discrete time: $\quad \rho(t) = \dfrac{1}{1+\delta_1} \cdot \dfrac{1}{1+\delta_2} \cdot \ldots \cdot \dfrac{1}{1+\delta_t}$

continuous time: $\quad \rho(t) = \exp\left(-\int_0^t r(s)\,ds\right)$

The reader should check that these formulas reduce to the previous expressions in the case of constant discount rates.

We now consider the form of the discrete- and continuous-time problems with present value objectives.

Consider the discrete-time problem

$$\text{maximize} \sum_{t=0}^{T-1} \rho^t V(x_t, y_t) + \rho^T F(x_T)$$
$$\text{subject to} \quad x_{t+1} - x_t = f(x_t, y_t) \tag{1.81}$$
$$x_0 = a \quad \text{given}$$

There are two ways one might formulate the Lagrangian expression for this problem. We take the following approach because it offers more straightforward interpretations. Define

$$L = \sum_{t=0}^{T-1} \rho^t \left\{ V(\cdot) + \rho\lambda_{t+1}[x_t + f(\cdot) - x_{t+1}] \right\} + \rho^T F(\cdot) \tag{1.82}$$

In (1.82) we premultiply the difference equation by λ_{t+1} as before but then premultiply the product by the discrete-time discount factor ρ. The multiplier λ_{t+1} can be interpreted as the value of an additional unit of x_{t+1} from the *perspective of period* $t+1$. The term $\lambda_{t+1}[\cdot]$ is thus a value in period $t+1$. The objective function $V_t = V(x_t, y_t)$, however, represents a value in period t. To make these two values comparable we discount $\lambda_{t+1}[\cdot]$ one period, thus the expression in $\{\cdot\}$ is a value from the perspective of period t, and it is discounted by ρ^t, then added to the discounted values from other periods to calculate the present value of the Lagrangian.

The discrete-time *current value* Hamiltonian is

$$\tilde{\mathcal{H}}(x_t, y_t, \lambda_{t+1}) = V(\cdot) + \rho\lambda_{t+1}f(\cdot) \tag{1.83}$$

and the first order conditions will require

$$\frac{\partial \tilde{\mathcal{H}}(\cdot)}{\partial y_t} = 0$$

$$\rho\lambda_{t+1} - \lambda_t = -\frac{\partial \tilde{\mathcal{H}}(\cdot)}{\partial x_t} \qquad x_{t+1} - x_t = \frac{\partial \tilde{\mathcal{H}}(\cdot)}{\partial(\rho\lambda_{t+1})}$$

$$\lambda_T = F'(\cdot) \qquad x_0 = a \tag{1.84}$$

The above conditions can be verified by rewriting the Lagrangian in terms of the discrete-time current value Hamiltonian. The term "current value" stems from the fact that the Hamiltonian as we have defined it represents a value from the perspective of period t. In comparing conditions (1.57) without discounting to (1.84) with discounting note the discount factor which premultiplies λ_{t+1} in (1.84).

Suppose, if instead of the finite horizon problem in (1.81), we had the infinite horizon problem

$$\text{maximize} \sum_{t=0}^{\infty} \rho^t V(x_t, y_t)$$

$$\text{subject to} \quad x_{t+1} - x_t = f(x_t, y_t)$$

$$x_0 = a \quad \text{given} \tag{1.85}$$

The current value Hamiltonian is again given by (1.83) and the first order conditions will imply

$$\frac{\partial V(\cdot)}{\partial y_t} + \rho \lambda_{t+1} \frac{\partial f(\cdot)}{\partial y_t} = 0 \tag{1.86}$$

$$\rho \lambda_{t+1} - \lambda_t = -\frac{\partial V(\cdot)}{\partial x_t} - \rho \lambda_{t+1} \frac{\partial f(\cdot)}{\partial x_t} \tag{1.87}$$

$$x_{t+1} - x_t = f(\cdot) \tag{1.88}$$

Suppose a steady state exists and is reachable from $x_0 = a$. Then evaluating (1.86) at steady state implies $\lambda = -(1+\delta)[V_y/f_y]$. Substituting this expression into (1.87) (also evaluated at steady state) and isolating δ on the RHS yields

$$f_x - \frac{V_x}{V_y} f_y = \delta \tag{1.89}$$

Equation (1.89) is a fundamental result to models of renewable resources and in the next chapter it will be given a capital-theoretic interpretation. Together with Equation (1.88), which evaluated at a steady state implies $f(\cdot) = 0$, we obtain a two equation system that may be solved for the steady-state optimum (x^*, y^*).

Let us next reconsider the mine manager's problem posed in Section 1.2, but now introduce discounting. The problem becomes:

$$\text{maximize} \, V = \sum_{t=0}^{9} \rho^t [1 - y_t/x_t] y_t$$

$$\text{subject to} \quad x_{t+1} - x_t = -y_t$$

$$x_0 = 1,000$$

The current value Hamiltonian is

$$\tilde{\mathcal{H}}(\cdot) = [1 - y_t/x_t]y_t - \rho \lambda_{t+1} y_t$$

and the first order conditions require

$$\frac{\partial \tilde{\mathcal{H}}(\cdot)}{\partial y_t} = 1 - 2y_t/x_t - \rho \lambda_{t+1} = 0 \qquad t = 0, 1, \ldots, 9$$

Table 1.1 *Solution to the mine manager's problem with discounting* $(\delta = 0.10)$.

t	x_t	y_t	λ_t
0	1,000	238.23	–
1	761.77	183.68	0.5759
2	578.09	141.82	0.5695
3	436.27	109.71	0.5603
4	326.56	85.09	0.5467
5	241.47	66.22	0.5267
6	175.25	51.74	0.4967
7	123.51	40.61	0.4505
8	82.90	32.03	0.3765
9	50.87	25.43	0.2500
10	25.44	0	0

$$\rho\lambda_{t+1} - \lambda_t = \frac{\partial \tilde{\mathcal{H}}(\cdot)}{\partial x_t} = -y_t^2/x_t^2 \qquad t = 1, 2, \ldots, 9$$

$$x_{t+1} - x_t = -y_t \qquad t = 0, 1, \ldots, 9$$

$$x_0 = 1,000, \qquad \lambda_{10} = F'(\cdot) = 0$$

The solution algorithm is the same, only now the discount factor will influence the values of $z_8, \ldots, z_0$; $\lambda_8, \ldots, \lambda_0$, and will thus affect the optimal values of y_t, $t = 0, 1, \ldots, 9$, and x_t, $t = 1, 2, \ldots, 10$, when solving forward for these values. If $\delta = 0.10$ the values for x_t and y_t are shown in Table 1.1. In each case, price is assumed constant, $p = 1$, and initial reserves are $x_0 = 1,000$. With discounting, the manager finds it optimal to produce more initially, driving remaining reserves down more quickly and producing less terminally (e.g., compare y_8 in Program 1.1 and Table 1.1). In this problem, discounting leads to greater production over the entire horizon (note $x_{10} = 25.4$ when $\delta = 0.1$). This tilting of production profiles toward the present (and the more rapid depletion of nonrenewable resources) is an all-but-universal feature of discounting. The higher the discount rate, the greater the tilt.

Discounting in the continuous-time model is also facilitated by introducing the current value Hamiltonian. Consider the following problem.

$$\text{maximize} \int_0^T V(x(t), y(t)) e^{-\delta t}\, dt + F(x(T)) e^{-\delta T}$$

$$\text{subject to} \quad \dot{x} = f(x(t), y(t))$$

$$x(0) = a \quad \text{given} \tag{1.90}$$

The Hamiltonian for this problem is

$$\mathcal{H}(\cdot) = V(\cdot) e^{-\delta t} + \lambda(t) f(\cdot) \tag{1.91}$$

The current value Hamiltonian is defined as

$$\tilde{\mathcal{H}} = \mathcal{H}(\cdot) e^{\delta t} = V(\cdot) + \mu(t) f(\cdot) \tag{1.92}$$

where $\mu(t) = e^{\delta t} \lambda(t)$. The necessary conditions given in (1.72) are in terms of the Hamiltonian and require, in part, that

$$\frac{\partial \mathcal{H}(\cdot)}{\partial y(t)} = \frac{\partial V(\cdot)}{\partial y(t)} e^{-\delta t} + \lambda(t) \frac{\partial f(\cdot)}{\partial y(t)} = 0 \tag{1.93}$$

$$\dot{\lambda} = -\frac{\partial \mathcal{H}(\cdot)}{\partial x(t)}$$

$$= -\frac{\partial V(\cdot)}{\partial x(t)} e^{-\delta t} - \lambda(t) \frac{\partial f(\cdot)}{\partial x(t)} \tag{1.94}$$

From the definition for $\mu(t)$ we note $\lambda(t) = \mu(t) e^{-\delta t}$ and $\dot{\lambda} = -\delta \mu(t) e^{-\delta t} + \dot{\mu} e^{-\delta t}$. Equations (1.93) and (1.94) may be rewritten in terms of $\mu(t)$ and $\dot{\mu}$ so that

$$\frac{\partial V(\cdot)}{\partial y(t)} + \mu(t) \frac{\partial f(\cdot)}{\partial y(t)} = 0 \tag{1.95}$$

$$\dot{\mu} = -\frac{\partial V(\cdot)}{\partial x(t)} + \mu(t) \left(\delta - \frac{\partial f(\cdot)}{\partial x(t)} \right) \tag{1.96}$$

The multipliers $\lambda(t)$ and $\mu(t)$ can be thought of as present-value and current-value shadow prices, respectively, where $\lambda(t)$ is the imputed value of an incremental unit in $x(t)$ from the perspective of $t = 0$, while $\mu(t)$ is the value of an additional unit of $x(t)$ at instant t. For problem (1.90) the complete set of first order conditions, expressed in terms of the current-value

Hamiltonian is

$$\frac{\partial \tilde{\mathcal{H}}(\cdot)}{\partial y_t} = 0$$

$$\dot{\mu} - \delta\mu(t) = -\frac{\partial \tilde{\mathcal{H}}(\cdot)}{\partial x(t)} \qquad \dot{x} = \frac{\partial \tilde{\mathcal{H}}(\cdot)}{\partial \mu(t)}$$

$$\mu(T) = F'(\cdot) \qquad x(0) = a \tag{1.97}$$

The infinite horizon problem with discounting becomes

$$\text{maximize} \int_0^\infty V(\cdot)e^{-\delta t}\, dt$$
$$\text{subject to} \quad \dot{x} = f(\cdot) \tag{1.98}$$
$$x(0) = a \quad \text{given}$$

Assume that a steady state exists and is reachable from $x(0) = a$. The current value Hamiltonian remains unchanged from (1.92). Evaluating Equation (1.95) in steady state implies $\mu = -(\partial V(\cdot)/\partial y)/(\partial f(\cdot)/\partial y)$. Evaluating (1.96) in steady state ($\dot{\mu} = 0$), substituting the expression for μ and isolating δ on the RHS yields:

$$f_x - \frac{V_x}{V_y}f_y = \delta \tag{1.99}$$

which is identical to the steady state expression (1.89) obtained from the analogous discrete-time problem. While discrete- and continuous-time analogues will typically produce identical expressions for steady state they may be subject to different dynamic behavior.

Consider the following problem, which is a simple special case of the above:

$$\text{maximize} \int_0^\infty U\Big(h(t)\Big)e^{-\delta t}\, dt$$
$$\text{subject to} \quad \dot{x} = F(x) - h(t)$$
$$x(0) \quad \text{given}$$

We will assume $U(\cdot)$ to be concave ($U'(\cdot) > 0$, $U''(\cdot) < 0$) and it may be thought of as social utility [or, perhaps, monopoly revenue, in which case $U(h(t)) = p(h(t))h(t)$, where $p(h(t))$ is the inverse demand function for $h(t)$].

The Hamiltonian is

$$\mathcal{H} = U(\cdot)e^{-\delta t} + \lambda(t)[F(\cdot) - h(t)]$$

while the current value Hamiltonian is

$$\tilde{\mathcal{H}} = U(\cdot) + \mu(t)[F(\cdot) - h(t)]$$

where $\mu(t) = \lambda(t)e^{\delta t}$. Using the first two conditions in (1.97)

$$\frac{\partial \tilde{\mathcal{H}}(\cdot)}{\partial h_t} = U'(\cdot) - \mu(t) = 0$$

$$\dot{\mu} - \delta\mu(t) = -\frac{\partial \tilde{\mathcal{H}}(\cdot)}{\partial x(t)} = -\mu(t)F'(\cdot)$$

Taking the time derivative of the first yields

$$U''(\cdot)\dot{h} - \dot{\mu} = 0$$

Substituting into the second and noting $\mu(t) = U'(\cdot)$ yields

$$\dot{h} = \frac{U'(\cdot)}{U''(\cdot)}[\delta - F'(\cdot)]$$

which along with the state equation constitutes a coupled nonlinear system of differential equations for the optimal control $h(t)$ and the state variable $x(t)$. This system can be analyzed by standard techniques for *plane* (two-dimensional) *dynamical systems*. Equilibrium occurs where $\dot{h} = \dot{x} = 0$ implying

$$F'(x^*) = \delta$$

$$h^* = F(x^*)$$

where (x^*, h^*) is a steady state equilibrium. Graphically this equilibrium is the intersection of two isoclines $\dot{x} = 0$ and $\dot{h} = 0$ which are drawn in Figure 1.6.

The isoclines divide the positive orthant into four *isosectors* labeled I, II, III, and IV. Each isosector has a *directional* indicating the movement of a point (x, h) over time. For example, a point in isosector I would move in a southwesterly direction under the influence of dynamics which reduce both $x(t)$ and $h(t)$ over time. How did we determine the directionals in isosector I?

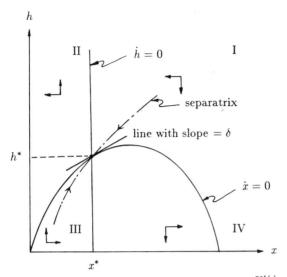

Figure 1.6   Phase plane diagram of the system: $\dot{h} = \dfrac{U'(\cdot)}{U''(\cdot)}[\delta - F'(x)]$ and
$\dot{x} = F(x) - h$ where $\dot{h} = 0$ when $F'(x^*) = \delta$ and $\dot{x} = 0$ when $h = F(x)$.

Along $x = x^*$, $\dot{h} = 0$. If $x > x^*$ the slope of $F(x)$ is less than δ and
$[\delta - F'(\cdot)] > 0$. Noting $U'(\cdot)/U''(\cdot) < 0$ (recall our concavity assumption)
then for $x > x^*$, $\dot{h} < 0$. For points above the $\dot{x} = 0$ isocline $h > F(x)$, thus
$\dot{x} < 0$ and we thus obtain the downward and leftward pointing directional
for isosector I. Similar analysis will permit one to determine the directionals
in the other sectors.

Isosectors I and III are *convergent* isosectors while isosectors II and IV
are *divergent*. The equilibrium (x^*, h^*) would be classified as a *saddle point*.
Isosectors I and III each contain a trajectory which converges to (x^*, h^*) and
is referred to as a *separatrix*. Taken together the two *separatrices* define
the optimal solution trajectories for our infinite horizon problem (since any
other trajectory converges either to $h = 0$ or $x = 0$ as $t \to \infty$).[13] If these
separatrix curves could actually be computed we would have an explicit
optimal harvest policy

$$h^* = h^*(x)$$

specifying the optimal harvest rate corresponding to any given stock level x.
Such a rule is called a *feedback* or *closed-loop control policy*, since h^* is

---

[13] The convergent separatrices are said to form the *stable manifold*. Isosectors II and
IV contain divergent separatrices which form the unstable manifold.

specified as a function of the current state x. A numerical procedure for computing the convergent separatrices will be given in Section 1.6.

In conclusion, let us remark that the situation shown in Figure 1.6 is typical for optimal control problems with a single state variable. With suitable concavity conditions, there exists a unique optimal equilibrium (x^*, h^*), which is a saddle point. The optimal approach to equilibrium follows the separatrix curves which specify a feedback control law.

Many things can go wrong, however, including nonconcavity effects, resulting in the nonexistence of a solution in the classical sense, and multiple equilibria. If the original control problem is time-dependent or if it has two or more state variables, the above phase plane methods do not apply. Normally one must fall back on purely numerical methods, but the subject bristles with difficulties of all kinds (some of the possibilities are discussed, for example, in Clark, 1976).

1.6 Some numerical and graphical techniques

1.6.1 Solution of equations: bisection

In infinite horizon problems we raised the possibility that the solution of the first order conditions might lead to a steady state. When evaluated at steady state the first order conditions reduced to a set of simultaneous equations with the unknowns being the equilibrium state, costate (or Lagrange), and control variables. By elimination, this set of equations might be further reduced to a single equation defining the optimal steady state value for a particular variable [see the discussion of Equation (1.89)].

Sometimes the steady state equation may be explicitly solved by algebra. In other instances it might only be written implicitly as, say, $g(x) = 0$. A steady state value, x^*, is thus a "zero" or root of $g(x)$, i.e., $g(x^*) = 0$. We will discuss two numerical techniques for solving for the zero of an equation. The first technique is interval bisection.

First we must "bracket" the desired solution $x^* \in (x_1, x_2)$ by determining two values x_1 and x_2 for which $g(x_1) < 0$ and $g(x_2) > 0$ (or vice versa). This situation is shown in Figure 1.7.

Define $z = (x_1 + x_2)/2$. Then we may approximate x^* by employing the following simple algorithm:

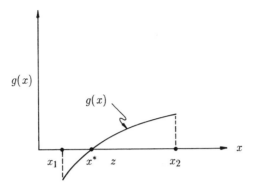

Figure 1.7   Interval bisection.

(a) $z = (x_1 + x_2)/2$

(b) if $|g(z)| \leq \epsilon$, stop (you've found x^* within some preassigned tolerance $\epsilon > 0$)

(c) if $|g(z)| > \epsilon$, then examine $g(z)$

(d) if $g(z) > 0$, redefine $x_2 = z$ otherwise $x_1 = z$ and return to (a).

It is clear from Figure 1.7 that the interval (x_1, x_2) will "zero in" on the solution x^*. The speed of convergence can be estimated by noting that each loop cuts the interval in half. Thus 10 loops will increase the accuracy by $(1/2)^{10} \approx 0.001$, or 3 decimals.

Program 1.2 solves $g(x) = x^3 + x + 1 = 0$. We start by trial and error until we find suitable x_1 and x_2. In our case $x_1 = -1$ and $x_2 = 0$, since $g(-1) = -1$ and $g(0) = +1$. The solution is $x^* = -0.682328$.

The second technique for finding a zero of $g(x)$, called Newton's method, is useful provided the first derivative, $g'(x)$, can be obtained.

1.6.2 Newton's method

If x^* is a zero of $g(x)$ then it is also a "fixed-point" of the function

$$f(x) = x + h(x)g(x) \tag{1.100}$$

in the sense that $f(x^*) = x^*$ since $g(x^*) = 0$. Here $h(x)$ is an arbitrary function. A zero of $g(x)$ may be found as the limit of an iteration sequence $\{x_t\}$ if the initial guess, x_0, is "close" to the zero, and if $f(x)$ is chosen so that $|f'(x^*)| < 1$. Convergence will be most rapid if we define $f(x)$ so that $f'(x^*) = 0$. Taking the derivative of (1.100) and setting it equal to

```
10 REM PROGRAM 1.2: INTERVAL BISECTION
20 EPS = .000001
30 X1 = -1: X2 = 0
40 LPRINT "    Z          G(Z)"
50 LPRINT "--------------------------"
60 Z = .5 * (X1 + X2)
70 G = Z^3 + Z + 1
80 LPRINT Z,G
90 IF G > 0 THEN X2 = Z ELSE X1 = Z
100 IF ABS(G) > EPS THEN GOTO 60
110 END
```

Z	G(Z)
-.5	.375
-.75	-.171875
-.625	.1308594
-.6875	-1.245117E-02
-.65625	6.112671E-02
-.671875	2.482987E-02
-.6796875	6.313801E-03
-.6835938	-3.037453E-03
-.6816406	1.646042E-03
-.6826172	-6.937981E-04
-.682129	4.765988E-04
-.6823731	-1.084805E-04
-.682251	1.841188E-04
-.682312	3.784895E-05
-.6823425	-3.528595E-05
-.6823273	1.311302E-06
-.6823349	-1.692772E-05
-.6823311	-7.867813E-06
-.6823292	-3.33786E-06
-.6823283	-9.536743E-07

Program 1.2   Interval bisection.

zero yields

$$f'(x) = 1 + h'(x)g(x) + h(x)g'(x) = 0 \qquad (1.101)$$

Since $g(x^*) = 0$ we obtain $f'(x^*) = 0$ if

$$h(x^*) = -1/g'(x^*) \qquad (1.102)$$

provided $g'(x^*) \neq 0$. The above result leads to the iteration equation

$$x_{t+1} = f(x_t) = x_t - g(x_t)/g'(x_t) \qquad (1.103)$$

Starting from some x_0 sufficiently close to x^* Equation (1.103) will ultimately lead to an $x_{t+1} \approx x^*$, with $|g(x_{t+1})| < \epsilon$ for any prescribed "tolerance" $\epsilon > 0$ (the tolerance can be included in the iteration program). The Newton method has a simple graphical interpretation. Equation

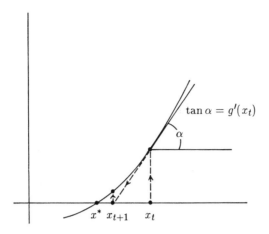

Figure 1.8   Graphical representation of Newton's method.

```
10 REM PROGRAM 1.3: NEWTON'S METHOD
20 LPRINT "   X                 G(X)":LPRINT "
30 X = -.5
40 EPS = .000001
50 G = X^3 + X + 1
60 LPRINT X,G
70 IF ABS(G) < EPS GOTO 110
80 DG = 3 * X^2 + 1
90 X = X - G / DG
100 GOTO 40
110 END
```

X	G(X)
-.5	.375
-.7142858	-7.871723E-02
-.6831798	-2.043366E-03
-.6823284	-1.430512E-06
-.6823278	0

Program 1.3   Newton's method

(1.103) implies

$$g'(x_t) = -g(x_t)/(x_{t+1} - x_t) \qquad (1.104)$$

and the sequence of convergence is shown in Figure 1.8.

As a simple example, let us again solve the equation

$$g(x) = x^3 + x + 1 = 0$$

Recall that $g(0) = 1$ and $g(-1) = -1$ and that from the method of interval bisection we obtained $x^* = -0.682328$. The first derivative is

```
10 REM PROGRAM 1.4: NEWTON'S METHOD
20 LPRINT "   X              G(X)":LPRINT "
30 X=3
40 EPS = .000001
50 G = (X-1) * EXP(-X)
60 LPRINT X,G
70 IF ABS(G) < EPS GOTO 110
80 DG = (2-X) * EXP(-X)
90 X = X - G / DG
100 GOTO 40
110 END
```

X	G(X)
3	9.957415E-02
5	2.695179E-02
6.333334	9.472552E-03
7.564103	3.405081E-03
8.743826	1.234697E-03
9.89211	4.496931E-04
11.01882	1.642118E-04
12.1297	6.006517E-05
13.22842	2.19959E-05
14.31748	8.061595E-06
15.39866	2.956432E-06
16.4733	1.084728E-06
17.54239	3.981398E-07

Program 1.4   Newton's method

$g'(x) = 3x^2 + 1$. The sequence $\{x_t\}$, starting, say, with $x_0 = -0.5$ can be easily obtained from a pocket calculator or a microcomputer. A BASIC program and its output are listed in Program 1.3; note the more rapid convergence to the solution $x^* = -0.682328$.

The speed of Newton's algorithm can be estimated from the fact (which can be proved) that Newton's method improves accuracy by about 2 decimals for each iteration. Thus Newton's method will take about 3 (or 4) steps for 6-figure accuracy, compared to about 20 steps for the bisection algorithm. Which method to use depends primarily on how hard it is to work out the derivative $g'(x)$. In some of the problems given later you'll probably be better off with bisection!

Newton's method can be extended to the solution of simultaneous equations (where it is usually called the Newton–Raphson method). Most computer centers have library routines using this method. The only difficulty will usually be in finding a good first approximation. An indication of what might go wrong is the following attempt to solve $g(x) = (x-1)e^{-x} = 0$ with

$x_0 = 3$, using Program 1.4. The only solution is $x = 1$. What happened? (Make a sketch.)

1.6.3 Eigenvalues

Once a steady state solution to a dynamic optimization model has been identified one would typically want to determine its "local" stability, that is, the dynamic behavior of the system near the steady state equilibrium. For nonlinear plane autonomous systems we could proceed by drawing the isoclines and identifying the directionals in the various isosectors as was done in Figure 1.6 for the nonlinear renewable resource problem posed at the end of the previous section. For numerical problems the local stability can be determined by calculating the characteristic roots or eigenvalues of the "linearized" dynamical system evaluated at steady state. Specifically, suppose the maximum principle, after a certain amount of manipulation, resulted in the following dynamical system for the state variable $x(t)$ and control variable $y(t)$

$$\left.\begin{array}{l} \dot{x} = F(x,y) \\ \dot{y} = G(x,y) \end{array}\right\} \tag{1.105}$$

Let (x^*, y^*) be an equilibrium, so that $F(x^*, y^*) = G(x^*, y^*) = 0$. Then if $F(\cdot)$ and $G(\cdot)$ are smooth we can approximate the system with

$$\begin{aligned} \dot{x} &= F_x(\cdot)(x - x^*) + F_y(\cdot)(y - y^*) + 0[(x - x^*)^2 + (y - y^*)^2] \\ \dot{y} &= G_x(\cdot)(x - x^*) + G_y(\cdot)(y - y^*) + 0[(x - x^*)^2 + (y - y^*)^2] \end{aligned} \tag{1.106}$$

where the partials of $F(\cdot)$ and $G(\cdot)$ are evaluated at (x^*, y^*) and where $0\{\cdot\}$ are terms of order two.

It can be shown that if the linear system obtained by omitting the higher order terms in (1.106) is structurally stable (node, saddle point, or a spiral) then the nonlinear system (1.105) has the same behavior in the neighborhood of (x^*, y^*) (see Birkhoff and Rota, 1969, p. 135, for the proof).

Let $a_{11} = F_x(x^*, y^*)$, $a_{12} = F_y(x^*, y^*)$, $a_{21} = G_x(x^*, y^*)$ and $a_{22} = G_y(x^*, y^*)$. Then the eigenvalues of the matrix

$$A = \begin{pmatrix} a_{11} & a_{12} \\ a_{21} & a_{22} \end{pmatrix} \tag{1.107}$$

are given by the characteristic equation [14]

$$\det[A - RI] = \begin{vmatrix} a_{11} - R & a_{12} \\ a_{21} & a_{22} - R \end{vmatrix}$$
$$= R^2 - (a_{11} + a_{22})R + (a_{11}a_{22} - a_{21}a_{12}) \qquad (1.108)$$
$$= 0$$

implying

$$R_1 = \frac{1}{2}\left(s + \sqrt{s^2 - 4d}\right) \qquad\qquad R_2 = \frac{1}{2}\left(s - \sqrt{s^2 - 4d}\right) \qquad (1.109)$$

where $s = (a_{11} + a_{22})$ and $d = (a_{11}a_{22} - a_{21}a_{12})$. R_1 and R_2 will be real and distinct (when $(s^2 - 4d) > 0$) or complex conjugates (when $(s^2 - 4d) < 0$) and the equilibrium (x^*, y^*) of the nonlinear system (1.105) may be locally classified as

(a) an unstable node if $R_1, R_2 > 0$
(b) a stable node if $R_1, R_2 < 0$
(c) a saddle point if $R_1 < 0 < R_2$ or $R_2 < 0 < R_1$
(d) an unstable spiral if R_1, R_2 are complex with positive real part
(e) a stable spiral if R_1, R_2 are complex with negative real part

Consider the following problem:

$$\text{maximize} \quad \int_0^\infty [20\ln x(t) - 0.10y(t)^2]\, dt$$
$$\text{subject to} \quad \dot{x} = y(t) - 0.10x(t)$$
$$x(0) = 10$$

The Hamiltonian for this problem is

$$\mathcal{H}(\cdot) = 20\ln x(t) - 0.10y(t)^2 + \lambda(t)[y(t) - 0.10x(t)]$$

---

[14] The characteristic equation arises from expansion of the determinant

$$\det(A - RI) = \begin{vmatrix} a_{11} - R & a_{12} \\ a_{21} & a_{22} - R \end{vmatrix} = 0$$

with first order necessary conditions requiring

$$\frac{\partial \mathcal{H}(\cdot)}{\partial y(t)} = -0.20y(t) + \lambda(t) = 0$$

$$\dot{\lambda} = -\frac{\partial \mathcal{H}(\cdot)}{\partial x(t)} = -\frac{20}{x(t)} + 0.10\lambda(t)$$

$$\dot{x} = \frac{\partial \mathcal{H}(\cdot)}{\partial \lambda(t)} = y(t) - 0.10x(t)$$

In steady state $\dot{x} = \dot{\lambda} = 0$, implying

$$\lambda = 0.20y$$

$$0 = -20/x + 0.10\lambda$$

$$y = 0.10x$$

The steady state equations are easily solved yielding $x = 100$, $y = 10$, $\lambda = 2$. What is the character of the equilibrium point? To evaluate the stationary state $(100, 10)$ in (x, y)-space we first solve for an expression for $\dot{y}$. Taking the time derivative of the maximum condition implies $\dot{\lambda} = 0.20\dot{y}$. Substituting into the second condition implies $0.20\dot{y} = -20/x(t) + 0.02y(t)$. Solving for $\dot{y}$ the first order conditions imply:

$$\dot{x} = -0.10x(t) + y(t) = F(x(t), y(t))$$

$$\dot{y} = -100/x(t) + 0.10y(t) = G(x(t), y(t))$$

The isoclines for this system are obtained by setting $\dot{x} = \dot{y} = 0$ implying

$$y = 0.10x \quad \text{when} \quad \dot{x} = 0$$

$$y = 1,000/x \quad \text{when} \quad \dot{y} = 0$$

The isoclines are drawn in the (x, y) phase plane and are shown in Figure 1.9. Note that the isoclines intersect at the steady state $(100, 10)$. The isoclines define four isosectors indicated by roman numerals. The directionals can be verified in a manner similar to that employed in the discussion of Figure 1.6. The linearized matrix is

$$A = \begin{pmatrix} -0.10 & 1 \\ 0.01 & 0.10 \end{pmatrix}$$

which leads to calculations of $s = 0$, $d = -0.02$ and eigenvalues of $R_1 = \sqrt{0.02}$, $R_2 = -\sqrt{0.02}$ confirming our qualitative analysis that $(100, 10)$ is a saddle point.

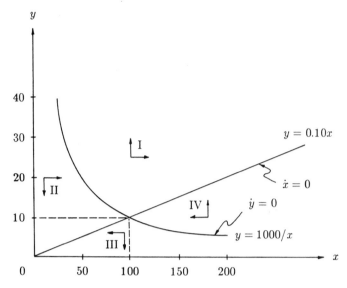

Figure 1.9   A phase plane analysis of the system $\dot{x} = -0.10x(t) + y(t)$, $\dot{y} = -100/x(t) + 0.1y(t)$.

1.6.4 Eigenvectors

Having solved for the eigenvalues of a matrix one can also solve for the associated *eigenvectors*. The eigenvectors are required if one wishes to diagonalize a symmetric matrix. Also, as we shall see, they can be used in solving for the saddle point separatrices in a two-dimensional nonlinear dynamical system.

By definition, R is an eigenvalue of the matrix A if

$$\det(A - RI) = 0$$

This means that the matrix $(A - RI)$ is "singular," i.e., that the linear system of equations

$$(A - RI)X = 0$$

has a nonzero solution vector X. Any such vector is called an *eigenvector* associated with R.

In the previous subsection we worked through an example where

$$A = \begin{pmatrix} -0.10 & 1 \\ 0.01 & 0.10 \end{pmatrix}$$

with eigenvalues $R_1 = \sqrt{0.02}$ and $R_2 = -\sqrt{0.02}$. Thus the eigenvector system for $R = R_1$ is

$$(A - R_1 I)X = \begin{pmatrix} -0.2414 & 1 \\ 0.01 & -0.0414 \end{pmatrix} \begin{pmatrix} x \\ y \end{pmatrix} = \begin{pmatrix} 0 \\ 0 \end{pmatrix}$$

The two rows of the matrix $(A - R_1 I)$ are *linearly dependent*. If x, y satisfy the single equation

$$-0.2414x + y = 0$$

then (x, y) will be an eigenvector. For example

$$V_1 = (x, y) = (1, 0.2414)$$

is one choice; any other eigenvector is a scalar multiple of V_1. By a similar calculation we find that

$$V_2 = (1, 0.0414)$$

is an eigenvector corresponding to the eigenvalue $R_2 = -\sqrt{0.02}$.

The problem of determining the eigenvalues and eigenvectors of a matrix arises in many areas of applied mathematics. Efficient computer algorithms are available for this problem; an excellent textbook is Strang (1980).

1.6.5 Numerical solution of differential equations

Frequently it is not possible to obtain closed form solutions for differential equation systems such as those obtained via the maximum principle. In numerical problems the computer can be used to obtain accurate approximate numerical solutions to such systems. Of the many known algorithms, we will discuss here only the popular Runge–Kutta method.

We consider an initial value problem

$$\frac{dy}{dt} = F(t, y) \qquad t_0 \le t \le t_1$$
$$y(t_0) = y_0 \quad \text{given} \qquad\qquad (1.110)$$

Here $y = (y^1, \ldots, y^N)$ in general denotes a vector of N unknown functions $y^i(t)$. We consider a uniform mesh on the interval $[t_0, t_1]$ given by

$$t_j = t_0 + jh \qquad h = \frac{t_1 - t_0}{n} \qquad j = 0, 1, \ldots, n$$

We wish to obtain approximate values for the solution $y(t)$ at each mesh point t_j. If n is sufficiently large (i.e., h sufficiently small), interpolation of these values will closely approximate the desired solution over $t_0 \leq t \leq t_1$.

The Runge–Kutta algorithm is given by

$$y_0 \quad \text{given}$$

$$y_{j+1} = y_j + \frac{h}{6}(k_{j1} + 2k_{j2} + 2k_{j3} + k_{j4}) \tag{1.111}$$

where

$$
\begin{aligned}
k_{j1} &= F(t_j, y_j) \\
k_{j2} &= F(t_j + h/2, y_j + hk_{j1}/2) \\
k_{j3} &= F(t_j + h/2, y_j + hk_{j2}/2) \\
k_{j4} &= F(t_j + h, y_j + hk_{j3})
\end{aligned}
\tag{1.112}
$$

This algorithm is easily coded for the computer (see Program 1.5).

As a first example, consider the logistic equation

$$\dot{y} = F(y) = ry(1 - y/K) \qquad 0 \leq t \leq 100 \tag{1.113}$$

where now y is one-dimensional. We take

$$y_0 = 10 \quad r = 0.10 \quad K = 200$$

The output of Program 1.5 compares the exact solution (Clark, 1976, p. 11)

$$y(t) = \frac{K}{1 + ce^{-rt}} \quad \text{where} \quad c = 19$$

with the values computed via Runge–Kutta, with $h = 10$ ($n = 10$), and also via the simplistic difference scheme

$$y_{j+1} = y_j + F(y_j)$$

Note that, in spite of the coarse mesh ($h = 10$), even the difference scheme is not bad (maximum relative error of about 6%), while the Runge–Kutta method is quite accurate (maximum error .006%). Of course, the real usefulness of Runge–Kutta (and other numerical methods) comes when no analytic solution is possible.

```
10 REM PROGRAM 1.5: RUNGE-KUTTA EXAMPLE
20 DIM YRK(100),YDIFF(100)
30 DATA 0.10,200,10
40 READ R,K,YRK(0)
50 C = K / YRK(0) - 1
60 YDIFF(0) = YRK(0) - 1
70 LPRINT" T            YEXACT(T)      YRK(T)           YDIFF(T)"
80 LPRINT
90 DEF FN F(X) = R * X * (1-X/K)
100 FOR T = 0 TO 99
110    Y = YRK(T)
120 K1 = FN F(Y)
130    K2 = FN F(Y + K1/2)
140    K3 = FN F(Y + K2/2)
150    K4 = FN F(Y + K3)
160    YRK(T+1) = Y + (K1 + 2*K2 + 2*K3 + K4) / 6
170    Y1 = YDIFF(T)
180    YDIFF(T+1) = Y1 + FN F(Y1)
190 NEXT
200 FOR T = 0 TO 100 STEP 10
210    YEXACT = K / (1 + C * EXP(-R*T))
220    LPRINT T,YEXACT,YRK(T),YDIFF(T)
230 NEXT
240 END
```

T	YEXACT(T)	YRK(T)	YDIFF(T)
0	10	10	9
10	25.0322	25.03219	21.90572
20	56.00091	56.00088	48.9288
30	102.7773	102.7773	92.88643
40	148.3683	148.3682	140.7811
50	177.3017	177.3016	173.8964
60	191.0044	191.0044	189.9599
70	196.5939	196.5939	196.3678
80	198.7333	198.7333	198.7167
90	199.5321	199.5321	199.5505
100	199.8276	199.8276	199.843

Program 1.5   Runge–Kutta example.

As a two-dimensional example, let us consider the classic Lotka–Volterra predator-prey model (Clark, 1976, p. 194):

$$\dot{x} = rx - \alpha xy$$
$$\dot{y} = \beta xy - sy$$

(1.114)

This has an equilibrium at the point

$$\bar{x} = \frac{s}{\beta} \qquad \bar{y} = \frac{r}{\alpha}$$

This point is a center of the corresponding linearized system, and it can

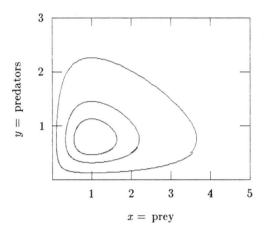

$x =$ prey

Figure 1.10   Lotka–Volterra curves plotted by microcomputer, using the Runge–Kutta method.

be shown that the trajectories of (1.114) consist of closed orbits circling counterclockwise around the equilibrium (Clark, ibid).

Figure 1.10 shows three such orbits computed via the Runge-Kutta scheme (see Program 1.6) using the parameter values

$$r = 1 \qquad s = 1 \qquad \alpha = 2 \qquad \beta = 1$$

(The listed program can be used to plot phase plane trajectories for general systems.)

For further discussion of numerical solution methods, see, e.g., Henrici (1982).

1.6.6 Computation of separatrices

Toward the end of Section 1.5 we posed the nonlinear renewable resource problem

$$\text{maximize} \quad \int_0^\infty U(h(t))e^{-\delta t}\, dt$$
$$\text{subject to} \quad \dot{x} = F(x) - h(t)$$
$$x(0) \quad \text{given}$$

whose analysis led to the phase plane diagram in Figure 1.6. In isosectors I and III of that diagram we identified two separatrices which defined the

```
10 REM PROGRAM 1.6: PHASE PLANE PLOTTER
20 REM   PLOTS PHASE PLANE DIAGRAM FOR THE FOLLOWING FUNCTIONS
30 DEF FN F(X,Y) = X - 2 * X * Y
40 DEF FN G(X,Y) = X * Y - Y
50 INPUT "HORIZONTAL RANGE";X1,X2
60 INPUT "VERTICAL RANGE";Y1,Y2
70 INPUT "HORIZONTAL BLIP SCALE";XB
80 INPUT "VERTICAL BLIP SCALE";YB
90 INPUT "NUMBER OF CURVES (MAX 3)";NCURVES
100 DIM X0(3),Y0(3),TF(3),DT(3)
110 FOR N = 1 TO NCURVES
120    PRINT "STARTING POINT FOR CURVE " N
130    INPUT X0(N),Y0(N)
140    INPUT "TIME LIMIT"; TF(N)
150    INPUT "MESH";DT(N)
160 NEXT
170 '  ***** DRAW WINDOW *****
180 SCREEN 2: CLS: KEY OFF: SCALE = 1.5
190 WINDOW (X1,Y1)-(SCALE*X2,SCALE*Y2)
200 LINE (X1,Y1)-(X2,Y2),,B
210 XL = (X2-X1) * .05: YL = (Y2-Y1) * .05
220 X = X1
230 WHILE X <= X2-XB
240    Y = Y1: X = X + XB: LINE (X,Y)-(X,Y+YL)
250    Y = Y2 - YL: LINE (X,Y)-(X,Y+YL)
260 WEND
270 Y = Y1
280 WHILE Y <= Y2 - YB
290    X = X1: Y = Y + YB: LINE (X,Y)-(X+XL,Y)
300    X = X2 - XL: LINE (X,Y)-(X+XL,Y)
310 WEND
320 '  ***** START GRAPHING *****
330 FOR NC = 1 TO NCURVES
340 N = TF(NC) / DT(NC)
350 X = X0(NC): Y= Y0(NC): H = DT(NC)
360 LINE (X,Y)-(X,Y)
370 FOR I = 1 TO N
380    KX1 = FN F(X,Y)
390    KY1 = FN G(X,Y)
400    XT = X + H * KX1 / 2: YT = T + H * KY1 / 2
410    KX2 = FN F(XT,YT)
420    KY2 = FN G(XT,YT)
430    XT = X + H * KX2 / 2: YT = Y + H * KY2 / 2
440    KX3 = FN F(XT,YT)
450    KY3 = FN G(XT,YT)
460    XT = X + H * KX3: YT = Y + H * DY3
470    KX4 = FN F(XT,YT)
480    KY4 = FN G(XT,YT)
490    X = X + (KX1 + 2 * (KX2 + KX3) + KX4) * H / 6
500    Y = Y + (KY1 + 2 * (KY2 + KY3) + KY4) * H / 6
510    LINE -(X,Y)
520 NEXT I
530 NEXT NC
540 DEF SEG=&HB000
550 BSAVE "PROG1-5.PIC",0,&HB000
560 END
```

Program 1.6   Phase plane plotter

optimal feedback control $h^* = h^*(x)$. A similar result holds for the example at the end of the last section. This subsection discusses how separatrices might be computed and graphed using a microcomputer.

The numerical solution of ordinary differential equations is simple and straightforward. The convergent separatrices, however, pose a slight problem since one does not know, a priori, where they "begin." An efficient approach is first to approximate the separatices in the neighborhood of the equilibrium point (x^*, y^*) by linearizing

$$\dot{x} = F(x) - h(t)$$
$$\dot{h} = \frac{U'(\cdot)}{U''(\cdot)}[\delta - F'(x)] \tag{1.115}$$

about that point.

To be explicit, we first expand the functions on the right side of (1.115) using Taylor's expansion:

$$G(x, h) = G(x^*, h^*) + G_x(x^*, h^*)(x - x^*)$$
$$+ G_h(x^*, h^*)(h - h^*) + \text{smaller order terms}$$

After a simple calculation, we obtain the linearized system (with $\xi = x - x^*$, $\eta = h - h^*$):

$$\left. \begin{array}{l} \dot{\xi} = \delta\xi - \eta \\ \dot{\eta} = c\xi \end{array} \right\} \tag{1.116}$$

where $c = -U'(h^*)F''(x^*)/U''(h^*) < 0$.

The linear system can be solved by elementary methods. First, the eigenvalues R are the solutions of

$$\det \begin{pmatrix} \delta - R & -1 \\ c & -R \end{pmatrix} = R^2 - \delta R + c = 0$$

so that

$$R_1 = \frac{1}{2}(\delta + \sqrt{\delta^2 - 4c}) \quad R_2 = \frac{1}{2}(\delta - \sqrt{\delta^2 - 4c})$$

Since $c < 0$, these eigenvalues are real and of opposite sign.[15] Hence (as we already know), the equilibrium point is a saddle point.

---

[15] It is of interest to note here that if $c > 0$ (as could happen if either U or F failed to be concave), then not only does the saddle point geometry disappear, but in fact the maximum principle does not work! Indeed, no optimal control even exists under these conditions.

Let V_1, V_2 denote the eigenvectors corresponding to R_1, R_2, respectively. The general solution of the linear system (1.116) is then

$$\begin{pmatrix} \xi \\ n \end{pmatrix} = aV_1 e^{R_1 t} + bV_2 e^{R_2 t} \qquad (a, b \text{ constant})$$

Since $R_2 < 0 < R_1$, the only trajectories which converge to the origin as $t \to +\infty$ are those for which $a = 0$. Thus the eigenvectors $\pm V_2$ determine the directions of the convergent separatrices. (A numerical example is worked out below.)

Returning now to the (x, h)-plane, we have shown that the eigenvectors $\pm V_2$ (with $R_2 < 0$) determine the directions along which the separatrices approach the equilibrium (x^*, h^*). The actual (curved) separatrices themselves may now be computed by numerical integration of the system (1.115). The best way to do this is to start with a point (x_0, h_0) near (x^*, h^*) and on the linearized separatrix found above; then solve (1.115) with time reversed (i.e., change the signs of the right sides).

Example. Assume that

$$F(x) = x(1 - x)$$
$$U(h) = h(1 - h)$$
$$\delta = 0.1$$

Then $F'(x) = 1 - 2x$, so that $\delta - F'(x^*) = 0$ implies $x^* = 0.45$ and $h^* = F(x^*) = 0.248$. [For the monopolist price $= p(h) = U(h)/h$ we have $p(0) = 1$ and $p(h^*) = 0.752$, i.e., the price at optimal sustained yield is only 75% of the choke-off price $p(0)$.]

The plane system (1.115) is

$$\dot{x} = x(1 - x) - h$$
$$\dot{h} = -(1 - 2h)(x - 1.45)$$

and the linearized version is

$$\dot{\xi} = 0.1\xi - \eta$$
$$\dot{\eta} = -0.504\xi$$

The eigenvalues of the matrix

$$\begin{pmatrix} 0.1 & -1 \\ -0.504 & 0 \end{pmatrix}$$

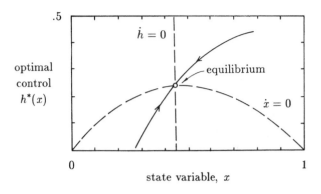

.5

$\dot{h} = 0$

optimal
control
$h^*(x)$

equilibrium

$\dot{x} = 0$

0   1

state variable, x

Figure 1.11   Convergent separatrices, defining optimal feedback policy $h^* = h^*(x)$, as obtained by numerical computation. The point (x^*, h^*) moves along the separatrix, from (x_0, h_0) to (x^*, h^*) as $t \to +\infty$.

are the solutions of the equation $R^2 - 0.1R - 0.504 = 0$, which are

$$R_1 = 0.762 \quad \text{and} \quad R_2 = -0.662$$

with corresponding eigenvectors

$$V_1 = (1, -0.662) \quad \text{and} \quad V_2 = (1, 0.762)$$

Thus the convergent separatrices have slope 0.762 at the equilibrium point (x^*, h^*). The resulting nonlinear separatrices (shown in Figure 1.11) were calculated in a few seconds using the Runge–Kutta algorithm.

1.7 Problems

P1.7.1. Consider the competitive (price-taking) firm which seeks to maximize profits subject to the following multiple-output production function:

$$\phi(Y_1, Y_2; X_1, X_2) \equiv 2Y_1^2 + Y_2^2 - 100X_1^{0.25}X_2^{0.75} \equiv 0$$

If $P_1 = 5$ is the per unit price for output Y_1, $P_2 = 10$ is the per unit price for output Y_2, $R_1 = 1$ is the per unit cost for input X_1, and $R_2 = 2$ is the per unit cost for input X_2, solve for the optimal values of Y_1, Y_2, X_1, and X_2. Note: Profit may be written as:

$$\pi = \sum_{i=1}^{2} P_i Y_i - \sum_{j=1}^{2} R_j X_j$$

Answer. $Y_1 = 42.37$, $Y_2 = 169.49$, $X_1 = 238.44$, $X_2 = 357.66$, $\lambda = 0.0295$.

P1.7.2. You have been appointed manager of a project with the objective of bringing 1,000 hectares under irrigation within 10 years $(t = 0, 1, \ldots, 9)$. At the present time there is no irrigated land in the project area. Let X_t represent the number of irrigated hectares in year t. Thus,

$$X_{t+1} = X_t + U_t$$

where U_t is the number of additional hectares irrigated in year t, and $X_0 = 0$, $X_{10} = 1,000$ are given.

You are asked to *minimize* the present value of project costs where you have determined that

$$C_t = cU_t^2 \qquad c = \text{constant}$$

is the cost of irrigating U_t additional hectares in period t. You are told that $c = 1$ and $\rho = 1/(1 + \delta)$, where $\delta = 0.10$, is the appropriate discount factor. Solve for the optimal time path for incremental and cumulative hectares under irrigation. Explain.

Answer

t	0	1	2	3	4	5	6	7	8	9	10
U_t	62.75	69.02	75.92	83.51	91.87	101.05	111.16	122.27	134.50	147.95	–
X_t	0	62.75	131.77	207.69	291.20	383.07	484.12	595.28	717.55	852.05	1000

Discounting implies that irrigation costs should be delayed to future periods, so the amount of irrigation increases with t. Also marginal costs discounted to $t = 0$ are all equal.

P1.7.3. Consider the following problem

$$\text{maximize} \quad J = \int_0^1 \{10q(t) - 0.01q(t)^2\}e^{-0.20t}\,dt$$

$$\text{subject to} \quad \dot{X}(t) = -q(t)$$

$$X(0) = 1 \qquad X(1) = 0$$

Solve for the optimal time path $X^*(t)$.

Answer. $X^*(t) = 2253.8e^{0.2t} - 500t - 2252.8$

P1.7.4. Consider the continuous-time version of the irrigation problem (Problem 1.7.2) which might be stated

$$\text{minimize} \quad C = \int_0^{10} U(t)^2 e^{-0.10t}\,dt$$

$$\text{subject to} \quad \dot{X}(t) = U(t)$$

$$X(0) = 0 \qquad X(10) = 1{,}000$$

Solve for the equation defining the optimal time path $X^*(t)$. Compare the values of $X^*(t)$ and X_t^* at $t = 3, 5, 7, 9$. Why is there a slight difference?

Answer. $X(t) = 581.98 \left(e^{0.10t} - 1\right)$

t	3	5	7	9
$X(t)$	203.61	377.54	589.98	849.46
X_t	207.69	383.07	595.28	852.05

Continuous discounting at 0.10 results in an *effective* annual discount rate that is greater than an annual discount rate of 0.10. If i is the annual (discrete-time) discount rate and δ is to be the corresponding continuous (or instantaneous) discount rate, then $\delta = \ln(1 + i)$. An $i = 0.10$ in Problem 1.7.2 would correspond to a $\delta = 0.0953$ in this problem. By solving the problem for $\delta = 0.10$ you have increased the effective discount rate and it is optimal to postpone some irrigation until just prior to $t = 10$. (If you solve it for $\delta = 0.0953$ you will get the same results as in Problem 1.7.2.)

P1.7.5. The rate at which natural gas is pumped from a deposit is given by

$$\dot{X} = -aXE$$

where $X(t)$ = amount of gas remaining in the deposit (million cu. ft.— MCF), $E(t)$ = input of pumping energy (kilowatts), and a = constant.

Let p denote the well-head price of gas and let $c(E)$ denote the cost of pumping. Given $a = .01$ /kw year, find the energy input $E(t)$ that

$$\text{maximizes} \quad J = \int_0^1 [paX(t)E(t) - c(E(t))]\, dt$$

$$\text{subject to} \quad \dot{X} = -aXE$$

$$X(0) = 1{,}000 \qquad x(1) = 500$$

(First use the maximum principle to show that $\dot{E} \equiv 0$.)

Given $p = \$2{,}000$ /MCF and $c(E) = 100E^2$ ($/yr), calculate the maximized profit objective J^*. Also determine explicitly the shadow price $\lambda(t)$. Why does $\lambda(t)$ decrease?

Answer. $E^* = 69.3$ kw, $J^* = \$520{,}000$, $\lambda(t) = \$(2{,}000 - 1{,}386e^{0.693t})$.

The shadow price represents the marginal value of gas in the deposit, and this decreases as the deposit is exploited.

(This example can be generalized to cover other aspects of exhaustible resource economics—see Chapter 3.)

P1.7.6. Assume the dynamics of two competing species may be characterized by the following dynamical system:

$$\dot{X}(t) = rX(t)(1 - X(t)/K) - \alpha X(t)Y(t)$$

$$\dot{Y}(t) = sY(t)(1 - Y(t)/L) - \beta X(t)Y(t)$$

Draw the isoclines, determine the directionals in each isosector and calculate the characteristic roots at the equilibrium when

(a) $r = 0.8$, $K = 200$, $\alpha = 0.002$
    $s = 0.5$, $L = 100$, $\beta = 0.001$
(b) As in part (a) except $\alpha = 0.02$, $\beta = 0.01$
(c) As in part (a) except $\beta = 0.01$

Answer

(a) Equilibrium at $X = 166.67$, $Y = 66.67$. Characteristic roots are $R_1 = -0.28$, $R_2 = -0.72$. The equilibrium is a stable node.

(b) There are actually *three* equilibria in this case
  (i) At $X = 33.33$, $Y = 33.33$ we obtain $R_1 = 0.32$, $R_2 = -0.62$, a saddle point.
  (ii) At $X = 200$, $Y = 0$ we obtain $R_1 = -0.80$, $R_2 = -1.5$, a stable node, and
  (iii) At $X = 0$, $Y = 100$ we obtain $R_1 = -0.50$, $R_2 = -1.2$, also a stable node.
  Whether you end up at $(33.33, 33.33)$, $(200,0)$ or $(0,100)$ depends on the initial conditions $(X(0), Y(0))$.

(c) Equilibrium at $X = 200$, $Y = 0$, same analysis as (b) (ii) above.

P1.7.7. Consider the following problem

$$\text{maximize} \quad \sum_{t=0}^{\infty} \rho^t Y_t$$

$$\text{subject to} \quad X_{t+1} = 100 X_t (1 + 0.18 X_t)^{-1} - Y_t$$

$$X_0 = 550 \qquad 0 \leq Y_t \leq 453$$

For $\rho = 1/(1 + \delta)$, $\delta = 0.10$ determine
  (a) the steady state optimum (X^*, Y^*), and
  (b) the optimal approach paths $\{Y_t^*\}, \{X_t^*\}$.
  Compare this to the MSY solution. Why are the two so close?

Answer

(a) $X^* = 47.41$, $Y^* = 449.87$
(b) MRAP is optimal. Since $X_0 > X^*$ and $Y_t = Y_{\max}$ reduces X_{t+1} as rapidly as possible we set $Y_t = 453$ for $t = 0, 1, \ldots, 6$ resulting in

t	1	2	3	4	5	6	7
X_t	97	72.46	62.99	57.53	53.63	50.41	47.41

The MSY solution is $X^* = 50$, $Y^* = 450$. This is close to the discounted case because the intrinsic growth rate $G'(0) - 1 = 99 >> \delta$.

P1.7.8. Use dynamic programming to solve the following problem for $T = 0, 1, 2$, and 3.

$$\text{maximize} \quad \sum_{t=0}^{T} \rho^t Y_t$$

$$\text{subject to} \quad X_{t+1} = G(X_t - Y_t) \quad t = 0, 1, \ldots, T - 1$$

$$0 \leq Y_t \leq X_t$$

$$\text{given} \quad \rho = 1/(1 + \delta), \qquad \delta = 0.1 \qquad X_0 = 1000$$

$$\text{and} \quad G(S) = \frac{2S}{1 + .001S}$$

If $J_n(X_0) = \max \sum_{t=0}^{n} \rho^t Y_t$ given X_0, show that

$$J_{n+1}(X_0) = X_0 + \max_{0 \leq S \leq X_0} [\rho G(S) - S]$$

Answer

(a) $T = 0$: $S_0^* = 0$, $Y_0^* = 1,000$, $J_0 = 1,000$

(b) $T = 1$: $S_0^* = 348.4$, $S_1^* = 0$, $Y_0^* = 651.6$ $Y_1^* = 516.76$, $J_1 = 1,121.38$

(c) $T = 2$: $S_0^* = S_1^* = 348.4$, $S_2^* = 0$, $Y_0^* = 651.6$, $Y_1^* = 168.36$, $Y_2^* = 516.76$, $J_2 = 1,231.73$.

(d) $T = 3$: $S_0^* = S_1^* = S_2^* = 348.4$, $S_3^* = 0$, $Y_0^* = 651.6$, $Y_1^* = Y_2^* = 168.36$, $Y_3^* = 516.76$, $J_3 = 1,332.04$

P1.7.9. What is the value of $J_\infty(X_0)$, $X_0 = 1,000$, for the preceding problem?

Answer. $J_\infty = 651.6 + 168.36(\rho + \rho^2 + \cdots) = 2,335.20$.

Chapter 2

Renewable resources

2.1 Growth functions

By a renewable resource we will mean a plant or animal population with the capacity for reproduction and growth [1] or an inanimate mass or energy source subject to constant or periodic flux. Grass, trees, fish, and game populations would be examples of the first type of renewable resource. Water (surface or groundwater), wind, and solar radiation would be examples of the latter type.

In building a model of a resource it is necessary to define a variable or variables which adequately describe the state of the resource at any point in time. Such variables were called state variables in the preceding chapter. For renewable resources they often describe a "standing stock," frequently the number of individuals in a population or the "biomass" of the population. If the age structure, sex ratio, or other population characteristics are important the model will require more than one state variable. While such models allow for greater biological detail and realism they typically become less tractable mathematically. For simplicity we will assume that the resource under consideration can be described by a single state variable.

Let us begin by considering the case of a biological resource stock, whose size at time t is denoted by X_t, or in continuous time, $X(t)$. In the absence of harvesting, the dynamics of the resource stock might be described by the difference equation

$$X_{t+1} - X_t = F(X_t) \qquad (2.1)$$

or by the differential equation

$$dX(t)/dt = \dot{X} = F\Big(X(t)\Big) \qquad (2.2)$$

The above equations assume that the change in the resource is dependent on the current stock size (X_t or $X(t)$); such growth is said to be *density-dependent*.

---

[1] Growth or flux is assumed to take place at a "significant" rate when viewed from man's economic time scale. If redwood trees regenerate, but at an insignificant rate, they might be regarded as a *non*renewable resource.

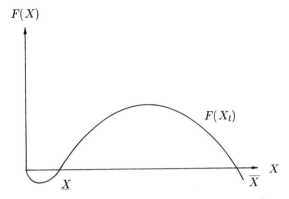

Figure 2.1 A growth function $X_{t+1} - X_t = F(X_t)$ or $\dot{X} = F(x(t))$.

The growth function $F(\cdot)$ is defined over the interval $X \geq 0$ and it is usually assumed that there exist two values $\underline{X} < \bar{X}$ for which

$$F(X) \leq 0 \qquad \text{if} \quad 0 \leq X \leq \underline{X}$$
$$F(X) > 0 \qquad \text{if} \quad \underline{X} < X < \bar{X} \qquad (2.3)$$
$$F(X) < 0 \qquad \text{if} \quad \bar{X} \leq X$$

A function exhibiting the properties in (2.3) is shown in Figure 2.1.

If $\underline{X} = 0$ and $F(\cdot)$ is strictly concave from below the growth function is said to be *purely compensatory*. For such a growth function, the relative growth rate $r(X) = F(X)/X$ is a decreasing function of X. If $\underline{X} = 0$ and $F(\cdot)$ is initially convex then concave (thus it has an inflection point), the growth function is said to be *depensatory*. If $\underline{X} > 0$ and $F(\cdot)$ is initially convex then concave (such as $F(X)$ in Figure 2.1) then the growth function exhibits *critical depensation*, and $\underline{X}$ is called the *minimum viable population*.[2] Whether a growth function is purely compensatory or exhibits depensation will be important in understanding the relationship between yield and effort (to be discussed shortly).

There are many possible functional specifications for $F(\cdot)$. One of the simplest and best known is the logistic model, which when written as a differential equation takes the form

$$\dot{X} = F(X(t)) = rX(t)(1 - X(t)/K) \qquad (2.4)$$

where r is called the intrinsic growth rate and K is the environmental

---

[2] Observe that by Equation (2.1) or (2.2) X_t or $X(t)$ approaches zero as $t \to \infty$ if $X_0 < \underline{X}$ in the case of critical depensation.

carrying capacity. As specified in (2.4) the logistic equation is purely compensatory ($\underline{X} = 0$, $F(\cdot)$ strictly concave) and $\bar{X} = K$ is a globally stable
equilibrium; that is, $X(t) \to K$ from any $X(0) > 0$ as $t \to \infty$. One can
solve (2.4) explicitly by the method of separation of variables, to obtain

$$X(t) = \frac{K}{(1 + ce^{-rt})}$$

where $c = \big(K - X(0)\big)/X(0)$ (we encountered the logistic equation previously in Section 1.6.5).

One might expect the discrete-time analogue

$$X_{t+1} - X_t = rX_t(1 - K/X_t) \tag{2.5}$$

to exhibit the same properties as (2.4). It is known, however, that nonlinear
difference equations are capable of producing much more complex behavior
(see May, 1975). Specifically:

(a) If $0 < r \leq 1$, the population steadily approaches K without
    overshooting it (e.g., Figure 2.2(a)),

(b) If $1 < r \leq 2$, the population overshoots but undergoes damped
    oscillations as it approaches K (e.g., Figure 2.2(b)),

(c) If $2 < r \leq 2.449$, then the population settles down to a two-
    point cycle (e.g., Figure 2.2(c)),

(d) If $2.449 < r \leq 2.570$, the population achieves a stable cycle
    with 2^n points, $n \geq 1$; the value of n depending on r (e.g.,
    Figure 2.2(d)), and

(e) If $r > 2.570$, the population size varies in a wholly irregu-
    lar, nonperiodic manner with different outcomes resulting from
    different values of X_0. This behavior, which has been much
    studied by mathematicians, is referred to as dynamic "chaos"
    (Figure 2.2(e) and 2.2(f)).

2.2 Production and yield functions

When a renewable resource is harvested it is usually assumed that the rate of
harvest (or yield) per unit time is a function of the economic inputs devoted
to harvesting, and of the available stock. Suppose a suitable aggregate
measure for the various economic inputs can be found, that it is referred to

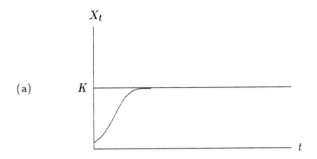

(a)

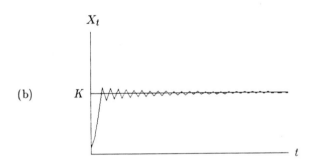

(b)

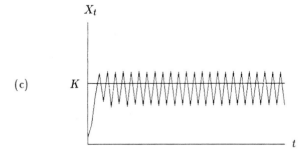

(c)

(continued)

(d)

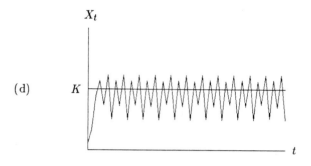

(e)

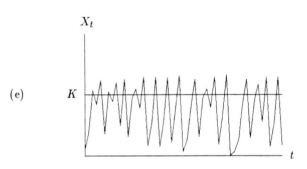

(f)

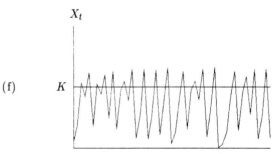

Figure 2.2   Simulation of discrete-time logistic model: (a) $r = 0.2$; (b) $r = 1.99$;
(c) $r = 2.2$; (d) $r = 2.5$; (e) $r = 2.7$; (f) $R = 3.0$.

as "effort" [3] and denoted by $E(t)$. The production function may be written explicitly as

$$Y(t) = H(E(t), X(t)) \tag{2.6}$$

where $Y(t)$ is the rate of harvest, measured in the same units as the resource stock $X(t)$.

A production function commonly used in fishery management is:

$$Y(t) = qE(t)X(t) \tag{2.7}$$

where $q = $ constant. This function is derived from two assumptions, namely (see Clark, 1985, Chap. 2)

(a) catch per unit effort (Y/E) is directly proportional to the density of fish in the sea, and

(b) the density of fish is directly proportional to the abundance $X(t)$.

If these assumptions are thought to be unrealistic, a more general form of production function may be preferable, such as

$$Y(t) = qE(t)^\alpha X(t)^\beta \tag{2.8}$$

The discrete-time analog of Equation (2.7) is

$$Y_t = X_t[1 - e^{-qE_t}] \tag{2.9}$$

where now E_t denotes total effort exerted during the period t. (A generalization of this equation is discussed in Problem 2.1.)

With harvesting, the rate of change in the resource stock must reflect growth *and* harvest, and Equations (2.1) and (2.2) are modified to become

$$X_{t+1} - X_t = F(X_t) - Y_t \tag{2.10}$$

and

$$\dot{X} = F(X(t)) - Y(t) \tag{2.11}$$

respectively.

The (sustained) *yield function* is an equilibrium concept expressing sustainable harvest (yield) as a function of effort. By sustained yield, we mean

---

[3] For example, in the case of commercial fisheries, annual fishing effort is often measured as the number of vessel days devoted to fishing during the particular year.

that X, Y, and E all remain constant over time. Hence for the continuous-time model we have, by Equations (2.11) and (2.6)

$$\left.\begin{array}{l} \dot{X} = F(X) - Y = 0 \\ Y = H(E, X) \end{array}\right\} \tag{2.12}$$

Eliminating X from these equations, we obtain the *sustained-yield function*

$$Y = Y(E) \tag{2.13}$$

Example. Assume that[4]

$$F(X) = rX(1 - X/K)$$
$$H(E, X) = qEX$$

Then (2.12) implies

$$Y = rX(1 - X/K) = qEX$$

Solving for X, we get

$$X = K\left(1 - \frac{qE}{r}\right)$$

Hence

$$Y = qEX = qKE\left(1 - \frac{qE}{r}\right) \tag{2.14}$$

This is the sustained-yield (or yield-effort) function for the Schaefer model; note that it is parabolic (Figure 2.3) and that for sufficiently high effort $(E > r/q)$ the yield is zero! If the relative rate of harvest (qE) exceeds the intrinsic growth rate of the population (r), then the population will be driven to extinction, and yield will become zero.[5]

Other functional forms for the growth function $F(X)$ and the harvest production function[6] $H(X, E)$ will, of course, give rise to other forms for the yield function $Y(E)$. For example, the Gompertz function takes the form

$$F(X(t)) = rX(t)\ln(K/X(t)) \tag{2.15}$$

---

[4] This particular model is called the Schaefer model, after the biologist, M.B. Schaefer, who first developed it for use in the Pacific tuna fisheries (Schaefer 1954).

[5] But note from Equation (2.11) that this would only occur asymptotically as $t \to \infty$.

[6] Fisheries biologists usually refer to $F(X)$ as the (natural) production function of the fish stock, and to $H(X, E)$ as the catch relationship. We will, however, retain the terminology used here, which is more familiar to economists.

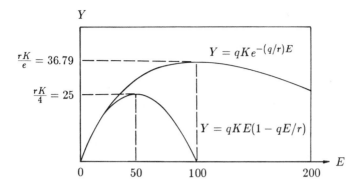

Figure 2.3   Yield functions derived from the logistic and Gompertz growth functions and the production function $Y = qEX$, where $q = 0.005$, $r = 0.500$, and $K = 200$. For the logistic-based function $Y_{\max} = rK/4$ at $E = r/2q$ declining to $Y = 0$ at $E = r/q$. For the Gompertz-based function $Y_{\max} = rK/e$ at $E = r/q$; as $E \to \infty$, $Y \to 0$.

Assuming the same production function (2.7), steady state equilibrium requires $Y = r\ln(K/X) = qEX$ and the sustained yield function becomes

$$Y = qKEe^{-(q/r)E} \qquad (2.16)$$

A plot of the two yield functions based on logistic and Gompertz growth functions is shown in Figure 2.3 for $q = 0.005$, $r = 0.5$, $K = 200$. (Question: why is it that the Gompertz relation requires $E \to \infty$ to obtain $Y = 0$?)

Fisheries data often consist of a time series of annual catches Y_t and effort levels E_t. These data can be used to obtain a crude estimate of the sustained yield curve. Note that the Schaefer and Gompertz yield curves of Equations (2.14) and (2.16) can be written in the forms

$$\frac{Y}{E} = qK - \frac{q^2 K}{r}E = a - bE \qquad (2.17)$$

and

$$\frac{Y}{E} = qKe^{-qE/r} = ae^{-bE} \qquad (2.18)$$

respectively. Thus the coefficients a, b of the Schaefer curve can be estimated by means of a linear regression of Y_t/E_t against E_t. Similarly, the coefficients for the Gompertz model can be obtained by regression of $\log(Y_t/E_t)$ vs. E_t. (In practice, these regressions perform poorly, in part because the equilibrium assumptions underlying the derivation of Equations

(2.17) and (2.18) are usually far from satisfied. Better estimation procedures
have been designed, but they are outside the scope of these notes.)

Only the two coefficients a, b are estimated from the regression approach, whereas three coefficients are needed for the original models. This
may not be a disadvantage if one is willing to accept the sustained yield
curves as a full description of the fishery, but all three coefficients are required for a dynamic, economic analysis. In these notes we will ignore the
technicalities of parameter estimation (which are a major part of fisheries
science), and assume that acceptable parameter estimates are available.
Similarly, we assume that appropriate function forms for $F(\cdot)$ and $H(\cdot)$
have been determined.

2.3 Objectives of management

A common objective of renewable resource management has been to maintain standing stock $X(t) \equiv X$ so as to afford a maximum sustainable
yield ("MSY"). Mathematically, in terms of the continuous-time model
(2.11), one seeks to maximize sustained yield $Y = F(X)$, which requires
$F'(X) = 0$. For the logistic growth function (Equation (2.4)), $F'(X) = 0$
at $X_{MSY} = K/2$ and $Y_{MSY} = rK/4$. For the Gompertz growth function
(Equation (2.15)) $F'(X) = 0$ at $X_{MSY} = K/e$ and $Y_{MSY} = rK/e$.

Alternatively, one can maximize the yield function $Y = Y(E)$ with
respect to E. It is easy to see that this gives the same results as before.

For many years MSY has been accepted as the proper objective for
management of forestry, fisheries, wildlife, and similar resources. In recent
years, however, maximum sustained yield policies have been criticized on a
number of grounds, including the following:

(1) MSY is unstable: if Y is set equal to MSY in Equation (2.16),
    then the resulting equilibrium becomes unstable; the slightest
    overestimate of MSY can lead to depletion or extinction of the
    resource stock.
(2) MSY is not actually sustainable over the long run, because of
    natural fluctuations in the resource stock. If MSY is allowed
    to be harvested in years when X is at a naturally low level,
    the resource may be seriously depleted.
(3) MSY does not make logical sense when two or more inter-
    dependent species are being harvested.

(4) MSY completely ignores all social and economic considerations of renewable resource management.

(5) MSY also ignores nonmarket "preservation" values derived from nonconsumptive uses of the resource stock.

Economists tend to view a renewable resource as simply a type of capital asset which should be managed so as to maximize its value to society. Biological considerations, in the form of growth equations, become constraints to a dynamic optimization problem. We will start out with a very general economic model, and then look at two special cases: (1) when per unit prices for the (harvested) resource and effort are constant, and (2) when the quantity harvested affects price per unit. We will also adopt the particular production function of Equation (2.7).

In its most general statement, we assume that society obtains net benefits from the resource which depend upon the harvest $Y(t)$ and the stock (or population) itself $X(t)$. Mathematically this may be expressed as

$$U(t) = U(Y(t), X(t)) \qquad (2.19)$$

where $U(t)$ is the flow of net social benefits (or utility) at instant t. The resource stock might appear as an argument of $U(\cdot)$ for a purely commercial reason: a larger stock may lower the cost of a given level of harvest. On the other hand, the dependence of $U(\cdot)$ on $X(t)$ may reflect preservation value for the stock X.

If discounting at some rate $\delta > 0$ is appropriate then maximization of the present value of net benefits involves solving for the time paths $Y(t)$ and $X(t)$ which

$$\text{maximize} \int_0^T U(Y(t), X(t)) e^{-\delta t} \, dt \qquad (2.20)$$

where in the infinite time horizon problem $T \to \infty$. The discrete-time analog when the discount factor is $\rho = 1/(1 + \delta)$ is

$$\text{maximize} \sum_{t=0}^{T} \rho^t U(Y_t, X_t) \qquad (2.21)$$

We now specify the net benefit function $U(\cdot)$ for two special cases.

2.3.1 Constant prices

Let p denote the per unit price for the resource after harvest and c the per unit cost of effort. With no preservation value, net benefits are equivalent to *net revenues*. Gross revenue will simply equal the per unit price times the rate of harvest, thus $R(t) = pY(t)$. Total cost is $C(t) = cE(t)$, that is, the per unit cost of effort times the amount of effort employed in harvesting the resource at instant t. Using the harvest production function (2.6), i.e., $Y = H(X, E)$, we can then express net benefits as

$$U(X, E) = pY - cE$$
$$= pH(X, E) - cE$$

Our optimization problem, therefore, becomes

$$\text{maximize} \int_0^T \{pH(X(t), E(t)) - cE(t)\} e^{-\delta t} \, dt \qquad (2.22)$$

$$\text{subject to} \quad \dot{X} = F(X(t)) - H(X(t), E(t)), \qquad X(0) = X_0 \qquad (2.23)$$

The discrete-time analog is

$$\text{maximize} \sum_{t=0}^T \rho^t \{pH(X_t, E_t) - cE_t\} \qquad (2.24)$$

$$\text{subject to} \quad X_{t+1} - X_t = F(X_t) - H(X_t, E_t) \qquad X_0 \quad \text{given} \qquad (2.25)$$

[Note that we have here expressed net benefits $U(\cdot)$ as a function of X and E, rather than as a function of X and Y as in Equation (2.19). Either formulation can be transformed into the other by substitution from the relationship $Y = H(X, E)$. Which form is used is simply a matter of convenience.]

2.3.2 Downward sloping demand

Suppose next that the price received per unit of harvest is no longer constant but varies according to the inverse demand curve $p(t) = D(Y(t))$ where $D'(\cdot) < 0$. If we assume that $D(\cdot)$ is a reasonable approximation to the income compensated demand curve, then the social benefit associated with harvest $Y(t)$ is the area under the demand curve from zero to $Y(t)$. This

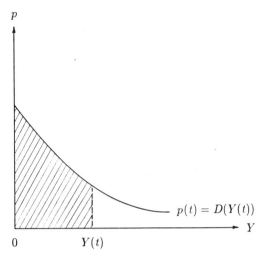

Figure 2.4   Benefit from harvest of $Y(t)$ when $p(t) = D(Y(t))$.

is shown graphically in Figure 2.4 and may be calculated according to

$$B(Y(t)) = \int_0^{Y(t)} D(s)\,ds \qquad (2.26)$$

If the cost per unit of effort remains constant at c and the production function is linear in effort, the net social benefit from harvest may be written as $N(t) = B(H(X(t), E(t))) - cE(t)$ and the maximization of the present value of net benefits seeks to

$$\text{maximize} \int_0^T \{B(H(X(t), E(t))) - cE(t)\}e^{-\delta t}\,dt \qquad (2.27)$$

For completeness the discrete-time analog is given as

$$\text{maximize} \sum_{t=0} \rho^t \{B(H(X_t, E_t)) - cE_t\} \qquad (2.28)$$

2.4 Optimal steady state and approach dynamics

Starting with the most general case, consider a problem comprised of objective (2.20) and a constraint in the form of Equation (2.11). This problem may be restated as

$$\text{maximize} \quad \int_0^T U(X(t), Y(t)) e^{-\delta t} \, dt$$

$$\text{subject to} \quad \dot{X} = F(X(t)) - Y(t) \tag{2.29}$$

$$X(0) \quad \text{given}$$

The current-value Hamiltonian for this problem is

$$\tilde{\mathcal{H}}(X, Y; \mu) = U(X, Y) + \mu[F(X) - Y] \tag{2.30}$$

and the necessary conditions of the maximum principle are:

(a) $Y(t)$ maximizes $\tilde{\mathcal{H}}(X, Y; \mu)$ for all t $\qquad$ (2.31)

(b) $\dot{\mu} = \delta\mu - \tilde{\mathcal{H}}_X = \delta\mu - U_X - \mu F_X$ $\qquad$ (2.32)

We will now apply these conditions to the two special cases under consideration.

2.4.1 Constant prices

In the case where prices are constant, we have

$$U(X, Y) = pY - cE$$

$$Y = qXE$$

or, therefore,

$$U(X, Y) = pY - \frac{cY}{qX} \tag{2.33}$$

Substituting into Equation (2.30), we obtain

$$\tilde{\mathcal{H}}(X, Y; \mu) = (p - \frac{c}{qX} - \mu)Y + \mu F(X) \tag{2.34}$$

Now consider condition (2.31): $Y \geq 0$ must be chosen to maximize $\tilde{\mathcal{H}}(X, Y; \mu)$. Obviously this implies that

$$Y(t) = \begin{cases} 0 & \text{if } \mu(t) > p - \frac{c}{qX(t)} \\ Y_{\max} & \text{if } \mu(t) < p - \frac{c}{qX(t)} \end{cases} \tag{2.35}$$

(where $Y_{\max}$ denotes some maximum feasible harvest rate). Recall that the function $\sigma(t) = \mu(t) - (p - \frac{c}{qX(t)})$ is called the "switching function" (see Section 1.4).

While condition (2.35) makes good economic sense (harvest the resource only if the net revenue per unit harvest, i.e., $p - c/qX(t)$, exceeds the shadow price $\mu(t)$), it is not an operational decision rule unless we can compute $\mu(t)$.

Note also that (2.35) does not say what to do in the event that

$$\mu(t) = p - \frac{c}{qX(t)} \qquad (2.36)$$

This in fact turns out to be the most important case. Assume that (2.36) holds for t in some interval. Then by differentiation we have

$$\dot{\mu} = \frac{c}{qX^2}\dot{X} = \frac{c}{qX^2}(F(X) - Y) \qquad (2.37)$$

But we also have the adjoint Equation (2.32):

$$
\begin{aligned}
\dot{\mu} &= \delta\mu - \tilde{\mathscr{H}}_X = \delta\mu - \frac{c}{qX^2}Y - \mu F'(X) \\
&= -\frac{c}{qX^2}Y + (p - \frac{c}{qX})(\delta - F'(X))
\end{aligned}
\qquad (2.38)
$$

by (2.34) and (2.36). Equating the right sides of (2.37) and (2.38) and simplifying gives

$$F'(X) + \frac{cF(X)}{X(pqX - c)} = \delta \qquad (2.39)$$

This is an implicit equation for the unknown X; any X which satisfies Equation (2.39) is called a *singular solution* of the original control problem.[7]

In most cases of interest, Equation (2.39) will have a unique solution $X = X^* > 0$, in which case X^* represents the *optimal equilibrium* stock level.[8] In the logistic case $F(X) = rX(1 - X/K)$, some simple if messy algebra reduces Equation (2.39) to a quadratic equation with solution

$$X^* = \frac{1}{4}\left[X_\infty + K(1 - \frac{\delta}{r}) + \sqrt{(X_\infty + K(1 - \delta/r))^2 + 8KX_\infty\delta/r}\,\right] \qquad (2.40)$$

where

$$X_\infty = c/pq$$

Problem 2.3 will ask you to compute X^* given appropriate data. The significance of X_∞ will be discussed in Section 2.7.

---

[7] In economics, Equation (2.39) would be called the "Golden Rule of Capital Accumulation."

[8] Cases can arise in which Equation (2.39) has multiple solutions, but this topic is perhaps more suited to research papers than to practical affairs.

Having determined the optimal equilibrium solution X^*, what can we conclude about the complete solution to our dynamic problem? Unless by fluke, $X_0 = X^*$, some initial stock adjustment will be necessary. It turns out that this is described by

$$Y(t) = \begin{cases} 0 & \text{whenever} \quad X(t) < X^* \\ Y_{\max} & \text{whenever} \quad X(t) > X^* \end{cases} \quad (2.41)$$

Such a policy, as discussed in Section 1.4, is the "most rapid approach path" (MRAP) to the long term equilibrium at X^*. Of course we also have

$$Y(t) = F(X^*) \quad \text{whenever} \quad X(t) = X^* \quad (2.42)$$

Thus we have completely specified the optimal solution to our original problem [see Clark (1976), Chap. 2, for a rigorous derivation]. Moreover, the solution is in "feedback" form—Equations (2.41) and (2.42) specify the optimal harvest *as an explicit function of the current state variable $X(t)$*. Such feedback, MRAP policies are extremely simple and elegant, but of course they only arise under special and possibly unrealistic circumstances. What are these circumstances? Look at Equation (2.35) again. This condition, which leads to the MRAP result, follows from the maximum principle, Equation (2.31), because for this model the Hamiltonian $\tilde{\mathscr{H}}(X, Y; \mu)$ in (2.34) is *linear in the control variable $Y(t)$*. This linearity condition is both necessary and sufficient for the optimality of singular MRAP solutions. In Problems 2.10.6 and 2.10.7 you will be asked to find the singular MRAP solution for a problem with time-varying parameters $p(t)$, $c(t)$, $\delta(t)$, etc. The procedure for any such problem is as follows:

(i) set the coefficient of the control variable (i.e., the switching function $\sigma(t)$) in the Hamiltonian equal to zero, and solve for $\mu(t)$;

(ii) differentiate this expression to obtain $\dot{\mu}$ (using the state equation);

(iii) find $\dot{\mu}$ from the adjoint equation, equate with $\dot{\mu}$ from (ii) and simplify. This gives the singular solution $X(t)$, which in general depends on time t;

(iv) use an MRAP path to adjust X from X_0 to the singular path.

[Further complications, called "blocked intervals," can sometimes confuse the issue, but we will by-pass them here; see Problem 2.10.7 and Clark (1976), Chap. 2.]

2.4.2 Downward sloping demand

In the case where the inverse demand function $D(Y)$ has negative slope we have seen that net social utility is given by

$$U(X,Y) = B(Y) - cE$$
$$= B(Y) - \frac{cY}{qX} \qquad (2.43)$$

where $B(Y)$ is given by Equation (2.26). Hence the current value Hamiltonian (2.30) becomes now

$$\tilde{\mathcal{H}}(X,Y;\mu) = B(Y) - \frac{cY}{qX} + \mu[F(X) - Y] \qquad (2.44)$$

Maximization with respect to Y now implies that $\partial\tilde{\mathcal{H}}/\partial Y = 0$, or

$$\mu = B'(Y) - \frac{c}{qX} = D(Y) - \frac{c}{qX} \qquad (2.45)$$

Differentiating with respect to t yields

$$\dot{\mu} = D'(Y)\dot{Y} + \frac{c}{qX^2}[F(X) - Y]$$

The adjoint Equation (2.32), on the other hand, implies

$$\dot{\mu} = \delta\mu - \tilde{\mathcal{H}}_X$$
$$= \delta\mu - \frac{cY}{qX^2} - \mu F'(X)$$
$$= [\delta - F'(X)][D(Y) - \frac{c}{qX}] - \frac{cY}{qX^2}$$

Equating and solving for $\dot{Y}$, and rewriting the state equation, we finally obtain the following system:

$$\dot{X} = F(X) - Y$$
$$\dot{Y} = \frac{1}{D'(Y)}\left\{[\delta - F'(X)]\left[D(Y) - \frac{c}{qX}\right] - \frac{c}{qX^2}F(X)\right\} \qquad (2.46)$$

The optimal harvest policy $Y(t)$, and corresponding stock level $X(t)$ must be solutions of this system of equations.

First we find the optimal equilibrium solution by setting the right sides of Equations (2.46) equal to zero. This gives

$$Y = F(X) \qquad (2.47)$$

$$F'(X) + \frac{cF(X)}{X[qXD(F(X)) - c]} = \delta \qquad (2.48)$$

Once again we obtain a single implicit equation for the optimal steady state $X = X^*$. Note the similarity of this to the previous Equation (2.39); indeed, the two equations become identical in the event that $D(Y) = p$. Given the necessary data, Equation (2.48) can be solved numerically to obtain the optimal steady state X^*.

The optimal approach path to the equilibrium solution (X^*, Y^*) can be obtained by solving the full system (2.46). It turns out (see Section 1.6.6) that (X^*, Y^*) is a saddle point equilibrium for this system. With an infinite time horizon, the optimal approach path follows the separatrix trajectories converging to (X^*, Y^*); these separatrices specify a feedback control policy $Y = Y(X)$. (Thus the optimal approach path is *not* an MRAP.) In general, the separatrices must be computed numerically; a simple method was described in Section 1.6.6.

2.5 Spawner-recruit models

Let us again consider the discrete-time model of Equation (2.10):

$$X_{t+1} - X_t = F(X_t) - Y_t$$

In order to write this in a form more familiar in fisheries management, we first write

$$X_{t+1} = G(X_t) - Y_t$$

where $G(X_t) = X_t + F(X_t)$. Next put $R_t = G(X_t)$; then

$$X_{t+1} = R_t - Y_t$$

so that, finally,

$$R_{t+1} = G(S_t) \qquad (2.49)$$

$$S_t = R_t - Y_t \qquad (2.50)$$

Equations (2.49), (2.50) define a *spawner-recruit* model, in which the symbols have the following interpretations

S_t = spawning escapement in year t

R_t = recruitment to the population in year t

Y_t = harvest extracted from R_t

Clearly Y_t must satisfy the constraint

$$0 \le Y_t \le R_t \tag{2.51}$$

The above model is appropriate for species that have nonoverlapping generations, and is used in the management of certain species of Pacific salmon. (The time between successive salmon generations is not one year, but a generation period of up to four or five years. For example, the famous Adams River sockeye salmon runs have a four-year cycle, and only the years 1980, 1984, 1988, ... produce major runs.)

Alternatively, the above model can be applied to species with overlapping generations, but which reach sexual maturity at one year's age. In this case, R_t denotes the adult, breeding stock. More complex age-structured models must be used when dealing with populations whose size, sexual maturity, or economic value depend upon age. Dynamic optimization of such age-structured models is difficult, and will not be discussed further here.

Consider now the optimal harvesting problem

$$\text{maximize} \quad \sum_{t=0}^{\infty} \rho^t U(R_t, S_t) \tag{2.52}$$

$$\text{subject to} \quad R_{t+1} = G(S_t) \tag{2.53}$$

$$0 \le S_t \le R_t \tag{2.54}$$

It can easily be shown (see Problem 2.10.9b) by the Lagrangian method that this problem possesses an optimal equilibrium solution $S = S^*$, $R = G(S^*)$, determined by

$$G'(S)\left[-\frac{\partial U/\partial R}{\partial U/\partial S}\right] = 1 + \delta \tag{2.55}$$

This equation is the discrete-time analog of the "golden rule" obtained previously for the continuous-time case—see Equations (2.39) and (2.48).

What about the optimal approach path—when is the MRAP optimal? Suppose we have

$$U(R, S) = \phi_1(R) + \phi_2(S) \tag{2.56}$$

for some functions $\phi_i(\cdot)$; such a utility function is called *separable*. We can then proceed to solve our optimization problem directly, as follows:

$$\sum_{t=0}^{\infty} \rho^t U(R_t, S_t) = \sum_{t=0}^{\infty} \rho^t [\phi_1(R_t) - \phi_2(S_t)]$$

$$= \sum_{t=1}^{\infty} \rho^t [\phi_1(G(S_{t-1})) - \phi_2(S_t)] + \phi_1(R_0) - \phi_2(S_0)$$

$$= \sum_{t=0}^{\infty} \rho^{t+1} \phi_1(G(S_t)) - \sum_{t=1}^{\infty} \rho^t \phi_2(S_t) + \phi_1(R_0) - \phi_2(S_0)$$

$$= \sum_{t=0}^{\infty} \rho^t [\rho \phi_1(G(S_t)) - \phi_2(S_t)] + \phi_1(R_0)$$

Writing

$$V(S) = \rho \phi_1(G(S)) - \phi_2(S) \qquad (2.57)$$

we see that our problem now becomes (since $\phi_1(R_0)$ = given constant)

$$\text{maximize} \quad \sum_{t=0}^{\infty} \rho^t V(S_t) \qquad (2.58)$$

$$\text{subject to} \quad 0 \leq S_{t+1} \leq G(S_t) \qquad t = 0, 1, 2, \ldots \qquad (2.59)$$

But now the complete solution seems to stare us in the face—simply choose S_t to maximize $V(S_t)$, subject to the constraint (2.59). Assume that $V(S)$ is concave, as in Figure 2.5. Writing $R_{t+1} = G(S_t)$, we conclude that the optimal escapement S_{t+1} is given by

$$S_{t+1} = \begin{cases} S^* & \text{if} \quad R_{t+1} \geq S^* \\ R_{t+1} & \text{if} \quad R_{t+1} < S^* \end{cases} \qquad (2.60)$$

where S^* is the unique maximizing point for $V(S)$. In terms of the harvest Y_{t+1}, the optimal policy is

$$Y_{t+1} = \begin{cases} R_{t+1} - S^* & \text{if} \quad R_{t+1} \geq S^* \\ 0 & \text{if} \quad R_{t+1} < S^* \end{cases} \qquad (2.61)$$

This is nothing other than the most rapid approach to the equilibrium S^*!

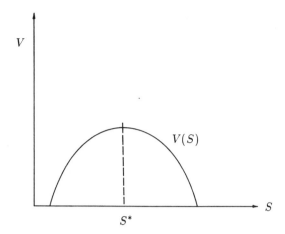

Figure 2.5   Concave objection function in a stock-recruitment model based on a separable utility function $U = \phi_1(R) + \phi_2(S)$.

From Equation (2.57) we also see that S^* satisfies

$$G'(S) \cdot \frac{\phi_1'(G(S))}{\phi_2'(S)} = \frac{1}{\rho} = 1 + \delta \qquad (2.62)$$

which is a special case of the general rule (2.55).

To summarize, we have shown that the discrete-time optimization problem (2.52)–(2.54) is solved by an MRAP to equilibrium escapement at $S = S^*$ given by Equation (2.62) provided that:

(i) $U(R, S)$ is separable, i.e., $U(R, S) = \phi_1(R) - \phi_2(S)$, and
(ii) $V(S) = \rho\phi_1(G(S)) - \phi_2(S)$ is quasi-concave.

For a discussion of what happens when (ii) fails see Spence and Starrett 1975. The assumption that $U(\cdot)$ is separable is analogous to the linearity assumption which was required in order to obtain MRAP solutions in the continuous-time case: see Section 2.4.1. Also, if $U(\cdot)$ is not separable, then the approach to S^* becomes asymptotic rather than the MRAP.

2.6 Optimal investment strategy

The renewable resource models described so far have all treated effort as a one-dimensional index of economic inputs to harvesting. Costs have been assumed directly proportional to effort. Since effort is variable, this means that only variable costs have been taken into consideration.

In many resource industries, however, fixed costs are highly significant. Fisheries require vessels, port facilities, and processing plants; logging requires machinery, roads, and sawmills; water resources are controlled by dams and irrigation systems, and so on. Such investments are highly "nonmalleable" in the sense that the initial costs of investment cannot be recovered later if equipment is no longer needed. For the case of an exhaustible resource deposit, it is clear that equipment used in recovering the resource will eventually become surplus, but this can also occur following an initial "running-down" phase of a renewable resource stock.

In the case of a fishery, an initial capital investment can be thought of as providing the fishery with harvesting and processing *capacity*. The following model (Clark et al. 1979) captures this idea:

$$\dot{X} = F(X) - qEX \qquad (2.63)$$

$$0 \leq E(t) \leq K(t) \qquad (2.64)$$

$$\dot{K} = I(t) - \gamma K \qquad (2.65)$$

Equation (2.63) is the usual fishery model, but Equation (2.65) describes the evolution of fishing capacity $K(t)$, which can be increased by investment at the rate $I(t)$, and which also depreciates at a constant relative rate $\gamma \geq 0$. The fishery owner wishes to determine an investment strategy $I(t)$, together with an effort strategy $E(t)$ constrained by Equation (2.64), so as to maximize the present value of net revenues:

$$\underset{E(t), I(t)}{\text{maximize}} \int_0^\infty e^{-\delta t}[(pqX - c)E - c_f I]\, dt \qquad (2.66)$$

where c_f denotes the unit cost of investment. The initial levels of $X(t)$ and $K(t)$ are known:

$$X(0) = X_0 \qquad K(0) = K_0 \qquad (2.67)$$

Observe that this model has *two* state variables $X(t)$, $K(t)$, and also two control variables $E(t)$, $I(t)$. Solution of the optimization problem is immeasurably more difficult than for the single-variable models discussed previously, and will only be partially described here (the full gory details are given in Clark et al. 1979).

First, what constraints should be imposed on investment $I(t)$? If investment is really nonmalleable we should assume that

$$I(t) \geq 0 \qquad (2.68)$$

There is no obvious upper bound on investment, so we will allow $I(t)$ to be arbitrarily large, even infinite. The latter case corresponds to an instantaneous jump in capacity K.

Observe next that our optimization problem is linear in both control variables. We therefore anticipate singular solutions, but there are several possibilities, depending on whether E or I is singular, or both. The calculations will be simplified if we write

$$E(t) = \phi(t)K(t) \qquad (2.69)$$

$$0 \leq \phi(t) \leq 1 \qquad (2.70)$$

The control variables are now $\phi(t)$ and $I(t)$.

The Hamiltonian becomes[9]

$$\begin{aligned}
\mathcal{H} &= e^{-\delta t}[(pqX - c)\phi K - c_f I] + \lambda(t)[F(X) - q\phi KX] + \mu(t)[I - \gamma K] \\
&= \left\{ e^{-\delta t}(pqX - c)K - \lambda qXK \right\} \phi(t) \\
&\quad + \left\{ -e^{-\delta t}c_f + \mu \right\} I(t) + \lambda F(X) - \mu\gamma K
\end{aligned}$$

$$(2.71)$$

A singular control variable arises when one or both of the expressions in curly brackets (i.e. the switching function) vanishes identically.

Case (i) $\phi(t)$ singular: then (2.71) implies that

$$\lambda(t) = e^{-\delta t}\left(p - \frac{c}{qX}\right)$$

$$\dot{\lambda} = e^{-\delta t}\left\{ -\delta\left(p - \frac{c}{qX}\right) + \frac{c}{qX^2}[F(X) - q\phi KX] \right\}$$

The adjoint equation for X is

$$\begin{aligned}
\dot{\lambda} &= -\mathcal{H}_X = -e^{-\delta t}pq\phi K + \lambda q\phi K - \lambda F'(X) \\
&= e^{-\delta t}\left\{ -pq\phi K + \left(p - \frac{c}{qX}\right)q\phi K - \left(p - \frac{c}{qX}\right)F'(X) \right\}
\end{aligned}$$

---

[9] In this problem $\mu(t)$ is the second costate variable associated with $K(t)$. Both $\lambda(t)$ and $\mu(t)$ are *discounted* shadow prices.

Equating and simplifying gives

$$F'(X) + \frac{cF(X)}{X(pqX - c)} = \delta \tag{2.72}$$

which is identical with Equation (2.39). Denote the solution of Equation (2.72) by X_1^*.

Case (ii) $\phi(t)$ and $I(t)$ both singular: besides the above we also have

$$\mu(t) = e^{-\delta t} c_f$$

Hence

$$\dot{\mu} = -\delta c_f e^{-\delta t} \tag{2.73}$$

But

$$\dot{\mu} = -\mathcal{H}_K = -[e^{-\delta t}(pqX - c) - \lambda qX]\phi + \mu\gamma \tag{2.74}$$

However, for ϕ singular the first term here vanishes, by Equation (2.71), so we just have

$$\dot{\mu} = \gamma\mu$$

But (2.73) implies that $\dot{\mu} = -\delta\mu$. Since $\delta > 0$ and $\gamma \geq 0$ this is a contradiction. Hence both ϕ and I cannot simultaneously be singular.

Case (iii) $\phi(t)$ singular, $I(t) \equiv 0$: this is allowed, and occurs for $X(t) = X_1^*$. But this can only be a temporary equilibrium, since with $I(t) \equiv 0$ we have $\dot{K}(t) = -\gamma K$ so that harvest capacity will eventually decline below the level needed to harvest the sustained yield $F(X_1^*)$.

Case (iv) $I(t)$ singular, $\phi(t) \equiv 0$: Equations (2.73) and (2.74) again imply, since $\phi = 0$, that $\dot{\mu} = \gamma\mu = -\delta\mu$, which rules this case out.

Case (v) $I(t)$ singular, $\phi(t) \equiv 1$: Equations (2.73) and (2.74) now imply

$$-\delta c_f e^{-\delta t} = -[e^{-\delta t}(pqX - c) - \lambda qX] + \gamma c_f e^{-\delta t}$$

so that

$$\lambda(t) = e^{-\delta t}\left\{ p - \frac{c + (\delta + \gamma)c_f}{qX} \right\} \tag{2.75}$$

Computing $\dot{\lambda}$ from this, and equating it with $-\mathcal{H}_X$ implies, exactly as in Case (i), that

$$F'(X) + \frac{c_{tot}F(X)}{X(pqX - c_{tot})} = \delta \qquad (2.76)$$

where

$$c_{tot} = c + (\delta + \gamma)c_f \qquad (2.77)$$

Let X_2^* denote the solution to Equation (2.76). Since $c_f > 0$ we clearly have

$$X_2^* > X_1^*$$

We have thus identified two (partially) singular solutions X_1^* and X_2^*; "all" that remains to be done is to deduce the optimal approach path using bang-bang controls $\phi = 0$ or 1, $I = 0$ or $= +\infty$. It might be fun to make a classroom exercise of doing this, by guessing, for example. Warning: it originally took three of us *eleven months* to come up with the right guess![10]

Considerable insight can be obtained, however, from our two singular solutions. Note that the formula for X_1^* involves only variable costs, c, of fishing, whereas X_2^* involves $c_{tot} = c + (\delta + \gamma)c_f$, which also includes interest and depreciation on capital. Which of the two singular solutions is "relevant" at a particular point in time depends upon the current level of fishing capacity.

If current capacity is so great that there will be no reason to increase it further, then fixed costs are irrelevant (they're "bygone"—even if interest on a loan has to be paid), and X_1^* is the optimal stock level. But if current capacity is small and additional investment is required, then the full costs c_{tot} become relevant to decision making, and X_2^* becomes the optimal stock level. Clearly, investment will occur only if $X \geq X_2^*$. Moreover, the level of invested capital K will be greater than or equal to $K_2^* = F(X_2^*)/qX_2^*$—i.e., at least sufficient to harvest the sustained yield at X_2^*.

Investment rule: invest up to some level $K = K(X) \geq K_2^*$ depending on current stock level X, but only if $X \geq X_2^*$.

For example, suppose the initial stock level X_0 is much larger than X_2^*; then one can expect that $K(X_0)$ will be much larger than K_2^*. The

---

[10] We got the singular solutions in one afternoon.

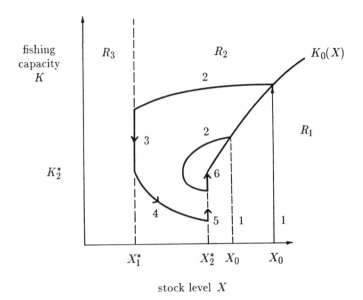

stock level X

Figure 2.6   Optimal sequences of investment and effort for two values of initial stock X_0: (1) initial investment; (2) MRAP; (3) temporary equilibrium at X_1^*; (4) MRAP to X_2^*; (5) reinvestment; (6) long-run equilibrium. [The phase (3) is actually oversimplified here; see Clark et al. 1979.]

result will be an *apparent* initial overcapacity; however, this will eventually depreciate (unless $\gamma = 0$).

Once the initial investment has been made, X_1^* becomes the target level, and an MRAP approach is used, $E(t) \equiv K(t)$ unless $X(t)$ is reduced to X_1^*. Actually there are two cases: if K_0 is small, $X(t)$ may never reach X_1^*, but if K_0 is large $X(t)$ will reach X_1^* and stay there temporarily (unless $\gamma = 0$). The entire sequence of investment and harvesting strategy is shown in Figure 2.6.

The overall strategy is rather complicated (and in fact Figure 2.6 over-simplifies it!), but it makes quite good sense. Consider the larger value of X_0 (this situation might seldom occur in practice). Six phases can be identified:

1. Initial investment increases capacity up to $K_0 = K(X_0)$.
2. Full capacity $E(t) = K(t)$ is used to reduce stock to X_1^* (MRAP); meanwhile $K(t)$ depreciates at rate γ.
3. Singular solution X_1^* is followed; $E(t) = E_1^* < K(t)$, so that capacity is temporarily "excessive."

4. Capacity is no longer excessive; full capacity is now used, but stock begins to recover.

5. Stock reaches X_2^*; additional investment up to K_2^* is made.

6. Long-run equilibrium at $X = X_2^*$, $K = K_2^*$, $E = K_2^*$, $I = \gamma K_2^*$ (investment covers depreciation).

Figure 2.6 also indicates the optimal policy if it happens that $X_0 < X_2^*$ (for example, a 200 mile zone is declared at $t = 0$ and the stock is initially in a depleted state). If $X_1^* \le X_0 < X_2^*$ just follow the same policy, utilizing any existing capacity (unless X falls to X_1^*) until reaching long-run equilibrium at X_2^*. For a severely depleted stock, $X_0 < X_1^*$, fishing would not take place at all until $X(t)$ had recovered to X_1^* (this is not quite true—see below).

Note that Figure 2.6 is in fact a *feedback control* diagram, specifying the optimal policies $E(t)$, $I(t)$ as functions of the current state variables $X(t)$, $K(t)$. The rules in the three regions are:

in R_1 invest (instantaneously) up to $K(X_0)$

in R_2 use full capacity $E = K$ but don't invest

in R_3 use $E = I = 0$.

Besides this there are the two singular solutions, one of which is the long-term equilibrium.[11]

How did the class do guessing? Our purpose in going through this rather complicated example is first to show that investment problems are important, and second to indicate how difficult dynamic optimization problems can become when more than one state variable is involved. A standard practice in the economic literature, unfortunately, is to throw in a bunch of Kuhn–Tucker multipliers, and then write down a long string of fancy looking necessary conditions. Such conditions are not helpful in solving the required problem. (Besides which, the process has not been justified mathematically, in general, and is known to lead to wrong conclusions in some cases.) Complete solution of a multidimensional control problem is usually a major research undertaking, and will normally require expert mathematical advice. The very difficulty of solving complicated optimization models

---

[11] The slight inaccuracy referred to in Figure 2.6 pertains to region R_3, where there is another switch-over curve $S(X)$, lying to the left of X_1^*. Optimal effort switches from $E = 0$ to $E = K(t)$ along $S(X)$; this happens because $X(t) = X_1^*$ is in fact "blocked" when $K(t) < K_1^* = F(X_1^*)/qX_1^*$. See Clark et al. (1979) for details.

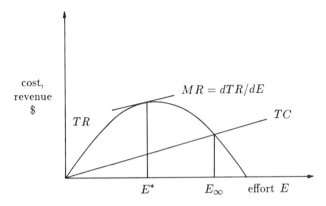

Figure 2.7　Gordon's model of the common-property fishery.

makes the study of simplified models all the more valuable. (For an application of this model to pelagic whaling, see Clark and Lamberson, 1982.)

2.7　Common-property resources

Few if any fish populations are, or ever have been optimally managed—although the advent of 200-mile fishing zones since 1977 has at least opened up the possibility of improved fishery management. However, most of these resources still remain "common property"—meaning that no individual or firm possesses exclusive rights to exploit these resources. Many other renewable resources, including water, air, wildlife, grazing areas, etc. are also exploited as common property.

The general rule is that common-property resources will become overexploited. Unfortunately this rule is almost as much misunderstood as it is well known. The result of this misunderstanding is a long history of ill-conceived advice to management authorities, which has often failed to achieve desirable or stated objectives.

An early model of the common-property fishery is due to H. S. Gordon (1954). This model, based on the yield-effort curve of the Schaefer model (Section 2.2), assumes a constant fish price p and effort cost c. Figure 2.7 shows Total Sustained Revenue, $TR = pY$, and Total Sustained Cost, $TC = cE$, as functions of effort E.

Gordon (1954) argues that, whereas the optimum point is at $E = E^*$, where marginal revenue equals marginal cost, the common-property fishery will instead reach equilibrium at $E = E_\infty$, where total revenue equals total cost (or, if you prefer, average revenue equals average cost). Resource rent $TR - TC$, which would be maximized at E^*, is in fact totally "dissipated" at $E = E_\infty$. With the geometry of Figure 2.7, moreover, the fish stock itself will be seriously depleted, since $E_\infty > E_{MSY}$. (Gordon makes much ado about the fact that $E^* < E_{MSY}$, but a dynamic analysis, of course, shows that this conclusion depends upon an assumption of zero discounting, which Gordon makes tacitly. Nevertheless it is always true, even for $\delta > 0$, that the optimal effort level is less than E_∞, which in fact corresponds to $\delta \to +\infty$.)

The argument behind Gordon's prediction is simple: clearly a sustained effort level $E > E_\infty$ will not occur, because then fishermen would be losing money and would give up fishing. Conversely, for $E < E_\infty$, fishermen would be making more than their opportunity costs cE, and hence additional fishermen would be attracted to the fishery (or existing fishermen would expand their effort). Thus an equilibrium can only be established at $E = E_\infty$; Gordon calls this the *bionomic* equilibrium of the common-property fishery.

Let us express this theory in terms of the model of Section 2.3.1:

$$\dot{X} = F(X) - Y \tag{2.78}$$

$$Y = qEX \tag{2.79}$$

$$U(X, E) = pY - cE = (pqX - c)E \tag{2.80}$$

Bionomic equilibrium occurs when net returns $U(X, E)$ are zero. By Equation (2.80) this becomes simply [12]

$$X = X_\infty = \frac{c}{pq} \tag{2.81}$$

Thus X_∞ is the stock level at which net returns from fishing become zero. The corresponding bionomic yield and effort levels are given by Equations (2.78) and (2.79):

$$Y_\infty = F(X_\infty) \tag{2.82}$$

$$E_\infty = \frac{Y_\infty}{qX_\infty} = \frac{F(X_\infty)}{qX_\infty} \tag{2.83}$$

Could common-property exploitation ever drive a renewable resource

---

[12] An exception: if X_∞ in (2.81) is greater than K (the carrying capacity), then $E = 0$ is the solution to (2.80). The fishery is simply not viable.

stock to extinction? According to (2.81) we have $X_\infty > 0$; if also $F(X_\infty)$ > 0 then bionomic equilibrium is indeed also a biological equilibrium at $X = X_\infty$. But in the case that $F(X_\infty) < 0$ (i.e., $X_\infty < \underline{X} = $ minimum viable population), extinction *will* result, although *exploitation* will cease when $X(t)$ falls below X_∞.

The fact that X_∞ is positive is itself a result of our model assumptions, namely, the form of the production function

$$Y = qEX$$

which implies that catch per unit effort $Y/E \to 0$ as $X \to 0$. Since price p is also assumed constant, it follows that revenues fall below effort costs at low but positive X levels. In fact, this model assumes that the cost of driving the resource to extinction is infinite—a rather strong assumption! An alternative model is given in Problem 2.10.10.

2.7.1 Overcapacity

The above simple theory of bionomic equilibrium assumes that fishermen enter or leave the fishery according to whether net revenues from fishing are positive or negative. Clearly this assumption overlooks fixed costs—a fisherman will buy a vessel and enter the fishery only if he expects to earn enough revenue to cover his opportunity costs *and to repay the cost of the vessel*. But the fisherman's future revenues depend upon how many other fishermen also enter the fishery.

Thus it is not possible to predict the number of vessels that will actually enter the fishery unless one assumes something about the ability of the fishermen themselves to predict the future. Two polar possibilities are:

(i) myopic decision rule: each potential fisherman assumes that the net revenues experienced by current fishermen will persist indefinitely into the future;

(ii) rational expectations: each fisherman predicts the total number of entrants, and the resulting time profile of net revenues per fisherman, and all these predictions turn out to be correct.

These two assumptions lead to quite different predictions regarding entry.

Consider first the myopic rule. Current net revenue flow per unit of effort is

$$pqX(t) - c$$

where $X(t) =$ current stock. If c_f denotes the cost of one unit of effort capacity, then capital costs per unit of capacity are

$$(\gamma + \delta)c_f$$

where γ is depreciation rate and δ the interest rate. Thus entry will occur if and only if

$$pqX(t) - c > (\gamma + \delta)c_f$$

or

$$X(t) > \frac{c_{tot}}{pq} = X_{\infty,tot}$$

where $c_{tot} = c + (\gamma + \delta)c_f$. The total *number* of vessels entering the fishery cannot be predicted from this assumption, but at least vessels will cease entering once $X(t) < X_{\infty,tot}$.

Next, when will vessels *exit* from the fishery? Assuming that vessel costs are "sunk" costs, i.e., that vessel capital is nonmalleable, as in Section 2.6, we can say that vessels will leave the fishery only when revenue falls below variable costs, i.e., when

$$pqX(t) - c < 0 \qquad \text{or} \qquad X(t) < X_{\infty} = \frac{c}{pq}$$

Thus there is a "gap" between the stock levels at which entry and exit occur; within the gap neither entry nor exit occurs. (You are asked to calculate such a gap in Problem 2.10.14.)

A common government policy in fisheries is to subsidize the construction of fishing vessels. This reduces c_f (from the fisherman's point of view) and thus narrows the entry-exit gap. It also encourages overcapacity, and may increase the number of fishermen who are ultimately unable to make a living from fishing.

The rational expectations assumption is more fruitful, since it leads to a prediction of total entry. Suppose that N vessels enter the common-property fishery at $t = 0$, and assume that each vessel exerts one unit of effort (this simply specifies effort units). Then our model becomes

$$\dot{X} = F(X) - qNX \qquad X(0) = X_0 \qquad (2.84)$$

$$U(t) = pqX(t) - c \qquad (2.85)$$

where $U(t)$ denotes net revenue flow per vessel. The present value of net revenue is

$$P_N = \int_0^\infty e^{-\delta t} U(t)\, dt \tag{2.86}$$

It is clear that P_N is a decreasing function of N (why?).

The flow of capital costs per vessel is $c_f(\gamma + \delta)$, and the present value of this is

$$C_N = \int_0^\infty e^{-\delta t} c_f(\gamma + \delta)\, dt = c_f(1 + \gamma/\delta) \tag{2.87}$$

That is, of course, independent of N.

Our entry prediction is that

$$P_N = C_N \tag{2.88}$$

which has a unique solution $N = N_0$ (depending, of course, on X_0). You are asked to compute N_0 for Antarctic whales in Problem 2.10.15.

(There is a slight additional complication. If N is sufficiently large, the population $X(t)$ may be driven below the break-even revenue level X_∞. If this occurs at time $t = t_0(N)$, the net revenues simply become zero for $t \geq t_0$.)

2.8 The theory of resource regulation

It was A.C. Pigou who first explored the use of taxes as a method of counteracting externalities. In the case of a common-property renewable resource, the primary externality can be identified as the "stock" externality: individual exploiters ignore the effect that their removals from a common stock have upon future productivity of that stock. (This should be distinguished from the "crowding" externality that interested Pigou. In the resource setting, crowding occurs when the activities of exploiters interfere with one another at a point in time.)

Mathematically speaking, the competitive resource exploiter behaves as if the shadow price $\mu(t)$ (sometimes called the "user cost" in this setting) of the resource were zero. A management agency can, in principle at least, force exploiters to recognize the shadow price by imposing it as a tax on harvests. Under this setup, the entire resource rent is captured for the public purse by means of the resource tax, and the management agency acts as a sole owner of the resource, charging "rent" for its use.

To put this in mathematical terms, suppose there are N potential exploiters of a renewable resource stock, with effort cost functions $c_i(E_i)$, $i = 1, \ldots, N$, and with identical production functions

$$h_i = \phi(X, E_i)$$

If the price of the harvested resource is p, each exploiter attempts to maximize his short-term net revenues:

$$\underset{E_i \geq 0}{\text{maximize}} \{p\phi(X, E_i) - c_i(E_i)\} \tag{2.89}$$

Thus the exploiter merely equates (short-term) marginal revenues and marginal costs:

$$c_i'(E_i) = p\frac{\partial \phi}{\partial E_i}(X, E_i) \tag{2.90}$$

Because of the stock externality, however, this is not a cooperative (or social) optimum.

The cooperative optimum would

$$\text{maximize} \int_0^\infty e^{-\delta t} \sum_i [p\phi(X, E_i) - c_i(E_i)] \, dt \tag{2.91}$$

$$\text{subject to} \quad \dot{X} = F(X) - \sum_i \phi(X, E_i) \tag{2.92}$$

The corresponding current-value Hamiltonian is

$$\tilde{\mathcal{H}} = \sum_i [p\phi(X, E_i) - c_i(E_i)] + \mu(t)[F(X) - \sum_i \phi(X, E_i)]$$

The necessary conditions include $\partial \tilde{\mathcal{H}} / \partial E_i = 0$, or

$$c_i'(E_i) = (p - \mu)\frac{\partial \phi}{\partial E_i}(X, E_i) \tag{2.93}$$

where μ is the shadow price.

Since μ equals the marginal value of the resource stock X, it is positive in all cases of interest. It therefore follows immediately from comparison of Equations (2.90) and (2.93) that the competitive resource exploiters always exert excessive levels of effort, relative to the cooperative optimum. It also follows that, if the price received by the individual is reduced by the amount of the shadow price, then the individual will exert the optimal level of effort. In other words, a tax on resource harvest equal to the shadow price causes competitive resource exploitation to coincide with the optimum. This is a dynamic version of Pigou's original theorem.

We trust that it goes without saying that the above simple model glosses over a plethora of built-in assumptions which may fail to hold in the real world. For example, the management authority's ability to compute the shadow price $\mu(t)$, and to impose it as a tax (varying over time!) may be far from perfect. While governments often do collect significant tax revenues from resource industries, it is seldom the case that such taxes are specifically thought of, or designed as externality foils, or methods of preventing overexploitation. Almost always, other forms of regulation are used as well, usually directly controlling the amount, time, place, and other details of the harvest. It should be evident that the idea of taxing away all the resource rent is not one that appeals to the resource industry itself.

For example, the U.S. Fisheries Management and Conservation Act of 1976 expressly forbids the federal government from collecting *any* taxes from fishermen, beyond those needed to cover the administrative costs of management. The question therefore arises whether alternative instruments of regulation can be used in place of taxes. A further question would be, what purpose is to be served by regulation? Is one to be satisfied with preventing the depletion of a common-property resource, or should economic objectives be considered as well? Does biological conservation necessarily imply economic efficiency, or vice versa?

The answer to the second question is obviously no, at least if economic "efficiency" is equated with the maximization of discounted net revenues. Likewise, the answer to the first question is also negative. Here is a simple way to model the economic perversity of purely biological conservation. Consider the original Gordon model—see Figure 2.8. Bionomic equilibrium is at E_∞, with a severely depleted stock and reduced catches. The management authority decides to control effort at E_{MSY} instead. What happens?

The answer depends very much on *how* effort is controlled. A common approach is to shorten the fishing season, so that total annual effort is reduced. Assume that the authorities are able to restrict E to E_{MSY} in this way. The depleted stock will begin to recover, eventually reaching the MSY level. It works!—catches increase and costs of fishing decrease. The fishermen are getting rich. Consequently *more* fishermen will enter the fishery—even though there were originally too many! The additional fish-

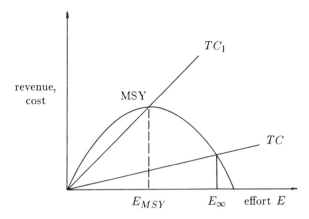

Figure 2.8   Effort regulation to achieve MSY.

ermen will mean that the season will have to be further shortened. Most of the year the fishermen and their vessels will be idle. Because of this idle capacity, the costs of fishing will have increased. A new equilibrium is reached when the cost curve has risen to the position TC_1 in Figure 2.8. Biological conservation has been achieved, but economic rent has again become zero. (And as a secondary effect, the expanded fishing fleet has greatly increased the difficulties of management—especially when the inevitable bad year comes and the fish don't show up.)[13]

Observe that Figure 2.8 could be used with a different interpretation. By charging for the *right* to fish, the management authority could adjust fishermen's costs to the TC_1 level, and thereby achieve MSY (this is just the taxation approach, but with the tax applied to effort). Since real fishing costs are not changed, no inefficiency is introduced. However, the entire resource rents now accrue to the management authority. Is there then no way to achieve both biological conservation and economic efficiency, while allowing the fishermen to enjoy some economic benefits?

Yes there is—but only if (i) the number of fishermen is limited, and (ii) each fisherman is prevented from expanding his effort capacity unduly. One way to achieve this result is to allocate individual catch quotas to specified fishermen. Then new fishermen can only enter by buying up existing quotas. Also, existing fishermen have no incentive to increase their harvest capacity. Such a system of *allocated* quotas is in a sense a system of "property rights"

---

[13] Short seasons and idle vessels may also cause boats to regear and enter other fisheries, perhaps contributing to overfishing of other species.

in the resource, albeit somewhat different from the usual property rights enjoyed, say, by farmers.

All of this can be expressed in mathematical form, on the basis of models like those developed in these notes. One interesting result is that a system of allocated individual catch quotas can be proved to be equivalent to a tax on catch, provided that the quotas are *transferable*. The market for quota transfers throws up a quota price equal to the optimizing tax. The details are gone through in Clark (1980).

2.9 Optimal forest rotation

In this section we discuss briefly the well known Faustmann model of optimal forest rotation period. $V(t)$ will denote the "stumpage" value for a given stand of trees of age t years. Typically we have

$$V(t) = 0 \qquad \text{for} \qquad 0 \le t \le t_1$$
$$V(t) > 0 \qquad \text{for} \qquad t > t_1$$

If the forest is clearcut at age t net revenue will be

$$V(t) - c$$

where c represents total cost of clearcutting and replanting. After clearcutting a new rotation is begun. We wish to determine the optimal rotation period $t = T$. We assume a discount rate δ, and suppose that all parameters remain constant over time (e.g., soil productivity, price, discount rate, and replanting cost).

Given these assumptions, it is obvious (from the principle of optimality) that all rotation periods will have the same length T. Then the total net present value of all future forest cuttings is

$$J = (V(T) - c) \cdot (e^{-\delta t} + e^{-2\delta T} + \ldots)$$
$$= \frac{V(T) - c}{e^{\delta T} - 1} \tag{2.94}$$

The optimal rotation period T is then obtained by setting $dJ/dT = 0$; the resulting equation is

$$\frac{V'(T)}{V(T) - c} = \frac{\delta}{1 - e^{-\delta T}} \tag{2.95}$$

This is called the Faustmann equation.

The growth rate of forests is usually quite low. One would expect, therefore, that the rotation period T is highly sensitive to the discount rate δ, and this is generally the case. Likewise, the average yield is also sensitive to δ. An alternative forestry model, which allows for continuous harvesting is given in Problem 2.10.18. A stochastic version of the Faustmann model, allowing for the risk of forest fires, is discussed in Chapter 5.

2.10 Problems

P2.10.1 Let $X(t)$ denote the number of fish in a certain population during a given fishing season $0 \le t \le T$, and write $R = X(0)$ as the initial "recruitment." If $M(t) = $ natural mortality rate and $F(t) = $ fishing mortality rate, we have

$$\frac{dX}{dt} = -(M(t) + F(t))X$$

(a) Show that the escapement $S = X(T)$ is given by

$$S = R \exp\left(- \int_0^T (M(t) + F(t)) \right) dt$$

(b) Find an expression for the total seasonal catch Y in numbers of fish. [Note $\dot{Y} = F(t)X(t) = $ instantaneous catch rate.]
(c) Simplify these results for the case M and F constant.

Answer
(a) Solve the differential equation to obtain $X(t) = R\exp(-\int_0^t (M(u) + F(u))\,du$ for any $t > 0$.
(b) Let $Y(t) = $ total catch up to time t; then $\dot{Y} = F(t)X(t)$ where $X(t)$ is given in (a). Hence

$$Y(T) = R \int_0^T F(t) \exp\left(- \int_0^t (M(u) + F(u))\,du \right) dt$$

(c) The equations are

$$S = X(T) = Re^{-(M+F)T}$$

and

$$Y = Y(T) = \frac{RF}{F+M}(1 - e^{-(M+F)T})$$

Note that if $M = 0$ we obtain Equation (2.9) of the text.

P2.10.2 Compute the MSY and corresponding effort levels for the following two examples, using the Schaefer model. Also find the level of effort just sufficient to drive the populations to extinction.
(a) Antarctic baleen whales: $r = .05$ per year, $K = 400,000$ BWU (blue-whale units), $q = 1.6 \times 10^{-3}$ per whale-catcher year.
(b) Pacific yellowfin tuna: $r = 2.6$ per year, $K = 250,000$ metric tons, $q = 3.8 \times 10^{-5}$ per standard fishing day (SFD).

Answer
(a) MSY $= 5,000$ BWU/yr, $E_{\text{MSY}} = 15.63$ catchers, $E_{\text{ext}} = 2E_{\text{MSY}}$ $= 31.26$ catchers.
(b) MSY $= 162,500$ metric tons/yr, $E_{\text{MSY}} = 17,100$ SFD/yr, $E_{\text{ext}} = 2E_{\text{MSY}}$.

P2.10.3 Continuing with Problem 2.10.2, compute the optimal stock levels X^*, optimal sustained biological yields Y^*, optimal effort levels E^*, optimal sustained economic rents $R^* = pY^* - cE^*$, and optimal initial economic yields Y_0 assuming that $X(0) = K$ (and that maximum effort is unconstrained), given:
(a) whales: $p = \$7,000$ per BWU, $c = \$600,000$ per whale-catcher year.
(b) tuna: $p = \$600$ per metric ton, $c = \$2,500$ per SFD.
Use the values $\delta = 0$ and $\delta = 10\%$ per year. Explain your results.

Answer. (The discounted results are in parentheses.)
(a) whales: $X^* = 226,800$ BWU (83,500 BWU), $Y^* = 4,910$ BWU/yr (3,300 BWU/yr), $E^* = 13.53$ catchers (24.73 catchers), $R^* = \$26.5$ million/yr (\$8.3 million/yr), $Y_0 = \$100$ million (\$162.8 million).
(b) tuna: $X^* = 179,880$ MT (178,000 MT), $Y^* = 131,200$ MT/yr (133,300 MT/yr), $E^* = 19,200$ SFD/yr (19,700 SFD/yr), $R^* = \$30.7$ million (same).
Discounting at 10% per annum has a strong effect on the whale results because $r = 5\%$ per annum for whales, but little effect on tuna, for which $r = 260\%$ per annum.
The formula for Y_0 is

$$Y_0 = \int_{X^*}^{X(0)} (p - \frac{c}{qx})\, dx = p(X(0) - X^*) - \frac{c}{q} \log \frac{X(0)}{X^*}$$

P2.10.4 Find the stock level X_∞, effort level E_∞, and sustained yield Y_∞ corresponding to bionomic equilibrium for the whale and tuna examples above. Explain why $Y_\infty > Y^*$ $(\delta = 0$ or $0.1)$ for the case of tuna.

(a) Whales: $X_\infty = 53{,}600$ BWU, $Y_\infty = 2{,}320$ BWU/yr, $E_\infty = 27.06$ catchers.

(b) Tuna: $X_\infty = 109{,}600$ MT, $Y_\infty = 160{,}700$ MT/yr, $E_\infty = 38{,}600$ SFD/yr. Tuna fishing is relatively expensive, with the result that X_∞ is only slightly less than X_{MSY}. Hence $Y_\infty \approx Y_{MSY} > Y^*$.

P2.10.5 The "skewed" logistic

$$F(x) = rx\left(1 - \frac{X}{K}\right)^\alpha \qquad (0 < \alpha \le 1)$$

has been proposed as an improved model of whale population dynamics.

(a) Find the MSY solution and the sustained yield curve. What happens as $\alpha \to 0$?

(b) Using the whale parameters of Problems 2 and 3, find X^* for $\alpha = 0.2$ and for a range of values of δ from 0 to 10% per annum, and compare with the logistic model $(\alpha = 1)$.

Answer

(a) $X_{MSY} = K/(1 + \alpha)$; $Y_{MSY} = rK\alpha^\alpha/(1 + \alpha)^{1+\alpha}$; the yield curve is $Y = qKE(1 - (qE/r)^{1/\alpha})$, which is also skewed to the right for $\alpha < 1$. As $\alpha \to 0$ we have $X_{MSY} \to K$, $Y_{MSY} \to rK$.

(b) Values of X^* (thousands of BWU):

δ	0	.01	.02	.03	.04	.05	.06	.07	.08	.09	.10
Skewed	342	328	308	281	245	203	166	139	120	108	99
Logistic	227	198	172	150	132	118	107	99	92	87	82

Note that the skewed logistic produces a larger X^*, but that the effect weakens as δ increases.

P2.10.6 Let $N(t)$ denote the number of fish in a given cohort (i.e., from the same spawning), and assume that

$$\dot{N} = -(M + qE(t))N(t) \qquad t \geq 0$$

$$N(0) \quad \text{given}$$

where $M =$ natural mortality rate and q, $E(t)$ are as usual. Consider the problem

$$\text{maximize} \quad \int_0^\infty e^{-\delta t}[pqN(t)w(t) - c]E(t)\, dt$$

where $w(t)$ is the weight of one fish at time ($=$ age) t.

(a) Find the equation of the singular solution $N^*(t)$. What happens as $\delta \to 0$? Sketch the curves $N^*(t)w(t)$ and $N_0(t)w(t)$ on the same graph, where

$$N_0(t) = N(0)e^{-Mt}$$

represents the size of the unfished cohort. (Assume that

$$\dot{w}(0) > Mw(0)$$

—this implies that the cohort biomass increases initially.)

(b) Given $M = 0.1$ per year, $N(0) = 3 \times 10^7$ fish, $p = \$1.50/\text{kg}$, $c = \$200/\text{SFD}$, $q = 1 \times 10^{-5}/\text{SFD}$, $\delta = 0.1$ per year, and

$$w(t) = w_\infty(1 - ae^{-kt})$$

with $w_\infty = 2.2$ kg, $a = 0.8$, $k = 0.4/\text{year}$, determine the complete optimal effort policy. In particular, determine the period during which $E(t) > 0$.

Answer

(a) The singular solution is

$$N^*(t) = \frac{c\delta}{pq[(M + \delta)w(t) - \dot{w}(t)]} \qquad t \geq t_\delta$$

where $(M + \delta)w(t_\delta) - \dot{w}(t_\delta) = 0$. The corresponding singular biomass curve $B^*(t) = N^*(t)w(t)$ is shown in Figure 2.9; note that $B^*(t_0) = c/pq$ (independent of δ). The optimal MRAP singular solution is

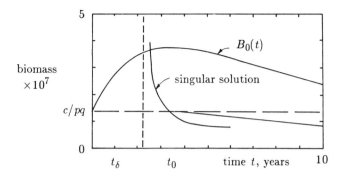

Figure 2.9   Natural biomass curve $N_0(t)$ and singular solution $N^*(t)$ for Problem 2.10.6.

given by

$$
E^*(t) = \begin{cases} 0 & \text{if} \quad t < t' \\ -\frac{1}{q}\left(\frac{\dot{N}^*(t)}{N^*(t)} + M\right) & \text{if} \quad t' < t < t_0 \\ 0 & \text{if} \quad t > t_0 \end{cases}
$$

where t' is determined by

$$
B_0(t) = N_0(t)w(t) = N^*(t)
$$

and t_0 satisfies $\dot{w}(t_0)/w(t_0) = \delta$. (Fishing clearly ceases at $t = t_0$ since net returns $pqN(t)w(t) - c$ become negative for $t > t_0$.)

(b) We have $E^*(t) > 0$ for $t' = 2.54 < t < t_0 = 3.47$ yrs. The above expression for $E^*(t)$ can be rewritten as

$$
E^*(t) = \frac{ak(M + \delta + k)}{q[(M + \delta)(e^{kt} - a) - ak]}
$$

which gives, for example, $E^*(2.54) = 265{,}100$ SFD/yr and $E^*(3.47) = 59{,}700$ SFD/yr. Taking one year $= 365$ days, this gives 762 vessels fishing on the first day of the season and 164 on the last day.

P2.10.7 In this problem you are asked to consider the case of a varying discount rate $\delta(t)$. It is easy to see that the discount factor now becomes

$$
\alpha(t) = \exp\left(-\int_0^t \delta(s)\,ds\right)
$$

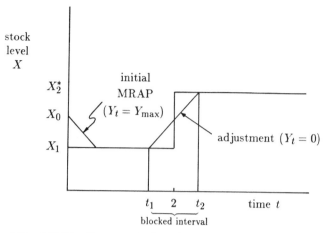

Figure 2.10   MRAP adjustment during a blocked interval; see Problem 2.10.7.

which reduces to the usual form $e^{-\delta t}$ in case $\delta = $ constant. It also turns out that the maximum principle, Equations (2.31) and (2.32), remain the same as before—except of course that now $\delta = \delta(t)$.

(a) Assuming that

$$\delta(t) = \begin{cases} \delta_1 = 0.15 & \text{for } 0 \leq t \leq 2 \\ \delta_2 = 0.05 & \text{for } t > 2 \end{cases}$$

find the singular solution to the problem

$$\text{maximize} \quad \int_0^\infty \alpha(t)Y(t)\,dt$$

$$\text{subject to} \quad \dot{X} = 0.5X(1 - X) - Y(t)$$

$$0 \leq Y(t) \leq Y_{\text{max}}$$

Also find the corresponding harvest rate $Y^*(t)$.

(b) Obviously the above singular solution cannot be used for t near $t = 2$ — why not? The optimal solution, in fact, requires an MRAP-type *adjustment* from X_1^* to X_2^*, with $Y_t = 0$ for $t_1 < t < t_2$ where the interval $[t_1, t_2]$ surrounds the discontinuity point $t = 2$ (see Figure 2.10). (The interval $[t_1, t_2]$ is called a *blocked interval*, because the constraint $Y(t) \geq 0$ blocks the singular path within this interval—see Arrow 1968, Clark 1976, Chap.2). Find the optimal blocked interval. (Hint. For simplicity assume $X_0 = X_1^*$; this doesn't affect the result. Now take

t_1 as a parameter and express the objective as a function of t_1 alone. Then maximize relative to t_1.)

Answer

(a) The singular solution is

$$X^*(t) = \begin{cases} X_1^* = 0.35 & \text{for} \quad 0 \le t < 2 \\ X_2^* = 0.45 & \text{for} \quad t > 2 \end{cases}$$

The corresponding harvest rates are $Y_1^* = 0.114$ and $Y_2^* = 0.124$.

(b) t_1 satisfies

$$Y_1^* e^{-\delta_1(t_1-2)} = Y_2^* e^{-\delta_2(t_2-2)}$$

$$t_2 - t_1 = \int_{X_1^*}^{X_2^*} \frac{dX}{0.5X(1-X)} = 0.84$$

This gives $t_1 = 1.58$, $t_2 = 2.42$.

P2.10.8 The island economy of Abalonia is based on the harvest of a single resource by native divers. The island chief is concerned about the resource stock left to unborn generations and has solicited your advice in resource management. After discussions with the chief, as well as some biological research, you determine the following:

$U(Y(t)) = Y(t)^{0.75} = $ utility of yield $Y(t)$

$\dot{X} = X(t) - 0.001X(t)^2 - Y(t)$ equation of motion

$\delta = 0.10 = $ the tribal discount rate

(a) What is the (continuous-time) current value Hamiltonian?

(b) What are the first order necessary conditions for a maximum. Solve for the steady state optimum (X, Y, μ).

(c) Plot the $\dot{X} = 0$ isocline. Locate the point defining the optimal stock and yield. What is the slope of the growth function at the optimal stock? Interpret your results.

Answer

(a) $\tilde{\mathcal{H}} = Y(t)^{0.75} + \mu(t)[X(t) - 0.001X(t)^2 - Y(t)]$

(b) $0.75Y(t)^{-0.25} = \mu(t)$

$\dot{\mu} = \mu(t)[0.002X(t) - 0.90]$

$\dot{X} = X(t) - 0.001X(t)^2 - Y(t)$

$X = 450$, $Y = 247.50$, $\mu = 0.189$

(c) The slope of the growth function $F(X)$ at $X = 450$ is $F'(450) = 0.10 = \delta$. With no cost function (thus no marginal stock effect) the resource's own rate of return is simply its marginal rate of growth, $F'(X)$. This is equated to the discount rate at the steady state optimum.

P2.10.9

(a) Use the Hamiltonian method to show that the problem

$$\text{maximize} \quad \int_0^\infty e^{-\delta t} U(X(t), Y(t)) \, dt$$

$$\text{subject to} \quad \dot{X}_t = F(X_t) - Y_t$$

has an equilibrium solution given by

$$F'(X) + \frac{\partial U/\partial X}{\partial U/\partial Y} = \delta$$

Show that Equations (2.39) and (2.48) are special cases.

(b) Use the Lagrangian method to show that the problem

$$\text{maximize} \quad \sum_{t=0}^\infty \rho^t U(R_t, S_t)$$

$$\text{subject to} \quad R_{t+1} = G(S_t)$$

has an equilibrium solution given by

$$G'(S) \cdot [-\frac{\partial U/\partial R}{\partial U/\partial S}] = 1 + \delta$$

Show that Equation (2.62) is a special case.

P2.10.10 The catch relation

$$Y = \gamma E \qquad (\gamma = \text{constant})$$

has been suggested as a more realistic production function for certain types of schooling fish, the schools of which are easily located by sonar and captured in purse seines. Adopting the model

$$\dot{X} = rX(1 - X/K) - Y$$

$$U(X, Y) = pY - cE$$

(a) determine optimal and common-property solutions. In particular, show
that there is a critical cost price ratio $c/p = \theta$ such that $X_\infty = K$ if
$c/p > \theta$ while $X_\infty = 0$ if $c/p < \theta$;

(b) find the optimal equilibrium solutions given parameter values

$$r = 0.15/\text{yr} \qquad K = 800{,}000 \text{ MT} \qquad \gamma = 50 \text{ MT/SFD}$$

$$p = \$200/\text{MT} \qquad c = \$1{,}000/\text{SFD}$$

$$\text{for} \quad \delta = 0.1/\text{yr} \quad \text{and} \quad \delta = 0.2/\text{yr}$$

Answer

(a) Since $U = (p\gamma - c)E$ we have $\theta = \gamma$ and $c/p < \gamma$ implies $E > 0$ until
X is driven to 0, while $c/p > \gamma$ implies $U < 0$ for any $E > 0$, so that
$X_\infty = K$.

For the optimal solution, clearly $E^* = 0$ and $X^* = K$ if $c/p > \gamma$. For
$c/p < \gamma$, the optimal stock level is given by

$$F'(X^*) = \delta \quad \text{provided that} \quad \delta < r$$

If $\delta \geq r$, this equation has no solution $X^* > 0$, and the optimal stock
level is $X^* = 0$.

(b) We have $c/p = 5 \text{ MT/SFD} < \gamma$, so that the fishery is viable (and
$X_\infty = 0$). From $F'(X^*) = \delta$ we get $X^* = \frac{K}{2}(1 - \frac{\delta}{r}) = 133{,}300 \text{ MT}$
($\delta = 0.1$) and $X^* = 0$ ($\delta = 0.2$).

P2.10.11 The following model of Antarctic blue whale harvesting is due to
M. Spence (1974). Let

X_t = number of blue whales in year t
E_t = number of catcher vessels in year t
Y_t = number of whales harvested in year t
U_t = net revenue in year t

Assume that

$$X_{t+1} = aX_t^b - Y_t$$

$$Y_t = aX_t^b(1 - e^{-qE_t})$$

$$U_t = pY_t - cE_t$$

Spence estimates the parameter values $a = 8.4$, $b = 0.82$, $q = 0.002$,
$p = \$7{,}000$, $c = \$875{,}000$.

(a) Perform the transformation given in Section 2.5, and then verify that conditions (i) and (ii) of that section are satisfied, so that an MRAP solution is valid.

(b) Show that the optimal steady state escapement S is given by

$$\frac{b(apqS^b - c)}{pqS - c} = 1 + \delta$$

If $\delta = 0.05$, solve for X^*, Y^*, and E^*.

(c) If $0 \leq E_t \leq 50$ and $R_0 = 8,000$, solve for the optimal approach to X^*. How long will this take?

(d) Spence's model is not likely to show the same strong dependence of S^* on δ as the logistic (or skewed logistic) model of Problem 2.10.4. Explain.

Answer

(a) Putting $R_t = aX_t^b$ and $S_t = R_t - Y_t$ gives

$$R_{t+1} = aS_t^b$$
$$U_t = \phi(R_t) - \phi(S_t)$$

where

$$\phi(R) = pR - \frac{c}{q}\log R$$

Direct calculation then verifies that $V''(S) < 0$ for the given parameter values.

(b) The formula for S^* follows directly from Equation (2.62); it gives $S^* = 88,200$.

(c) Since $R_0 < S^*$ we have $Y_t = 0$ until $R_t > S^*$. Simulation of the equation $R_{t+1} = aR_t^b$, $R_0 = 8,000$ shows that this requires 9 years.

(d) The intrinsic growth rate, $G'(0+) - 1$ for Spence's model is $= \infty$; a logistic model based on whale reproductive biology would have an intrinsic growth rate of about 5-10% per annum (or less—some whale scientists now propose 2%). Thus discounting will have a stronger effect for the logistic model.

Another feature of Spence's model is that bionomic equilibrium escapement $S_\infty = c/pq = 62,500$. Current population estimates for Antarctic blue whales are about 8,000 (some estimates range down to 1,000).

By the way, the logistic model, $r = 0.05$, predicts a recovery period of 68 years, rather than Spence's 9 years. (For $r = 0.10$, recovery takes 34 years.)

P2.10.12 Consider again the logistic model of Antarctic baleen whales (Problems 2.10.2, 2.10.3), in both continuous and discrete time:

continuous time

$$\text{maximize} \quad \int_0^\infty e^{-\delta t}(pqX - c)E\,dt$$

$$\text{subject to} \quad \dot{X} = F(X) - qEX = rX(1 - X/\bar{X}) - qEX$$

discrete time

$$\text{maximize} \quad \sum_{t=0}^\infty \rho^t U_t$$

$$U_t = PY_t - cE_t = \int_{S_t}^{R_t} \left(p - \frac{c}{qx}\right) dx$$

$$\text{subject to} \quad R_{t+1} = G(S_t) = S_t + rS_t(1 - S_t/\bar{X})$$

$$S_t = R_t(1 - e^{-qE_t}) = R_t - Y_t$$

parameter values: $r = 0.05$\$/year, $\bar{X} = 400{,}000$ BWU, $q = 1.6 \times 10^{-3}$ /catcher year, $p = \$7{,}000$/BWU, $c = \$600{,}000$/catcher year, $\delta = 0.1$/year.

(a) Calculate the optimal equilibrium stock X^*, and the optimal equilibrium escapement S^*, and also Y^* and E^*, for the two models. (Be sure to adjust the values of ρ and δ to take care of instantaneous vs. annual growth and discounting.)

(b) Now introduce fixed cost, $c_f = \$1.5 \times 10^6$/catcher. With $\gamma = 0.15$/year calculate X_2^* and S_2^* for total cost $c_{tot} = c + (\gamma + \delta)c_f$.

Answer

	X_1^*	Y_1^*	E_1^*	X_2^*	Y_2^*	E_2^*
continuous time	83479	3303	24.7	129106	4280	21.6
discrete time	83229	3353	24.9	125323	4412	21.6

(The differences in the results are relatively much smaller than the probable errors in parameter estimates.)

P2.10.13 Find the optimal investment $K_0(\bar{X})$ for the whale model of the preceding problem. Do this by simulation, using the discrete-time model, and simply determine the optimal K_0 by trial-and-error search. (For simplicity, ignore any temporary equilibrium at X_1^*; your simulation program can tell you if this is relevant, and the necessary correction could be included.)

Answer. $K_0(X) \cong 220$ whale catchers, and the cycle to long-run equilibrium takes about 27 years; the total discounted present value of net revenues is $1.24 billion. The population level X_1^* is not reached. See Program 2.1.

YEAR	X	K	Y
0	400000	220	118688
1	285591.7	184.3965	72966.96
2	217731.4	154.5549	47701.48
3	175041.9	129.5427	32767.56
4	146974.3	108.5782	23438.3
5	127913.7	91.00659	17333.03
6	114682.9	76.27863	13176.17
7	105390.4	63.93416	10247.79
8	98860.35	53.58744	8123.062
9	94334.16	44.91517	6541.395
10	91306.06	37.64637	5337.387
11	89429.05	31.5539	4402.857
12	88458.91	26.44741	3665.116
13	88219.66	22.16732	3074.108
14	88581.78	18.57989	2594.589
15	89448.12	15.57303	2201.226
16	90744.44	13.05279	1875.498
17	92413.03	10.9404	1603.583
18	94408.34	9.169874	1375.023
19	96693.82	7.685877	1181.803
20	99239.71	6.442041	1017.642
21	102021.4	5.3995	877.5906
22	105018.3	4.525677	757.6969
23	108212.8	3.793269	654.7769
24	111589.8	3.179389	566.2161
25	115135.9	2.664855	489.8687
26	118839.4	2.233591	423.9401
27	122689.4	1.87212	366.9591

K0 = 220 NET PV = 1.240463E+09

```
10 REM PROGRAM 2.1 : PROB. 2.10.13
20 READ R,XB,Q,P,C,CF,GAMMA,DELTA
30 DATA .051271,4E5,1.6E-3,7000,6E5,1.5E6,.161834,.105171
40 READ X0,K0
50 DATA 4E5,220
60 DEF FN F(X) = X * (1+R*(1-X/XB))
70 ALPHA = 1/(1+DELTA)
80 GAMMA1 = 1 - GAMMA
90 CTOTAL = C + (GAMMA+DELTA)*CF
100 XINFTOT = CTOTAL/(P*Q)
110 TERM = (1-DELTA/R)*XB + XINFTOT
```

(continued)

```
120 XSTAR = .25*(TERM + SQR(TERM*TERM+8*XINFTOT*XB*DELTA/R))
130 HSTAR = FNF(XSTAR) - XSTAR
140 KSTAR = HSTAR/(Q*XSTAR)
150 PSTAR = P*HSTAR - (C + GAMMA*CFR) * KSTAR
160 X = X0
170 K = K0
180 I = 0
190 DISCFACT = 1
200 SUM = 0
210 LPRINT "YEAR              X              K              Y"
220 LPRINT""
230 WHILE (K > KSTAR) OR (X < XSTAR)
240   H = X*(1-EXP(-Q*K))
250   LPRINT I,X,K,H
260   PROFIT = P*H - C*K
270   SUM = SUM +DISCFACT*PROFIT
280   X = FNF(X-H)
290   K = GAMMA1 * K
300   I = I + 1
310   DISCFACT = ALPHA * DISCFACT
320 WEND
330 PV = SUM + PSTAR * DISCFACT / (1-ALPHA)
       - CF * (K0+DISCFACT*(KSTAR-K))
340 LPRINT "K0 = "K0;"NET PV =";PV
350 END
```

Program 2.1

P2.10.14 Determine the entry-exit "gap," on the basis of the myopic entry rule, for the Antarctic whale model.

Answer. $X_\infty = c/pq = 53{,}600$ BWU; $X_{\infty,\text{tot}} = c_{\text{tot}}/pq = 87{,}100$ BWU.

P2.10.15 Consider the following discrete-time, rational expectations model:

$$R_{t+1} = G(S_t)$$
$$S_t = R_t - Y_t = R_t(1 - e^{-Nq})$$
$$U_t = pY_t/N - c$$
$$NR = \sum_{t=0}^{T(N)} \rho^t U_t - c_f$$

The symbols have the same interpretation as in Section 2.5, except that:

$N =$ number of vessels entering the fishery at $t = 0$

$U_t =$ net revenue per vessel in period t

$NR =$ total discounted net revenue per vessel.

Also

$$T(N) = \begin{cases} T & \text{if } R_t > \bar{R} = c/pq \text{ for } t = 0, \ldots, N \\ \text{first } t \text{ such that } R_{t+1} \leq \bar{R} \text{ otherwise} \end{cases}$$

and T is a given time horizon.

The rational expectations assumption is that $\bar{N}$ will be such that

$$NR = 0$$

Determine $\bar{N}$ (by simulation) given the Antarctic whale parameters:

$$G(S) = S + .05S(1 - S/400{,}000)$$

$$q = 1.6 \times 10^{-3} \qquad p = \$7{,}000 \qquad c = \$825{,}000 \qquad c_f = \$1.5 \times 10^6$$
$$\rho = 1/1.1 \qquad T = 25 \text{ years}$$

Answer. $N \cong 840$ whale catchers, which reduce the stock to $\bar{R}$ in two whaling seasons. See Program 2.2.

```
10 REM PROGRAM 2.2: RATIONAL EXPECTATIONS MODEL (PROBLEM 2.10.15)
20 READ R,XB,Q,P,C,CF,D
30 DATA .05,4E5,1.6E-3,7000,8.25E5,1.5E6,.1
40 READ T,X0
50 DATA 25,4E5
60 INPUT "N";N
70 DEF FN F(X) = X + R * X * (1-X/XB)
80 RHO = 1 / (1+D)
90 RINF = C / (P*Q)
100 X = X0
110 DISCFACT = 1
120 SUM = 0
130 LPRINT ""
140 LPRINT "N ="N
150 LPRINT "YEAR             X             U"
160 T1 = T + 1
170 FOR I = 1 TO T1
180    H = X * (1 - EXP(-Q*N))
190    U = P * H / N - C
200    LPRINT I-1,X,U
210    SUM = SUM + DISCFACT * U
220    X = FNF(X-H)
230    IF (X <= RINF) THEN GOTO 260
240    DISCFACT = RHO * DISCFACT
250 NEXT
260 NR = SUM - CF
270 LPRINT "NET REVENUE ="NR
280 END
```

(continued)

```
N = 300
YEAR              X                  U
 0            400000             2733021
 1            252231.2           1418610
 2            160835.3           605638.8
 3            103260.2           93505.38
NET REVENUE = 3093447

N = 500
YEAR              X                  U
 0            400000             2258758
 1            184680.3           598772.9
 2            86270.56           -159906.3
NET REVENUE = 1170943

N = 800
YEAR              X                  U
 0            400000             1701869
 1            115229.6           -97074.75
NET REVENUE = 113619.5

N = 825
YEAR              X                  U
 0            400000             1662298
 1            110769.6           -136207.3
NET REVENUE = 38473.38

N = 840
YEAR              X                  U
 0            400000             1638999
 1            108175.8           -158637.3
NET REVENUE =-5216.875

N = 900
YEAR              X                  U
 0            400000             1549003
 1            98386.96           -241072.8
NET REVENUE =-170154.4
```

Program 2.2

P2.10.16 Consider the common-property fishery model in dynamic form:

$$\dot{X} = rX(1 - X/K) - \sum_{i=1}^{N} h_i$$

$$h_i = qXE_i$$

$$U_i = (pqX - c)E_i$$

$$0 \le E_i \le E_{\max}$$

Here N, the number of identical fishing vessels, is assumed fixed, X is measured in tons, and E_i in hours fishing per year.

Parameter values: $r = 0.8$/yr, $K = 50{,}000$ tons, $N = 40$ vessels, $q = 0.0002$/hour fishing, $p = \$200$/ton, $c = \$400$/hour fishing, $E_{max} = 500$ hours fishing/year.

(a) Find the bionomic equilibrium if fishing is unregulated (except for N being held constant). What is the yearly catch per vessel at equilibrium? Also, determine the length of time that the fleet of N vessels will take in reducing the biomass from $X_0 = K$ to bionomic equilibrium, if they fish at the maximum rate.

(b) Devise a taxation policy that will cause the fleet of 40 vessels to pursue the optimal fishing policy. Use $\delta = 8\%$ per annum. What individual vessel quota would achieve the same result? How much "excess capacity" is there, at equilibrium?

Answer

(a) $X_\infty = c/pq = 10{,}000$ tons; $H_\infty = rX_\infty(1 - X_\infty/K) = 6{,}400$ tons/year, so average individual catch $= 160$ tons/year, requiring effort $E_i = h_i/qX_\infty = 125$ hours fishing/year. Time T satisfies $\dot{X} = rX(1 - X/K) - NqE_{max}X$, $X(0) = K$, $X(T) = X_\infty$. Separating variables and integrating gives

$$T = \int_{10{,}000}^{50{,}000} \frac{dX}{1.2X + 1.6 \times 10^{-5}X^2} = 1.29 \text{ years}$$

(b) First, from Equation (2.40) we get $X^* = 28{,}340$ tons, $H^* = 9{,}820$ tons/year, and $E^* = 1{,}730$ hours fishing/year. At equilibrium, the necessary tax τ is such that

$$X^* = \frac{c}{(p - \tau)q}$$

Hence, $\tau = \$129.50$/ton.

Since the MRAP is optimal, no tax needs to be applied during the initial phase, when $X(t) > X^*$. However, assuming that all vessels continue to fish as long as net returns are positive, we see that any tax $\tau(t)$ for which

$$(p - \tau(t))qX(t) - c > 0$$

can be charged during the initial phase. Thus the management authority can capture an arbitrarily large portion of the economic rent. (The fact that the optimizing tax does not have to equal the adjoint variable during the initial phase is a consequence of the constrained linearity of our model.)

An individual vessel quota $Q_i^* = H^*/40 = 245.5$ tons/year at equilibrium would achieve the same result, as would an effort quota of $E_i^* = Q_i^*/qX^* = 43.2$ hours fishing/year. Again no quota need be set during the initial phase.

Optimal fishing at equilibrium requires $E^*/E_{\max} = 3.46$ vessels, "excess capacity" is 36.5 vessels. However, according to the present model there is no inefficiency associated with using all 40 vessels, since costs are just proportional to total effort. (Question: what kind of costs should be included in order to make excess capacity inefficient? List two examples.)

P2.10.17 The Bureau of Land Management is trying to determine the appropriate number of cattle to permit to graze on a federally owned range. The production function for annual beef production has been estimated to be

$$B_t = aG_t \frac{H_t}{H_t + b} \qquad a = .01 \qquad b = 8,000$$

where B_t = beef produced (tons), G_t = amount of grazable grass (tons), and H_t = number of beef cattle allowed to graze. If left ungrazed, the range contains $G_0 = 100,000$ tons.

The wholesale price of beef is $1.00 per pound (i.e., $2,000/ton), and the cost of herding, transporting, and processing one head of cattle is $200.

(a) On ungrazed land, what is the maximum possible beef production? What number of cattle will maximize short-term profit? How many cattle will be placed on the range by a large number of independent cattle owners?

(b) The amount of grass available in year $t + 1$ is given by

$$G_{t+1} = g_0 e^{-qH}t \qquad g_0 = 100,000 \text{ tons} \qquad q = 2 \times 10^{-4}$$

Determine the equilibrium herd size, beef and grass production under short-term profit maximization, and under open access. (Also, what is MSY?)

(c) Determine the equilibrium solution for long-term profit maximization, discounted at 10% per annum.

(d) Does the optimal dynamic solution in (c) have an MRAP? Explain.

(e) Write out the dynamic programming formulas for the dynamic problem in (c). (These formulas could be iterated numerically to obtain the optimal dynamic policy, but you aren't expected to do that.)

Answer

(a) Maximum production, as $H_t \to \infty$ is 1,000 tons. The profit maximizing herd is 940 head of cattle, while the "open access" herd reaches 2,000 head.

(b) Under open access $\bar{H} = 697$, $\bar{G} = 87,000$ tons, and $\bar{B} = 69.7$ tons; under short-term profit maximization $\bar{H} = 504$, $\bar{G} = 90,400$ tons, and $\bar{B} = 53.6$ tons, MSY is at $B = 151$ tons, $H = 3,483$, $G = 49,800$ tons.

(c) $H = 348$, $G = 93,300$ tons, $B = 38.9$ tons.

(d) No. The objective function is

$$\sum_{t=0}^{\infty} \rho^t \left[paG_t \frac{H_t}{H_t + b} - cH_t \right] \qquad G_{t+1} = g_0 e^{-qH_t}$$

which does not satisfy the separability condition.

(e)

$$J_0(G) = \max_{H \geq 0} \left[\frac{paGH}{H + b} - cH \right]$$

$$J_{n+1}(G) = \max_{H \geq 0} \left[\frac{paGH}{H + b} - cH + J_n(g_0 e^{-qH}) \right]$$

P2.10.18 The growth rate of a stand of trees satisfies

$$\frac{dV}{dt} = \frac{a}{1 + bt} V \left(1 - \frac{V}{k} \right) \qquad V(0) = V_0$$

where $V(t)$ represents the volume of merchantable timber at time t.

(a) Solve the equation for $V(t)$, and show that $\lim_{t \to \infty} V(t) = K$.

(b) Solve

$$\text{maximize} \atop h(t) \qquad \int_0^T e^{-\delta t} h(t)\, dt \qquad (T \text{ fixed})$$

$$\text{subject to} \quad \frac{dV}{dt} = \frac{a}{1 + bt} V \left(1 - \frac{V}{K} \right) - h(t) \qquad V(0) = V_0$$

$$0 \leq h(t) \leq +\infty \qquad V(t) \geq 0$$

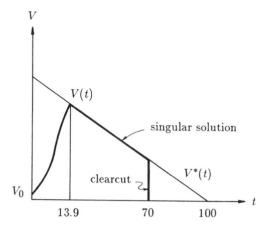

Figure 2.11 Optimal volume over time for the forest model of Problem 2.10.18.

Use the parameter values $a = 0.2$ per year, $b = 0.01$ per year, $K = 500$ TCF (thousand cubic feet), $V_0 = 10$ TCF, $\delta = 0.1$ per year, $T = 70$ years.

(c) Same for $\delta = 0$.

Answer

(a) $V(t) = K / \left[1 + \frac{K-V_0}{V_0} (1 + bt)^{-a/b} \right]$

(b) The singular solution is

$$V^*(t) = K/2 \left(1 - \frac{\delta}{a} (1 + bt) \right) = 125 - 1.25t$$

The optimal harvest rate $h(t)$ is

$$h(t) = \begin{cases} 0 & \text{for} \quad 0 < t < t_1 = 13.9 \text{ years} \\ h^*(t) & \text{for} \quad t_1 < t < 70 \text{ years} \\ +\infty & \text{for} \quad t = 70 \text{ years} \end{cases}$$

where $h^*(t) = \frac{a}{1+bt} V^*(t)[1 - V^*(t)/K] - \dot{V}^*(t)$ is the singular control. The final clearcut at $t = 70$ reduces V from $V^*(70)$ to 0; see Figure 2.11.

(c) For $\delta = 0$ the singular solution is $V^*(t) = \frac{K}{2} = 250$. The optimal harvest is

$$h(t) = \begin{cases} 0 & \text{for} \quad 0 < t < 21.5 \text{ years} \\ h_0^*(t) & \text{for} \quad 21.5 < t < 70 \\ \infty & \text{for} \quad t = 70 \end{cases}$$

where the singular control is

$$h_0^*(t) = \frac{a}{1 + bt} V^*(1 - V^*/K) = \frac{25}{1 + .01t} \text{ TCF/yr}$$

(Note: one could treat T as a parameter, and then determine the optimal rotation period $T = T^*$, as in the Faustmann model.)

Chapter 3

Nonrenewable resources

3.1 Depletion and discovery

In contrast to renewable resources, nonrenewable resources exhibit no growth or regenerative processes. Early models, dating back to the seminal work by Hotelling (1931), typically presumed a model of *pure depletion* where if $R(t)$ represented remaining reserves and $q(t)$ production, then

$$\dot{R}(t) = -q(t) \tag{3.1}$$

With search and discovery of new reserves, Pindyck (1978) makes the distinction between *exhaustible* and *nonrenewable* resources by noting that while the latter do not exhibit growth or regeneration, new reserves can be acquired through exploratory effort and discovery. Denoting $X(t)$ as *cumulative discoveries*, $w(t)$ as *exploratory effort*, we model the dynamics of the nonrenewable resource with exploration by the system

$$\begin{aligned} \dot{R}(t) &= \dot{X}(t) - q(t) \\ \dot{X} &= f(w(t), X(t)) \end{aligned} \tag{3.2}$$

where $f(w(t), X(t))$ is a discovery function relating new discoveries $(\dot{X})$ to exploratory effort and past, cumulative discoveries. It is usually assumed that $f_w > 0$ and $f_x < 0$. "Thus as exploration and discovery proceed over time it becomes more and more difficult to make new discoveries" (Pindyck 1978, p. 844).

To review some of the classical results attributable to Hotelling we will first return to the case of pure depletion characterized in Equation (3.1). This model also permits an analysis of production and price paths for the competitive and monopolistic mining industry. Later we shall return to the model with exploration.

3.2. Pure depletion:
competitive and monopolistic mining industries

What is the simplest meaningful model of exhaustible resource exploitation? Hotelling (1931) begins his study by assuming that the per unit price for ore, $p(t)$, will be a function of the form $p(t) = p(0)e^{\delta t}$, since "it is a matter of indifference to the owner of a mine whether he receives for a unit of his product a price $p(0)$ now or a price $p(0)e^{\delta t}$ after time t" (Hotelling 1931, p. 140).[1]

Under competition, Hotelling assumes that extraction at instant t will be determined according to the demand function

$$q(t) = D(p(t)) \tag{3.3}$$

Suppose, for the moment, that there are no costs to extraction. Then the initial reserves R will be exhausted, i.e.,

$$\int_0^T q(t)\, dt = R \tag{3.4}$$

At $t = T$, $q(T) = 0$ and we also have

$$q(T) = D(p(0)e^{\delta T}) = 0 \tag{3.5}$$

Equations (3.3)–(3.5) determine $p(0)$, T, and the entire time-path of extraction.

For example, suppose that $D(\cdot)$ is linear,

$$q(t) = D(p(t)) = a - bp(t) \tag{3.6}$$

Then

$$q(t) = a - bp(0)e^{\delta t} \tag{3.7}$$

and

$$q(T) = a - bp(0)e^{\delta T} = 0$$

The last equation implies $p(0) = ae^{-\delta T}/b$ and thus

$$q(t) = a(1 - e^{\delta(t-T)}) \tag{3.8}$$

Exhaustion of initial reserves implies

$$\int_0^T a(1 - e^{\delta(t-T)})\, dt = R \tag{3.9}$$

---

[1] Dasgupta and Heal (1979) discuss Hotelling's "rule" in considerable detail, showing that it can be justified by assuming perfect forward markets for resource stocks and flows. We will discuss the rule further below.

Integration yields

$$aT - a(1 - e^{-\delta T})/\delta = R \qquad (3.10)$$

which may be solved numerically for T (via bisection or Newton's method) and our solution is complete.

Now consider the rate of extraction if the mining industry were monopolistic. Retaining our assumption of zero extraction costs the monopolist would wish to maximize

$$\pi = \int_0^{T_m} P(q(t))q(t)e^{-\delta t}\, dt \qquad (3.11)$$

where $P(q(t))$ is the inverse of $D(p(t))$. We may formulate the monopolist's problem as an optimal control problem by letting $R(t)$ denote remaining reserves so that:

$$\frac{dR(t)}{dt} = \dot{R} = -q(t) \qquad R(0) = R \qquad (3.12)$$

The monopolist's current value Hamiltonian may be written as

$$\tilde{\mathcal{H}}(t) = P(q(t))q(t) - \mu(t)q(t) \qquad (3.13)$$

and the first order necessary conditions require

$$\frac{\partial \tilde{\mathcal{H}}}{\partial q(t)} = P(\cdot) + P'(\cdot)q(t) - \mu(t) = 0 \qquad (3.14)$$

$$\dot{\mu} - \delta\mu(t) = -\frac{\partial \tilde{\mathcal{H}}}{\partial R(t)} = 0 \qquad (3.15)$$

$$\dot{R} = \frac{\partial \tilde{\mathcal{H}}}{\partial \mu(t)} = -q(t) \qquad (3.16)$$

The expression $P(\cdot) + P'(\cdot)q(t)$ is recognizable as marginal revenue which we will denote as $MR(t)$. Equation (3.15) implies $\dot{\mu}/\mu = \delta$, that is, the current value shadow price rises at the rate of interest. But by (3.14) the current value shadow price is equated to marginal revenue at each instant t. Thus for the monopolist we have

$$\frac{M\dot{R}(t)}{MR(t)} = \delta \qquad (3.17)$$

implying that the monopolist extracts ore so that marginal revenue rises at the rate of interest.[2]

Suppose the monopolist faced the same linear demand curve as in (3.6). The inverse is

$$p(t) = a/b - q(t)/b \qquad (3.18)$$

and the monopolist's marginal revenue schedule is

$$MR(t) = a/b - 2q(t)/b \qquad (3.19)$$

Also $\tilde{y}(T_m) = 0$ implies $q(T_m) = 0$. Evaluating (3.14) at $t = T_m$ given our inverse demand curve implies

$$a/b = \mu(T_m) \qquad (3.20)$$

But $\mu(t) = \mu(0)e^{\delta t}$ and $\mu(T_m) = \mu(0)e^{\delta T_m}$. Thus from (3.20), $\mu(0) = ae^{-\delta T_m}/b$, finally yielding

$$\mu(t) = ae^{\delta(t-T_m)}/b \qquad (3.21)$$

Equating (3.19) with (3.21) and solving for $q(t)$ yields

$$q(t) = \frac{a}{2}(1 - e^{\delta(t-T_m)}) \qquad (3.22)$$

[Compare (3.22) with (3.8).] As before, the condition on total reserves gives

$$\int_0^{T_m} q(t)\,dt = aT_m/2 - a(1 - e^{-\delta T_m})/2 = R \qquad (3.23)$$

Let us now compare the exploitation profiles of the competitive and monopolistic resource industries. If T_c denotes the competitive exhaustion date, we obtain from (3.10) and (3.23):

$$T_c - (1 - e^{-\delta T_c})/\delta = R/a$$
$$T_m - (1 - e^{-\delta T_m})/\delta = 2R/a$$

Now the function $T - (1 - e^{-\delta T})/\delta$ is obviously an increasing function of T, so it follows immediately that

$$T_c < T_m \qquad (3.24)$$

---

[2] Note that, in contrast to the competitive model, no ad hoc price path $p(t) = p_0 e^{\delta t}$ has to be assumed here.

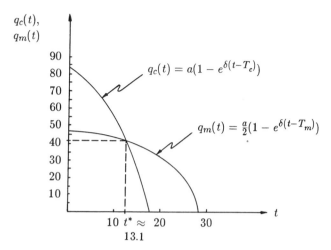

$q_c(t)$,
$q_m(t)$

$q_c(t) = a(1 - e^{\delta(t-T_c)})$

$q_m(t) = \frac{a}{2}(1 - e^{\delta(t-T_m)})$

Figure 3.1   Time-paths of extraction for competitive ($q_c(t)$) and monopolistic ($q_m(t)$) mining industries for the parameter values $a = 100$, $b = 10$, $\delta = 0.10$, and $R = 1000$. Equation (3.10) was solved for $T = T_c = 18.41$ and Equation (3.23) for $T_m = 29.48$.

Comparison of (3.22) and (3.8) then shows also that

$$q_c(0) > q_m(0)$$

In other words, the competitive industry initially exploits the resource at a higher rate, and also ultimately exhausts the resource more rapidly than the monopolist. This is not very surprising—the monopolist restricts production so as to maintain a higher price level [think of OPEC!].

A numerical example with $a = 100$, $b = 10$, $\delta = 0.10$, and $R = 1,000$ tons is shown in Figure 3.1. The values of T are $T_c = 18.41$ years and $T_m = 29.48$ years. The production rates $q_c(t)$ and $q_m(t)$ are given in the figure. The corresponding price paths are

$$p_c(t) = a - bq_c(t)$$
$$p_m(t) = a - bq_m(t)$$

The monopoly price path $p_m(t)$ starts out higher than $p_c(t)$, but cuts across it at $t \approx 13.1$ years (see Figure 3.1) and is below $p_c(t)$ until it reaches the choke-off price $a/b = 10$ at $T_m = 29.48$.

Thus, the monopolist might be seen as something of a "conservationist," restricting production initially and stringing it out over a longer horizon. The monopolist, of course, is not motivated out of altruism or a concern for future generations, but simply increases present value by restricting production early on. In the simple model just considered, the competitive extraction path is also socially optimal (in the usual sense), and the monopolistic path is dynamically inefficient in the sense that current generations could more than compensate future generations for an increase in current (near term) extraction and a reduction in future extraction.

To see this, assume that the social welfare from production $q(t)$ is given by the area under the inverse demand curve, so that

$$U(q(t)) = \int_0^{q(t)} P(z)\,dz \qquad (3.25)$$

The "social" mine manager would wish to

$$\text{maximize} \int_0^T U(q(t))e^{-\delta t}\,dt$$
$$\text{subject to} \quad \dot{R} = -q(t) \qquad (3.26)$$
$$R(0) = R \text{ given}$$

The current value Hamiltonian is

$$\tilde{\mathcal{H}} = U(q(t)) - \mu(t)q(t) \qquad (3.27)$$

with necessary conditions

$$\frac{\partial \tilde{\mathcal{H}}}{\partial q(t)} = U'(q(t)) - \mu(t) = 0 \qquad (3.28)$$

$$\dot{\mu} - \delta\mu(t) = -\frac{\partial \tilde{\mathcal{H}}}{\partial R(t)} = 0 \qquad (3.29)$$

$$\dot{R} = \frac{\partial \tilde{\mathcal{H}}}{\partial \mu(t)} = -q(t) \qquad (3.30)$$

and boundary conditions $R(0) = R$ and $q(T) = 0$. If one notes that $U'(q(t)) = P(q(t)) = p(t)$ then $\mu(t) = p(t)$ from (3.28) and $\dot{\mu}/\mu(t) = \dot{p}/p(t) = \delta$ from (3.29). The welfare maximizing extraction path is identical to the competitive extraction path, assuming identical initial reserves and rates of discount.

How reasonable is the assumption that competitive price $p(t)$ grows at the rate of interest? Theoretically this would require each mine owner to accurately estimate the date of depletion and choke-off price. Also, all owners must use the same discount rate. These assumptions may not be very realistic in the mining industry, which is characterized by volatile prices and other forms of uncertainty. Also, processes of exploration, discovery, and technological change suggest the possibility of alternative price paths (see Section 3.4). Smooth exponentially increasing price paths have not in fact been observed empirically in mining industries.

In the following sections we shall consider various modifications of the basic Hotelling model, including extraction costs, competitive exploitation, and finally exploration.

3.2.1 Extraction costs: the case of a single mine

Suppose initially that the cost of mining depends only on the rate of extraction. Specifically let

$$C(t) = C(q(t)) \tag{3.31}$$

be the cost of extracting at rate $q(t)$. Assume $p(t)$ is exogenous and known in advance to the mine owner. (This assumption will be relaxed later.) Then the mine owner would want to

$$\underset{q(t) \geq 0}{\text{maximize}} \int_0^T [p(t)q(t) - C(q(t))]e^{-\delta t}\, dt$$

$$\text{subject to} \quad \dot{R}(t) = -q(t) \tag{3.32}$$

$$R(0) \quad \text{given} \qquad R(t) \geq 0$$

The current value Hamiltonian is

$$\tilde{\mathcal{H}}(t) = p(t)q(t) - C(q(t)) - \mu(t)q(t) \tag{3.33}$$

with first order necessary conditions that imply

$$p(t) - C'(\cdot) - \mu(t) = 0 \tag{3.34}$$

$$\dot{\mu} = \delta\mu(t) \tag{3.35}$$

If $C(\cdot)$ is convex, the first order conditions are also sufficient; we will thus assume $C'(\cdot) > 0$, $C''(\cdot) > 0$. Following the usual procedure it can be shown that

$$\frac{\frac{d}{dt}(p(t) - C'(q(t)))}{p(t) - C'(q(t))} = \delta \tag{3.36}$$

which implies that *price net of marginal cost* rises at the rate of interest.

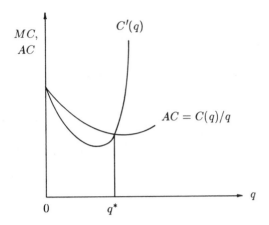

Figure 3.2   Marginal and average cost curves of extraction q.

However, this says nothing about the growth of the price itself, which we have assumed exogenously given (but see Section 3.2.2).

As we shall see later, the corresponding condition for the monopolist (who *controls* price) is

$$\frac{\frac{d}{dt}(R'(\cdot) - C'(\cdot))}{(R'(\cdot) - C'(\cdot))} = \delta \qquad (3.37)$$

where $R(q(t)) = p(q(t))q(t)$ is the monopolist's revenue function and $R'(\cdot)$ is marginal revenue. Equation (3.37) implies that marginal revenue net of marginal cost is rising at the rate of interest.

While Equation (3.36) gives us some abstract insight into the competitive mine owner's problem, we have yet to show how the actual time path of extraction $q(t)$ is determined. For this, let us first assume a U-shaped cost curve as shown in Figure 3.2. From elementary microeconomics we know that the mine owner will never produce at a rate q with $0 < q < q^*$. At q^* marginal cost equals average variable cost. Hence, unless the mine shuts down temporarily,[3] we will have

$$q^* \leq q(t) \quad \text{for} \quad 0 \leq t < T \qquad (3.38)$$

At time $t = T$ the mine shuts down permanently and q jumps to zero.

The transversality condition for free terminal time problems implies

$$\tilde{\mathcal{H}} = 0 \quad \text{at} \quad t = T \qquad (3.39)$$

---

[3] A shut down could occur if price $p(t)$ temporarily falls to a low level, but we will assume that this does not happen. Namely, we assume $p(t) > C(q^*)/q^*$ for all t.

From Equation (3.33) we obtain

$$\mu(T) = p(T) - \frac{C(q(T))}{q(T)} \qquad (3.40)$$

while Equation (3.34) implies that

$$\mu(T) = p(T) - C'(q(T))$$

Hence

$$C'(q(T)) = \frac{C(q(T))}{q(T)} \qquad (3.41)$$

so that

$$q(T) = q^* \qquad (3.42)$$

Notice that *if* we knew the value of T then our problem would be completely solved. For then Equation (3.40) would determine $\mu(T)$, from which by Equation (3.35)

$$\mu(t) = e^{\delta(t-T)}\mu(T) \qquad 0 \leq t \leq T \qquad (3.43)$$

Hence by Equation (3.34)

$$C'(q(t)) = p(t) - \mu(t)$$

from which $q(t)$ is determined for $0 \leq t \leq T$.

The value of T is determined from the condition that $R(T) = 0$ [our assumption that $p(t) > C(q^*)/q^*$ for all t obviously implies that the mine will eventually be exhausted].

As an example, suppose that price $p(t) = p$ (constant), and assume that

$$C(q) = a + bq^2$$

Then $q^* = \sqrt{a/b}$ (why?) and Equations (3.34)–(3.43) imply the conditions

$$\mu(T) = p - C'(q^*) = p - 2\sqrt{ab}$$
$$\mu(t) = e^{\delta(t-T)}\mu(T) \qquad 0 \leq t \leq T$$
$$C'(q(t)) = 2bq(t) = p - \mu(t)$$
$$q(t) = \frac{1}{2b}[p - e^{\delta(t-T)}(p - 2\sqrt{ab})]$$

$$\int_0^T q(t)\, dt = \frac{pT}{2b} - \frac{p - 2\sqrt{ab}}{2b} \frac{1 - e^{-\delta T}}{\delta} = R$$

It is easy to see geometrically that the last equation has a unique solution $T > 0$, so that the problem is solved. (A numerical illustration is given in Problem 3.5.4.)

Let us also reconsider the discrete-time version of the "mine-manager's problem." We solved the problem for *given* terminal time T in Section 1.5. Now let us consider varying T to find the free-time solution. The problem is:

$$\begin{aligned}
\underset{\{q_t\}}{\text{maximize}}\, V &= \sum_{t=0}^{T-1} \rho^t [1 - q_t/R_t] q_t \\
\text{subject to}\quad R_{t+1} - R_t &= -q_t \\
R_0 &= 1{,}000
\end{aligned}$$
(3.44)

For $T = 10$ and $\delta = 0.10$ the time paths for q_t, R_t, and λ_t are given in Table 1.2 (where in its earlier appearance $q_t = y_t$ and $x_t = R_t$). If one were to calculate the value of the objective function, i.e., the present value of net revenues, one would obtain $V_{10} = 580.2956$, where the subscript on V indicates $T = 10$. In the discrete free-time problem, because T assumes integer values, there is no derivative condition. To determine whether it is optimal to lengthen or shorten the mining horizon, one needs to increase or decrease the horizon, solve for the optimal production schedule $\{q_t\}$, calculate the present value of net revenues V_T, and compare it to earlier calculations. This was done via Program 3.1; the results are listed in Table 3.1.

When moving from $T = 10$ to $T = 40$, present net value increases from 580.2956 to 590.3423. Extending the horizon to $T = 50$ only increases V by 0.0002. Extending the horizon from $T = 10$ to $T = 20$ captures 97% of the increase in present net value. With the longer horizon, optimal extraction is lower initially as seen from a comparison of $\{q_t^*\}$ when $T = 10$ and $T = 40$.[4]

---

[4] An alternative method for solving this problem is to use dynamic programming. Using this method, it can be shown that the optimal solution has $T = \infty$ and

$$q_t = \text{const} \times R_t = \frac{\rho - 1 + \sqrt{1 - \rho}}{\rho} \times R_t$$

Thus a fixed portion of the remaining reserves are mined in each period. Note that

$$\lim_{\rho \to 0} \frac{\rho - 1 + \sqrt{1 - \rho}}{\rho} = \frac{1}{2}$$

Thus as $\rho \to 0$ the portion of reserves mined in each period approaches 50%, which is the single-period optimum.

```
10 REM PROGRAM 3.1: MINE MANAGER'S PROBLEM (TABLE 3.1)
20 D = .1
30 INPUT "TIME HORIZON";N
40 R = 1 / (1+D)
50 DIM L(N),X(N),Y(N),Z(N)
60 L(N) = 0
70 FOR T = N-1 TO 0 STEP -1
80    Z(T) = (1 - R * L(T+1)) / 2
90    L(T) = R * L(T+1) + Z(T)^2
100 NEXT
110 X(0) = 1000
120 FOR T = 0 TO N-1
130    Y(T) = X(T) * Z(T)
140    X(T+1) = X(T) - Y(T)
150 NEXT
160 U = 0: DF = 1
170 FOR T = 0 TO N-1
180    U = U + DF * (1 - Z(T)) * Y(T)
190    DF = DF * R
200 NEXT
210 PRINT "HORIZON="N
220 PRINT "T                X(T)              Q(T)              L(T)"
230 PRINT "------------------------------------------------------------"
240 FOR T = 0 TO N
250    PRINT T,X(T),Y(T),L(T)
260 NEXT
270 PRINT "------------------------------------------------------------"
280 PRINT "PRESENT VALUE ="U
290 END
```

Program 3.1   Mine manager's problem (Table 3.1).

Table 3.1 *The mine manager's problem revisited: present value maximization in a discrete free-time problem.*

T	10	20	30	40	50
V_T	580.2956	590.0675	590.3349	590.3423	590.3425

3.2.2 The competitive mining industry: a more detailed analysis

Consider a mining industry comprised of a large number of price-taking mine owners. Let $C_i(q_i(t))$ be the cost of extraction for the ith mine with initial reserves R_i, $i = 1, 2, \ldots, N$ ($N \gg 1$). The price $p(t)$ is determined by aggregate production according to

$$p(t) = P\left(\sum_{i=1}^{N} q_i(t)\right) \tag{3.45}$$

Each firm attempts to maximize its profits given by the expression

$$\pi = \int_0^{T_i} [p(t)q_i(t) - C_i(q_i(t))]e^{-\delta t}\, dt \tag{3.46}$$

subject to the reserves constraint

$$\dot{R}_i = -q_i(t) \qquad R_i(0) = R_i \qquad R_i(T_i) \geq 0 \tag{3.47}$$

But how does the firm know what price $p = p(t)$ to assume in the objective (3.46)? In the case of a monopoly (see below), $N = 1$, the firm has complete control over price, and our optimization problem is unambiguous. Here, however, we adopt the assumption of pure competition: The ith firm is a price taker, treating p as an exogenous variable.

In the static theory of the firm, we can proceed on the basis of this competitive assumption alone. Unfortunately, in the dynamic setting, we must assume that *the firm can predict the entire price profile $p(t)$* over time! Moreover, we must assume that it does so *correctly*. This is called the assumption of *rational expectations*; it is often not brought out explicitly in the literature. The rational expectations assumption may seem extreme, but let us note that the firm will be motivated to estimate $p(t)$ as accurately as it can, for any mistake in predicting $p(t)$ will lead to a sub-optimal policy, and hence to a loss of profit. Of course, with discounting, near-term price predictions are more important than long-term predictions, but serious losses may still result from errors in economic prediction.

The ith firm's Hamiltonian (*not* current value) is

$$\mathcal{H}_i = [p(t)q_i(t) - C_i(q_i(t))]e^{-\delta t} - \lambda_i(t)q_i(t) \tag{3.48}$$

with necessary conditions that imply

$$p(t) - C_i'(q_i(t)) = \lambda_i(t)e^{\delta t} \tag{3.49}$$

and

$$\dot{\lambda}_i = -\frac{\partial \mathcal{H}_i}{\partial R(t)} = 0 \tag{3.50}$$

Thus $\lambda_i(t) = \lambda_i$, a constant. The transversality condition $\mathcal{H}_i(T_i) = 0$ implies

$$\lambda_i = [p(T_i) - C_i(q_i(T_i))/q_i(T_i)]e^{-\delta T_i} \tag{3.51}$$

But, evaluating (3.49) at $t = T_i$ also implies

$$\lambda_i = [p(T_i) - C_i'(q_i(T_i))]e^{-\delta T_i} \tag{3.52}$$

and thus $q_i(T_i) = q_i^*$ is the level of production where

$$C_i'(q(T_i)) = C_i(q_i(T_i))/q_i(T_i) \tag{3.53}$$

that is, where the average variable cost of the ith mine is minimized.
Substituting (3.52) back into (3.49) implies

$$C_i'(q_i(t_i)) = p(t) - [p(T_i) - C_i'(q_i(T_i))]e^{\delta(t-T_i)} \tag{3.54}$$

At this stage we have $2N + 1$ unknowns $T_1, \ldots, T_N$, $q_1(t), \ldots, q_N(t)$, and $p(t)$ [since $\lambda_1, \ldots, \lambda_N$ can be determined from (3.51)] and $2N + 1$ equations consisting of (3.54) with $q_i(T_i) = q_i^*$ plus (3.45) and

$$\int_0^{T_i} q_i(t)\, dt = R_i$$

Solution of these equations is certainly nontrivial in general; the special case in which the N firms have identical costs and reserves is considered in Problem 3.5.5.

3.2.3 The social optimum with N firms

Since there are no externalities between mines (i.e., no stock or "common pool" externalities) we should expect that, as before, the perfectly competitive industry would be socially optimal in the usual sense of maximizing discounted social welfare (utility). This is easily verified as follows.

The social objective is to

$$\text{maximize} \int_0^T \left[U(\sum_{i=1}^N q_i(t)) - \sum_{i=1}^N C_i(q_i(t)) \right] e^{-\delta t}\, dt$$

$$\text{subject to} \quad \dot{R}_i = -q_i(t) \tag{3.55}$$

$$R_i(0) = R_i$$

$$R_i(t) \geq 0$$

The Hamiltonian is

$$\mathcal{H} = \left[U(\sum_{i=1}^{N} q_i(t)) - \sum_{i=1}^{N} C_i(q_i(t))\right]e^{-\delta t} - \sum_{i=1}^{N} \lambda_i(t)q_i(t) \qquad (3.56)$$

Each $\lambda_i(t) = \lambda_i = $ constant (since $\partial \mathcal{H}/\partial R_i = 0$) and we have

$$\lambda_i = [U'(Q(t)) - C_i'(q_i(t))]e^{-\delta t} \qquad (3.57)$$

where $Q(t) = \sum_{i=1}^{N} q_i(t)$, thus $\partial U/\partial q_i = dU/dQ \cdot \partial Q/\partial q_i = U'(Q)$. Also
$U'(Q(t)) = P(Q(t)) = p(t)$.

Suppose that all N firms have identical reserves and costs. Then $T_i = T$
and $H(T) = 0$ implies

$$\lambda_i = \lambda = [p(T) - C(q(T))/q(T)]e^{-\delta T} \qquad (3.58)$$

and $q_i^* = q^* = q(T)$ is the level of output which minimizes average variable
cost [recall Equations (3.51) and (3.52) implied (3.53)]. The rest of the
solution is identical to the competitive case.

In the case where the N firms are not identical, it can be shown that

$$\lambda_i = [p(T_i) - C(q_i(T_i))/q_i(T_i)]e^{-\delta T_i} \qquad (3.59)$$

and the same system of equations is obtained as in the competitive model
with rational expectations. Two problems therefore lead to the same solution.

3.3 Scarcity from an economic perspective

To an economist, scarcity is not a physical concept but a value concept. This
difference in perspective has often put economists at odds with biologists
and geologists when evaluating whether a resource is becoming more or less
scarce. For a nonrenewable resource the rent (royalty or shadow price) is
given by the costate variable

$$\mu(t) = p(t) - MC(t) \qquad (3.60)$$

along the *optimal* trajectories for $q(t)$ and $R(t)$. It reflects the difference
between the current market price and the marginal cost of extraction at
instant t. In a competitive market, this difference would equal the difference

between what society would be willing to pay for an additional unit of $R(t)$ and the cost incurred in extraction. If this difference is positive and large, then the resource is scarce. If the difference increases over time ($\dot{\mu} > 0$) then the resoure is becoming more scarce in a relative sense, while if it is decreasing over time ($\dot{\mu} < 0$), the resource is becoming less scarce.

Recall the mine manager's problem as posed in (3.44). In this problem λ_{t+1} is the value (in period $t+1$) of an additional unit of the resource. The discounted value of an additional unit of the resource is equated to the price net of marginal cost in period t; thus $\rho\lambda_{t+1} = 1 - 2q_t/R_t$. For $T = 10$ (or any other positive integer) we saw that λ_{t+1} (thus $\rho\lambda_{t+1}$) declined over time. From an economic perspective, the resource was becoming *less scarce* (see Table 1.2). This occurred even though R_t (or x_t in Table 1.2) was declining (becoming physically more scarce).[5]

Which notion is correct? In the mine manager's problem, we stacked the deck because we fixed $p_t = 1$, that is, market price did not increase even as production (q_t) declined to zero. This is probably unrealistic for the natural resources that underpin developed (industrial) economies. However, if an abundant resource can substitute for a resource that is becoming physically scarce, that resource may no longer be viewed as scarce from an economic perspective. This scenario has probably occurred for copper where aluminum has become a substitute in electrical transmission and plastic a substitute in plumbing. There is strong indication that λ_{t+1} has fallen for copper and from an economic viewpoint it is now more "abundant" than it used to be.

3.4 Exploration

With exploration and discovery it is possible to augment reserves, perhaps at a rate that exceeds depletion. We have seen in previous models that there may be an economic incentive to add to the known reserves if extraction costs are lowered when mining from a larger reserve base (e.g., $C(q, R_2) < C(q, R_1)$; $R_1 < R_2$).

The following model is due to Pindyck (1978). Let

$$\dot{R} = f(w(t), X(t)) - q(t) \tag{3.61}$$

---

[5] Recall, however, that with t not specified in advance, the optimal policy has $q_t/R_t =$ constant, so that λ_t is also constant (see footnote 4). In this case, the "scarcity" of the resource remains constant!

$$\dot{X} = f(w(t), X(t)) \tag{3.62}$$

where, as noted in Section 3.1, $f(\cdot)$ is a discovery-rate function with arguments $w(t)$, exploratory effort, and $X(t)$, cumulative discoveries. Assume initially that extraction costs are linear in $q(t)$ and that the total cost of extraction per unit time is $C_1(R(t))q(t)$ where $C_1(\cdot)$ is a *unit* extraction cost function dependent on remaining reserves. The cost of exploration is assumed to be a convex function $C_2(w(t))$ and net revenue at instant t is

$$p(t)q(t) - C_1(R(t))q(t) - C_2(w(t)) \tag{3.63}$$

where $p(t)$ is the per unit price of ore. We will consider the case of a competitive mining industry, consisting of a large number of identical mining firms. The individual firm takes price $p(t)$ as exogenous (rational expectations), and attempts to

$$\text{maximize} \int_0^T [p(t)q(t) - C_1(R(t))q(t) - C_2(w(t))]e^{-\delta t}\, dt$$

$$\text{subject to} \quad \dot{R} = f(w(t), X(t)) - q(t) \tag{3.64}$$

$$\dot{X} = f(w(t), X(t))$$

$$R(0), X(0) \quad \text{given}$$

This problem has two state variables R, X and two control variables q, w and is thus considerably more difficult than most of the problems we have discussed until now.

The current-value Hamiltonian is

$$\tilde{\mathcal{H}} = p(t)q(t) - C_1(R)q(t) - C_2(w) + \mu_1[f(\cdot) - q(t)] + \mu_2 f(\cdot) \tag{3.65}$$

and the first-order conditions include [6]

$$\frac{\partial \tilde{\mathcal{H}}}{\partial q(t)} = p(t) - C_1(\cdot) - \mu_1(t) = 0 \tag{3.66}$$

$$\frac{\partial \tilde{\mathcal{H}}}{\partial w(t)} = -C_2'(\cdot) + (\mu_1(t) + \mu_2(t))f_w = 0 \tag{3.67}$$

$$\dot{\mu}_1 - \delta\mu_1(t) = -\frac{\partial \tilde{\mathcal{H}}}{\partial R(t)} = C_1'(\cdot)q(t) \tag{3.68}$$

---

[6] Equation (3.66) actually specifies the singular solution for $q(t)$. Pindyck argues that market clearing will ensure that this solution is followed. See Problem 3.5.6 for a simpler case.

$$\dot{\mu}_2 - \delta\mu_2(t) = -\frac{\partial\tilde{\mathcal{H}}}{\partial X(t)} = -(\mu_1(t) + \mu_2(t))f_x \qquad (3.69)$$

where f_x and f_w are partials of $f(\cdot)$ with respect to $X(t)$ and $w(t)$. Taking the time derivative of (3.66) implies $\dot{\mu}_1 = \dot{p} - C_1'(\cdot)\dot{R}$. Substituting this expression into (3.68) yields

$$\dot{p} - C_1'(\cdot)\dot{R} = \delta(p(t) - C_1(\cdot)) + C_1'(\cdot)q(t)$$
$$\dot{p} = \delta(p(t) - C_1(\cdot)) + (\dot{R} + q(t))C_1'(\cdot)$$
$$\dot{p} = \delta(p(t) - C_1(\cdot)) + f(\cdot)C_1'(\cdot) \qquad (3.70)$$

Equation (3.67) may be solved for $\mu_2(t)$ yielding

$$\mu_2(t) = C_2'(\cdot)/f_w - p(t) + C_1(\cdot)$$

Taking the time derivative of this expression yields

$$\dot{\mu}_2 = C_2''(\cdot)\dot{w}/f_w - C_2'(f_w)^{-2}[f_{w,w}\dot{w} + f_{w,x}\dot{X}] - \dot{p} + C_1'(\cdot)\dot{R} \qquad (3.71)$$

Substituting the expression for $\mu_2(t)$ into (3.69) and noting from (3.67) that $(\mu_1(t) + \mu_2(t)) = C_2'(\cdot)/f_w$ we also obtain

$$\dot{\mu}_2 = \delta[C_2'(\cdot)/f_w - p(t) + C_1(\cdot)] - C_2'(\cdot)f_x/f_w \qquad (3.72)$$

Equating (3.71) and (3.72), solving for $\dot{w}$, substituting expression (3.70) for $\dot{p}$, and simplifying will finally produce

$$\dot{w} = \frac{[(f_{w,x}/f_w)f(\cdot) + \delta - f_x]C_2'(\cdot) + q(t)C_1'(\cdot)f_w}{C_2''(\cdot) - C_2'(\cdot)f_{w,w}/f_w} \qquad (3.73)$$

Equations (3.61), (3.62), (3.70), and (3.73) form a four-equation dynamical system for the five unknown functions $R(t)$, $X(t)$, $w(t)$, $p(t)$, and $q(t)$. The latter function may be eliminated via the demand equation

$$q(t) = D(p(t)) \qquad (3.74)$$

The terminal conditions for $\dot{p}$ and $\dot{w}$ will depend on $C_2'(\cdot)/f_w(\cdot)$ as $t \to T$. This expression defines the ratio of marginal exploration costs to the marginal product of exploratory effort, and is referred to as the "marginal discovery cost." If $C_2'(0)/f_w(0, X) = 0$ then $w(T) = q(T) = 0$ and more specifically they must fall to zero *simultaneously* at $t = T$. It will also be the case that $\mu_2(T) = 0$ and $\mu_1(T) = p(T) - C_1(R(T)) = 0$ so that no additional profit can be obtained from further extraction.

If $C_2'(0)/f_w(0, X) = \phi > 0$ then exploratory effort will become zero before extraction, that is, there will exist an interval $T_1 \leq t \leq T$ where $w(t) = 0$ but $q(t) > 0$. At $t = T_1$, $\mu_2(T_1) = 0$ and with $w(t) = 0$, $\dot{\mu}_2 = 0$. Then for $t \geq T_1$, $p(t) - C_1(\cdot) = \mu_1(t) = \phi$. This implies $\dot{\mu}_1 = 0$ and further that $-C_1'(\cdot)q(t)/\delta \to \phi$ as $t \to T$. Thus for $t \geq T_1$ both $p(t) - C_1(\cdot)$ and $C_1'(\cdot)q(t)$ remain constant implying $p(t)$, $C_1(\cdot)$, and $C_1'(\cdot)$ rise as $q(t)$ falls. The last unit of reserves should be discovered when its marginal discovery cost (ϕ) equals the *sum* of the net revenue obtained upon extraction and sale and the value of cost savings after discovery but before extraction. This sum represents the present value of net revenues of the marginal discovery.

The system $\dot{R}, \dot{X}, \dot{p}$, and $\dot{w}$ leads to several dynamic possibilities, two of which are shown in Figure 3.3. First, if initial reserves R_0 are high, then exploratory effort w will initially be low (Figure 3.3a). As reserves fall, exploratory effort w increases, but eventually both R and w fall to zero. This case is qualitatively similar to the standard Hotelling result, with price $p(t)$ steadily increasing with t.

The case in which initial reserves are low is shown in Figure 3.3b. Exploratory effort begins at a high level, reserves increase [and hence price $p(t)$ falls]. Eventually the situation reverts to that given in Figure 3.3a (or alternatively, exploration may decline monotonically). In this second scenario, the price of the resource follows a U-shaped profile over time, in contrast to the Hotelling rule.

In an appendix, Pindyck (1978) gives a numerical example relating to the Permian oil region of Texas. Pindyck estimates the following model:

$$p_t = a - bq_t \qquad\qquad a = \$33 \qquad\qquad b = 0.05$$

$$C_1(R_t) = c/R_t \qquad\qquad c = 8{,}960$$

$$C_2(w_t) = m + nw_t \qquad\qquad m = 103.2 \qquad\qquad n = 0.067$$

$$f(w_t, X_t) = rw_t^s e^{-uX_t} \qquad\qquad r = 0.871 \qquad\qquad s = 0.599$$

$$u = 0.0002258$$

He then employs difference equation approximations to the equations for $\dot{X}$, $\dot{R}$, $\dot{p}$ (or $\dot{q}$), and $\dot{w}$. By specifying values for T, p_0, and w_0 one can simulate the system forward in time. The values of T, p_0, and w_0 are adjusted until q_T, w_T, and π_T (net revenue) all go to zero simultaneously.

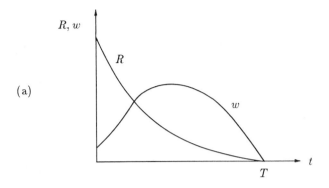

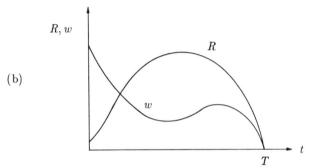

Figure 3.3 Exploratory activity and proven reserves: (a) high initial reserves; (b) low initial reserves.

The results for the competitive industry are given in Table 3.2. Exploratory effort leads to discoveries which augment reserves (slightly) and briefly allows production to increase and price to fall (see Figure 3.3b).

3.5 Problems

P3.5.1. Consider the mine manager's problem, but with cost independent of remaining reserves. Specifically, you wish to

$$
\underset{\{q_t\},T}{\text{maximize}} \quad V = \sum_{t=0}^{T-1} \rho^t [1 - aq_t] q_t
$$

$$
\text{subject to} \quad R_{t+1} - R_t = -q_t
$$

$$
R_0 \text{ given}
$$

Table 3.2 *The Competitive solution of the exploration/extraction problem*
(Source: Pindyck 1978, p. 858).

Year	Production (10^6 brl/yr)	Price ($/brl)	Rent[a] ($/brl)	Wells drilled	Reserves (10^6 brl)	Cumulative discoveries (10^6 brl)	Profits (10^6 $/yr)
1965	552.0	5.40	4.150	9,353	7,170	0	1,556
1966	557.0	5.15	4.177	4,779	9,243	2,630	1,901
1967	554.9	5.25	4.284	4,120	9,648	2,630	2,019
1968	551.9	5.40	4.488	3,794	9,801	3,590	2,019
1969	548.5	5.57	4.661	3,612	9,822	4,295	2,118
1970	544.7	5.76	4.842	3,511	9,763	4,865	2,209
1975	522.1	6.89	5.883	3,554	8,892	5,350	2,298
1980	493.6	8.32	7.147	4,014	7,659	7,138	2,729
1985	458.8	10.05	7.990	4,681	4,361	8,433	3,154
1990	417.0	12.14	10.391	5,411	5,117	9,500	3,550
1995	368.1	14.59	12.350	5,978	3,994	10,428	3,867
2000	312.4	17.37	14.413	6,012	3,031	11,247	4,039
2005	251.0	20.44	16.452	5,062	2,243	11,960	3,996
2010	185.4	23.72	18.201	2,968	1,623	12,552	3,684
2015	113.6	27.31	19.584	670	1,159	12,993	3,071
2020	22.0	31.89	22.120	3	917	13,308	384
2021	0.2	32.99	23.233	3	918	13,309	99

[a] Marginal discovery cost and opportunity cost of additional cumulative discoveries

(a) Write the expression for the Hamiltonian $\mathcal{H}$ (*not* the current value
    Hamiltonian $\tilde{\mathcal{H}}$).

(b) Derive the first order necessary conditions in terms of the partials of
    $\mathcal{H}$ and show that they imply

$$\lambda_{t+1} = \lambda_t = \lambda = (T - 2aR_0) \Big/ \sum_{k=0}^{T-1} (1+\delta)^k$$

assuming $\displaystyle\sum_{t=0}^{T-1} q_t = R_0$.

(c) Solve for the optimal horizon and extraction path when $a = 0.001$, $\delta = 0.1$, and $R_0 = 1,000$.

Answers

(a) $\mathcal{H} = \rho^t[1 - aq_t]q_t - \lambda_{t+1}q_t$

(b) $\dfrac{\partial \mathcal{H}}{\partial q_t} = \rho^t[1 - 2aq_t] - \lambda_{t+1} = 0$

$\lambda_{t+1} - \lambda_t = -\dfrac{\partial \mathcal{H}}{\partial R_t} = 0 \qquad R_{t+1} - R_t = \dfrac{\partial \mathcal{H}}{\partial \lambda_{t+1}} = -q_t$

The above imply $\lambda_{t+1} = \lambda_t = \lambda$ and $q_t = (1 - (1 + \delta)^t\lambda)/(2a)$. With $\sum_{t=0}^{T-1} q_t = R_0$ you obtain $\lambda = (T - 2aR_0)\Big/\left(\sum_{k=0}^{T-1}(1 + \delta)^k\right)$.

(c) $T = 7$ (see Program 3.2).

```
10 REM PROGRAM 3.2: PROBLEM 3.5.1
20 DATA .001,.1
30 READ A,D
40 INPUT "TIME HORIZON";T
50 DIM Q(T),R(T)
60 S = 0
70 FOR I = 0 TO T-1
80    S = S + (1+D)^I
90 NEXT
100 R(0) = 1000
110 L = (T-2 * A * R(0)) / S
120 V = 0
130 FOR I = 0 TO T-1
140    DI = (1+D)^I
150    Q(I) = (1 - L * DI) / (2 * A)
160    V = V + (1 - A * Q(I)) * Q(I) / DI
170    R(I+1) = R(I) - Q(I)
180 NEXT
190 LPRINT "HORIZON=" T"
200 LPRINT "K                Q(K)           R(K)
210 LPRINT "---------------------------------------------"
220 FOR K = 0 TO T
230    LPRINT K,Q(K),R(K)
240 NEXT
250 LPRINT "PRESENT VALUE=";V
260 END
```

```
HORIZON= 7
K              Q(K)           R(K)
---------------------------------------------
0              236.4863       1000
1              210.1349       763.5138
2              181.1484       553.379
3              149.2632       372.2306
4              114.1895       222.9674
5              75.60846       108.7779
6              33.1693        33.16943
7              0              1.373291E-04
---------------------------------------------
PRESENT VALUE= 680.0307
```

Program 3.2

P3.5.2. Suppose the inverse demand for an exhaustible resource is given by

$$p(t) = q(t)^{-0.5}$$

Suppose further that the costs of extraction are zero, that initial reserves are $R = 1$ and $\delta = 0.10$.

(a) Solve for the time-path of extraction for the competitive mining industry.

(b) Solve for the time-path of extraction for the monopolistic mining industry. How does it compare to that obtained for the competitive industry in part (a)? Explain your answer.

(c) What are the values for T_c and T_m?

Answers

(a) $q_c(t) = e^{-0.2t}$

(b) $q_m(t) = e^{-0.2t}$. They are the same. The elasticity of demand is constant (-2) and $\dot{p}/p = \dot{MR}/MR = \dot{q}/q = -0.2$. Thus the time-paths for extraction are identical (see Stiglitz 1976).

(c) $T_c = T_m = 1.1157$

P3.5.3. You have inherited R_0 bottles of wine. Because of aging the demand for this wine is expected to shift over time according to $p(t) = ae^{\gamma t} - bq(t)$ where $q(t)$ is the number of bottles sold at instant t and a, γ, and b are positive constants. The cost of storage is given as $C(t) = cR(t)$ where $R(t)$ is the number of bottles left in the cellar and c is a positive constant. Assume the instantaneous discount rate is $\delta > \gamma > 0$.

(a) Write the current-value Hamiltonian for the problem which maximizes the present value of net revenues over the finite (but unknown) horizon $0 \le t \le T$.

(b) From the first order necessary conditions derive an equation for $\dot{q}(t)$.

(c) What are the transversality conditions?

(d) Use the transversality conditions to solve for $q(t)$, the optimal sale of wine from inventory.

(e) Use the transversality conditions to obtain an equation that may be used to solve for the optimal horizon, T.

Answers

(a) $\tilde{\mathcal{H}} = [ae^{\gamma t} - bq(t)]q(t) - cR(t) - \mu(t)q(t)$

(b) $\dot{q} - \delta q(t) - [(\gamma - \delta)ae^{\gamma t} - c]/(2b) = 0$

(c) $\tilde{\mathcal{H}}(T) = 0$ implies $q(T) = 0$ and $R(T) = 0$

(d) $q(t) = -\dfrac{e^{(t-T)\delta}(ae^{\gamma T} + c/\delta)}{2b} + \dfrac{ae^{\gamma t}}{2b} + \dfrac{c}{2b\delta}$

(e) $a\delta e^{\gamma T}(\delta - \gamma) + c\gamma(\delta T - 1) + a\delta\gamma e^{-(\delta-\gamma)T} + c\gamma e^{-\delta T} - a\delta^2 - 2b\delta^2\gamma R_0 = 0$

P3.5.4. Solve the mine owner's problem:

$$\text{maximize} \quad \int_0^T e^{-\delta t}(pq(t) - C(q(t)))\, dt$$

$$\text{subject to} \quad \dot{R} = -q(t) \qquad R(0) = R_0 \qquad R(T) = 0$$

given $p = \$50/\text{ton}$, $R_0 = 200{,}000$ tons, and $C(q) = 1000 + \frac{1}{2}q^2$ \$/day.
(a) Take $\delta = 0$; find $q^* = $ optimal production rate, and $T = $ lifetime of mine, and also total net mine income. Also determine q for the short-term profit maximizer.
(b) Take $\delta = 10\%/\text{year}$, and assume 250 mining days/year [with $C(q) = 0$ on closed days]. Find T, λ, and $q(0)$.

Answers

(a) $C'(q^*) = C(q^*)/q^*$ gives $q^* = 44.72$ tons/day or 11,180 tons/year. Hence $T = 17.89$ years. Net mine income is $\$50 \times 200{,}000 - 2{,}000 \times 4{,}472 = \$1{,}056{,}000$. The short-term maximizer sets $C'(q) = p$, or $q = 50$ tons/day.

(b) From $C'(q) = q = p - \lambda e^{\delta t}$ and $q(T) = q^*$ we get $\lambda = e^{-\delta T}(p - q^*)$ and $q(t) = p - (p-q^*)e^{\delta(t-T)}$. Integrating between $t = 0$ and T gives the equation

$$pT - (p - q^*)\dfrac{(1 - e^{-\delta T})}{\delta} = R$$

Here T is in days, so $\delta = (\log 1.1)/250 = 3.81 \times 10^{-4}$. The solution is $t = 4{,}222$ mining days, or 16.86 years. Hence $\lambda = 1.06$ and $q(0) = 48.94$ tons/day.

P3.5.5. Consider a competitive mining industry consisting of N identical mines. Assume rational expectations; each mine owner attempts to

$$\text{maximize} \quad \int_0^T e^{-\delta t}[p(t)q(t) - C(q(t))]\, dt$$

subject to $\dot{R} = -q(t)$ $R(0) = R_0$ $R(T) = 0$

Assume that $C(q) = a + bq^2$ $(q > 0)$, and that price $p(t)$ is determined by aggregate demand:

$$p(t) = P\left(\sum_{i=1}^{N} q_i(t)\right) = P(Nq(t))$$

with linear demand function

$$P(Q) = \alpha - \beta Q$$

Obtain the solution in general, and apply it to the parameter values $a =$ \$1,000/day, $b =$ \$0.5 days/ton^2, $\alpha =$ \$100/ton, $\beta =$ \$0.02 days/ton^2, $\delta =$ 0.10/year, $N = 20$, and $R = 200,000$ tons. There are 250 mining days per year.

Answer. $q^* = \sqrt{a/b}$ $p(T) = \alpha - \beta N q^*$

$$q(t) = \frac{\alpha}{2b + N\beta} - \left[\frac{\alpha}{2b + N\beta} - q^*\right] e^{\delta(t-T)} = c_1 - c_2 e^{\delta(t-T)}$$
$$p(t) = \alpha - \beta N q(t)$$

and T is determined by

$$c_1 T - c_2 (1 - e^{-\delta T})/\delta = R$$

The numerical results are $q^* = 44.72$ tons/day, $p(T) = 82.12/ton, $T = 14.07$ years, and

$$q(t) = 71.43 - 8.73 e^{\delta t} \text{ tons/day}$$
$$p(t) = 71.43 + 3.49 e^{\delta t} \text{ \$/ton}$$

Note that $p(t)$ has a *component* which grows at the rate of interest.

P3.5.6. Consider a mine owner whose costs of production are linear in q but depend on reserves R:

$$c(q, R) = c(R)q$$

Solve the problem

$$\underset{q(t)\geq 0}{\text{maximize}} \int_0^T e^{-\delta t}[p(t) - c(R(t))]q(t)\, dt$$

$$\text{subject to} \quad \dot{R} = -q(t) \qquad R(0) = R_0$$

for the case of an exogenous price $p(t) = p_0 e^{\gamma t}$. Use the parameter values

$$R_0 = 100{,}000 \text{ tons}$$

$$p_0 = \$200/\text{ton}$$

$$c(R) = \frac{6 \times 10^6}{R + 1.5 \times 10^4} \ \$/\text{ton}$$

$$\delta = 10\% \text{ per annum}$$

with three values for γ: 5%, 10% and 15% per annum.

Answer. The singular solution is given by

$$c(R) = p(t) - \frac{1}{\delta}\dot{p}(t) = p_0\big(1 - \frac{\gamma}{\delta}\big)e^{\gamma t}$$

This equation has no solution $0 < R < \infty$ if $\gamma \geq \delta$. In fact, the optimization problem also has no solution if $\gamma \geq \delta$; if $\gamma > \delta$ then price is growing faster than the rate of interest, and production should be postponed arbitrarily far into the future. If $\gamma = \delta$, the discounted price is constant, but discounted costs approach zero as $T \to \infty$. [Of course if T is fixed, the optimal solution exists: produce the entire deposit at $t = T$, at least if $p(T) > c(0)$.]

For $\gamma < \delta$ the singular solution exists, and is given by

$$R(t) = \frac{ae^{-\gamma t}}{p_0(1 - \gamma/\delta)} - b$$

$$= 1.5 \times 10^4 (2e^{-.05t} - 1)$$

Hence the optimal production schedule is: produce 70,000 tons at $t = 0$ and follow the singular path for $0 \leq t \leq T = 13.86$ years, using

$$q(t) = -\dot{R} = \frac{a\gamma e^{-\delta t}}{p_0(1 - \gamma/\delta)} = 1500e^{-.05t} \quad \text{tons/year}$$

P3.5.7. Solve the monopolistic version of Problem 3.5.5.

Answer.
$$q^* = 33.33 \text{ tons/day}$$
$$p(T) = \$86.67/\text{ton}$$
$$T = 15.97 \text{ years}$$
$$q(t) = 55.6 - 2.21e^{\delta t} \text{ tons/day}$$
$$p(t) = 77.78 + .89e^{\delta t} \$/\text{ton}$$

P3.5.8. Consider the discrete-time problem of optimal extraction and exploration which may be stated as

$$\underset{q_t, w_t}{\text{maximize}} \quad V = \sum_{t=0}^{T-1} \rho^t [p_t q_t - C_1(R_t)q_t - C_2(w_t)]$$

$$\text{subject to} \quad R_{t+1} - R_t = f(w_t, X_t) - q_t$$
$$X_{t+1} - X_t = f(w_t, X_t)$$
$$R_0, X_0 \text{ given}$$

(a) Write the discrete-time current-value Hamiltonian.
(b) Eliminate the Lagrange multipliers from the first order conditions to obtain four difference equations.
(c) Assume the following specification and parameter values:

$$p_t = a - bq_t \qquad a = 33 \qquad b = 0.05$$
$$C_1(R_t) = c/R_t \qquad c = 8960$$
$$C_2(w_t) = nw_t^2 \qquad n = 0.0001$$
$$f(w_t, X_t) = rw_t^s e^{-uX_t} \qquad r = 0.871 \qquad s = 0.599 \qquad u = 0.0002258$$
$$R_0 = 10{,}000 \qquad X_0 = 0 \qquad \delta = 0.05$$

Write the four difference equations for X_{t+1}, R_{t+1}, q_{t+1}, and w_{t+1} corresponding to this specification. Can you write an explicit equation for w_{t+1}?
(d) What are the transversality conditions?
(e) Write an interactive program which will permit you to select arbitrary values for T, q_0, and w_0 and then search for the *optimal* values of T, q_0, and w_0 which satisfy the difference equations, transversality conditions, and maximize V.
(f) Construct the phase plane diagram for w, R.

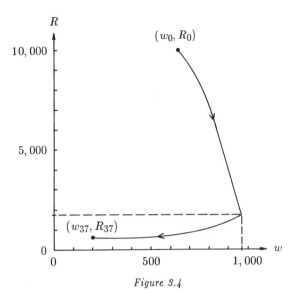

Figure 3.4

Answers

(a) $\tilde{\mathcal{H}} = p_t q_t - C_1(R_t) q_t - C_2(w_t) + \rho \lambda_{1,t+1}[f(w_t, X_t) - q_t] + \rho \lambda_{2,t+1} f(w_t, X_t)$

(b) $X_{t+1} = X_t + f(w_t, X_t)$

$R_{t+1} = R_t + (X_{t+1} - X_t) - q_t$

$P_{t+1} - C_1(R_{t+1}) - (1 + \delta)(p_t - C_1(R_t)) - C_1'(R_{t+1}) q_{t+1} = 0$

$C_2'(w_{t+1})/f_w(w_{t+1}, X_{t+1}) - p_{t+1} + C_1(R_{t+1})$

$\quad -(1 + \delta)[C_2'(w_t)/f_w - p_t + C_1(R_t)] - C_2'(w_{t+1}) f_{x_{t+1}}/f_{w_{t+1}} = 0$

(c) $X_{t+1} = X_t + r w_t^s e^{-u X_t}$

$R_{t+1} = R_t + (X_{t+1} - X_t) - q_t$

$q_{t+1} = [(1 + \delta)(a - b q_t - c/R_t) - a + c/R_{t+1}] R_{t+1}^2/(c - b R_{t+1}^2)$

$2 n w_{t+1}^2 (w_{t+1}^{-s} e^{u X_{t+1}}/r - u)/s - a + b q_{t+1} + c/R_{t+1}$

$\quad -(1 + \delta)[2 n w_t^{2-s} e^{u X_t}/(sr) - a + b q_t + c/R_t] = 0$

You can't solve for w_{t+1} explicitly and need to incorporate a bisection or Newton method in your solution algorithm.

(d) $\tilde{\mathcal{H}} = 0$ implying q_T and w_T must become (approximately) zero simultaneously.

(e) See Program 3.3. $T = 37$, $q_0 = 493$, $w_0 = 666$ $Z = 68{,}584.24$

(f) See Figure 3.4.

```
10 REM PROGRAM 3.3: PROBLEM 3.5.8 EXPLORATION AND EXTRACTION
20 DATA 33,0.05,8960,0.0001,0.871,0.599,0.0002258,0.05
30 READ A,B,C,N,R,S,U,D
40 INPUT "HORIZON LENGTH";T
50 DIM X(T),R(T),Q(T),P(T),W(T),V(T)
60 X(0) = R:R(0) = 10000
70 PRINT "Q(0)=":INPUT Q(0)
80 PRINT "W(0)=":INPUT W(0)
90 P(0) = A - B*Q(0)
100 V(0) = P(0) * Q(0) - C*Q(0)/R(0) - N*(W(0)^2)
110 V = V(0)
120 FOR I = 0 TO T-1
130 X(I+1) = X(I) + R*(W(I)^S) * EXP(-U*X(I))
140 R(I+1) = R(I) + X(I+1) - X(I) - Q(I)
150 Q(I+1) = ((1+D)*(A-B*Q(I)-C/R(I))-A+C/R(I+1))
              *(R(I+1)^2)/(C-B*(R(I+1)^2))
160 W(I+1) = W(I) + 1
170 G1 = 2*N*(W(I+1)^2)*((W(I+1)^-S)*EXP(U*X(I+1))/R-U)/S-A+B
              *Q(I+1)+C/R(I+1)
180 G0 = -(1+D)*(2*N*(W(I)^(2-S))*EXP(U*X(I))/(S*R)
              -A+B*Q(I)+C/R(I))
190 G = G1 + G0
200 DG = 2*(2-S)*N*(W(I+1)^(1-S))*EXP(U*X(I+1))/(S*R)
              -4*N*U*W(I+1)/S
210 IF ABS(G) <.00001 GOTO 230
220 W(I+1) = W(I+1) - G/(DG): GOTO 170
230 P(I+1) = A - B*Q(I+1)
240 V(I+1) = ((1/(1+D))^(I+1))*(P(I+1)*Q(I+1)-C*Q(I+1)/R(I+1)
              -N*(W(I+1)^2))
250 V = V + V(I+1)
260 NEXT I
270 LPRINT "    T      Q(T)      P(T)     W(T)     R(T)     X(T)"
280 LPRINT "---------------------------------------------------"
290 FOR I = 0 TO T
300 LPRINT USING "######.#";I,Q(I),P(I),W(I),R(I),X(I)
310 NEXT I
320 LPRINT "---------------------------------------------------"
330 LPRINT "PRESENT VALUE = ";V
340 END
```

T	Q(T)	P(T)	W(T)	R(T)	X(T)
0.0	493.0	8.4	666.0	10000.0	0.9
1.0	485.7	8.7	683.2	9549.8	43.6
2.0	478.0	9.1	700.6	9107.1	86.7
3.0	470.0	9.5	718.1	8672.4	129.9
4.0	461.7	9.9	735.9	8245.8	173.4
5.0	453.0	10.3	753.7	7827.8	217.0
6.0	444.0	10.8	771.6	7418.7	260.9
7.0	434.6	11.3	789.4	7018.7	305.0
8.0	424.9	11.8	807.2	6628.3	349.2
9.0	414.7	12.3	824.8	6247.8	393.6
10.0	404.2	12.8	842.1	5877.6	438.0
11.0	393.2	13.3	859.0	5518.0	482.7
12.0	381.9	13.9	875.4	5169.5	527.3
13.0	370.1	14.5	891.1	4832.3	572.1
14.0	358.0	15.1	905.9	4506.9	616.8
15.0	345.4	15.7	919.7	4193.7	661.6
16.0	332.5	16.4	932.1	3893.0	706.3
17.0	319.1	17.0	942.8	3605.1	750.9
18.0	305.4	17.7	951.6	3330.5	795.4
19.0	291.3	18.4	958.0	3069.4	839.6

(continued)

T	Q(T)	P(T)	W(T)	R(T)	X(T)
20.0	276.9	19.2	961.5	2822.1	883.7
21.0	262.2	19.9	961.8	2588.9	927.3
22.0	247.3	20.6	958.1	2369.9	970.6
23.0	232.2	21.4	950.0	2165.3	1013.3
24.0	216.9	22.2	936.5	1975.3	1055.4
25.0	201.6	22.9	917.2	1799.7	1096.7
26.0	186.3	23.7	891.0	1638.6	1137.2
27.0	171.1	24.4	857.3	1491.7	1176.6
28.0	156.0	25.2	815.2	1358.8	1214.8
29.0	141.2	25.9	764.2	1239.5	1251.5
30.0	126.6	26.7	703.8	1133.3	1286.5
31.0	112.2	27.4	633.9	1039.8	1319.6
32.0	97.9	28.1	555.0	958.4	1350.4
33.0	83.4	28.8	468.7	888.8	1378.7
34.0	68.3	29.6	378.9	830.7	1404.1
35.0	52.0	30.4	293.3	784.6	1426.3
36.0	33.7	31.3	226.7	751.6	1445.3
37.0	12.9	32.4	201.5	734.1	1461.4

PRESENT VALUE = 68584.5

Program 3.3

Chapter 4

Environmental management

4.1 Residuals management

The traditional economic theory of production views the firm striving to maximize profits subject to technology (characterized by a production function) and market conditions. The multiproduct firm sought the best combination of inputs to produce the best constellation of outputs (recall Problem 1.7.1). The consumer was thought to maximize ordinal utility subject to a budget (or income) constraint. The fact that production and consumption generate *residuals* or wastes was not explicitly considered or was dismissed by assuming "free" disposal. Situations where waste disposal resulted in pollution were known to violate the conditions for optimality of a competitive economy, but such instances of *negative externality* or *social cost* were, prior to 1960, seen as a minor distortion within a larger economic system and perhaps handled best via negotiation or tort law (Coase 1960).

It was not until the middle to late 1960s that economists came to view externality as something more "pervasive" (Ayres and Kneese 1969) and, in fact, the inevitable result of the first law of thermodynamics which requires the conservation of mass and energy within a closed system (Boulding 1966). In combination with a growing scientific and medical literature documenting the decline in air and water quality and the possible risks to public health, economists and other policy analysts became convinced of the need for a broader, "materials balance" approach to environmental management (Kneese, Ayres, and d'Arge 1970). In theory, such an approach would simultaneously consider (1) the extraction of raw materials and allocation of inputs, (2) the production of outputs ("goods") and residuals ("bads"), (3) the demand for goods by other firms and households, and finally (4) the treatment, storage and disposal of *all* residuals into or onto air, water, or land resources. The latter resources become receiving or storage *media* and the problem may be likened to a large general equilibrium problem. Rules for allocation and disposal emerge from first order conditions which might produce the following prescriptions:

1. Allocate an input or a raw material so as to equate its net marginal value across all activities.
2. Distribute (purely private) output so the marginal value among consumers with positive consumption is equal.
3. Dispose of waste so as to equate marginal social damage across all receiving media.

The problem will take on dynamic and spatial dimensions if the receiving media fluctuate in their assimilative capacity or if a residual accumulates, decomposes, or is dispersed within a receiving medium. Thus, the timing and location of disposal, as well as prior treatment, take on strategic significance.

In the next section we will briefly review some of the static models of externality and the (economic) incentive-based policies for controlling the production, treatment, and disposal of the more benign (biodegradable) residuals. Section 4.3 will consider certain dynamic aspects of a single residual that might accumulate or degrade over time. This dynamic analysis is followed by a model of spatial dispersion, again for a single residual. Section 4.5 presents problems and answers for the interested (and numerically inclined) reader.

4.2 Static externality

A central concept to the static theory of externality and residuals management will be the multiple-output production function (Hasenkamp 1976). Let

$y_{j,k} \geq 0$ be the level of the jth output produced by the kth firm,
$j = 1, \ldots, J, \ k = 1, \ldots, K$

$x_{i,k} \geq 0$ be the level of the ith input (or raw material) employed by the kth firm, $i = 1, \ldots, I$, and

$r^k_{m,n} \geq 0$ be the level of the nth residual produced by the kth firm, $n = 1, \ldots, N$ discharged in the mth medium, $m = 1, \ldots, M$.

It is assumed that the technology embodied by the fixed inputs may be characterized by the twice differentiable, convex production function:

$$F_k(y_{1,k}, \ldots, y_{J,k}; x_{1,k}, \ldots, x_{I,k}; r^k_{1,1}, \ldots, r^k_{1,N}, \ldots, r^k_{M,1}, \ldots, r^k_{M,N}) \leq 0$$

$$(4.1)$$

with $\partial F_k(\cdot)/\partial y_{i,k} > 0$, $\partial F_k(\cdot)/\partial x_{i,k} < 0$ and $\partial F_k(\cdot)/\partial r_{m,n}^k < 0$. Implicit in (4.1) is the possibility of *intra*firm reallocation of inputs, $x_{i,k}$, to change the mix of outputs and residuals. In particular, the level of residual $\underline{n}$ might be *reduced* if resources within the firm were reallocated so as to *reduce* the level of one or more outputs $y_{j,k}$ or to *increase* the level of some other residual(s) $r_{m,n}^k$ ($n \neq \underline{n}$). Thus, within the multiproduct firm inputs may be used to increase output or reduce residuals.

A firm may be limited in the possible disposal media for certain residuals. For example, SO_2 from the burning of coal might be disposed via a smoke stack into the air or collected in the form of sludge by "scrubbers" and disposed via landfill.

By reducing residuals we really mean rendering them innocuous or environmentally benign. From a materials balance point of view there is a mass of inputs and raw materials inside the plant. These materials are transformed into goods which fetch a positive market price and two types of residuals: those which cause a negative externality (damage) upon discharge and those which do not. The mass of goods plus detrimental and innocuous residuals must ultimately balance with the mass of raw material inputs. In our notation $r_{m,n}^k$ will represent the production of detrimental residuals.

To keep the analysis reasonably manageable we will assume that the residuals discharged by firm $\underline{k}$ do not adversely affect itself or any other firm. The damage or social cost of the nth residual disposed via the mth medium will be the collective damage imposed on the set of consumers. For simplicity it is also assumed that the mass of goods "consumed" by individuals are economically and environmentally costless to dispose of after they have outlived their economic life. Neither assumption is usually valid in practice, but allowing for interfirm externality and consumer residuals would only add to notational complexity without providing additional insight.

Let

$Y_{j,l}$ be the amount of the jth good consumed by the lth individual $l = 1, \ldots, L$, and

$R_{m,n}$ be the amount of the nth residual disposed via the mth medium, $m = 1, \ldots, M$.

Then the utility or welfare of the lth individual is assumed to be representable by the twice differentiable, quasi-concave function:

$$U_l = U_l(Y_{1,l}, \ldots, Y_{J,l}; R_{1,1}, \ldots, R_{1,N}; \ldots; R_{M,1}, \ldots, R_{M,N}) \qquad (4.2)$$

where $\partial U_l(\cdot)/\partial Y_{j,l} > 0$ and $\partial U_l(\cdot)/\partial R_{m,n} < 0$.

Let x_i denote the amount of the ith resource used in the economy. Then the following balancing equations must hold

$$x_i - \sum_{k=1}^{K} x_{i,k} = 0 \qquad i = 1, \ldots, I \qquad (4.3)$$

$$\sum_{k=1}^{K} y_{j,k} - \sum_{l=1}^{L} Y_{j,l} = 0 \qquad j = 1, \ldots, J \qquad (4.4)$$

and

$$R_{m,n} - \sum_{k=1}^{K} r_{m,n}^{k} = 0 \qquad n = 1, \ldots, N; \; m = 1, \ldots, M \qquad (4.5)$$

A Pareto optimal allocation of inputs and production and distribution (disposal) of outputs (residuals) may be found by arbitrarily fixing the level of welfare for $(L-1)$ of the individuals and maximizing the welfare of the unconstrained individual (see Baumol 1972 or Baumol and Oates 1975). Suppose we fix the welfare of the last $(L-1)$ individuals at $U_l^* > 0$ and maximize $U_1(\cdot)$ subject to the previous functions, balancing equations and

$$U_l(\cdot) - U_l^* = 0 \qquad (4.6)$$

for $l = 2, \ldots, L$.[1] The Lagrangian for this problem may be written as

$$\mathcal{L} = \sum_{l=1}^{L} \lambda_l [U_l(\cdot) - U_l^*] - \sum_{k=1}^{K} \mu_k F_k(\cdot) + \sum_{i=1}^{I} \omega_i \left[x_i - \sum_{k=1}^{K} x_{i,k} \right]$$

$$+ \sum_{j=1}^{J} \eta_j \left[\sum_{k=1}^{K} y_{j,k} - \sum_{l=1}^{L} Y_{j,l} \right] + \sum_{m,n} \tau_{m,n} \left[R_{m,n} - \sum_{k=1}^{K} r_{m,n}^{k} \right] \quad (4.7)$$

where $\lambda_1 = 1$ and $U_1^* = 0$, and the last summation is over all possible combinations of m and n.

─────────────────────

[1] This procedure is equivalent to maximizing a Bergson welfare function of the form

$$W = U_1(\cdot) + \sum_{l=2}^{L} \lambda_l U_l(\cdot)$$

We will assume that each firm uses a positive amount of each input to produce a positive amount of each output while residual production/disposal is nonnegative. Thus $x_{i,k} > 0$, $y_{j,k} > 0$, and $r_{m,n}^k \geq 0$. For the time being we will assume that $Y_{j,l} > 0$ and $R_{n,m} > 0$. With our convexity and concavity assumptions on $F_k(\cdot)$ and $U_l(\cdot)$ the first order conditions are necessary and sufficient and can be shown to imply the following:

$$\frac{\partial U_l(\cdot)/\partial Y_{j,l}}{\partial U_l(\cdot)/\partial Y_{\underline{j},l}} = \frac{\eta_j}{\eta_{\underline{j}}} = \frac{\partial U_{\underline{l}}(\cdot)/\partial Y_{j,l}}{\partial U_{\underline{l}}(\cdot)/\partial Y_{\underline{j},\underline{l}}} \tag{4.8}$$

which says the rate of commodity substitution (RCS) for any two goods j and $\underline{j}$ must be the same for all individuals, $j, \underline{j} = 1, \ldots, J$, $j \neq \underline{j}$, $l, \underline{l} = 1, \ldots, L$, $l \neq \underline{l}$,

$$\frac{\partial F_k(\cdot)/\partial y_{j,k}}{\partial F_k(\cdot)/\partial y_{\underline{j},k}} = \frac{\eta_j}{\eta_{\underline{j}}} = \frac{\partial F_{\underline{k}}(\cdot)/\partial y_{j,k}}{\partial F_{\underline{k}}(\cdot)/\partial y_{\underline{j},\underline{k}}} \tag{4.9}$$

which says the rate of product transformation (RPT) for any two goods j and $\underline{j}$ must be the same for all firms, $k, \underline{k} = 1, \ldots, K$, $k \neq \underline{k}$, and

$$\frac{\partial F_k(\cdot)/\partial x_{i,k}}{\partial F_k(\cdot)/\partial x_{\underline{i},k}} = \frac{\omega_i}{\omega_{\underline{i}}} = \frac{\partial F_{\underline{k}}(\cdot)/\partial x_{i,k}}{\partial F_{\underline{k}}(\cdot)/\partial x_{\underline{i},\underline{k}}} \tag{4.10}$$

which says the rate of technical substitution (RTS) between any two inputs i and $\underline{i}$ must be the same for all firms, where $i, \underline{i} = 1, \ldots, I$, $i \neq \underline{i}$. For firms k and $\underline{k}$ disposing positive levels of residuals n and $\underline{n}$ in medium m we obtain

$$\frac{\partial F_k(\cdot)/\partial r_{m,n}^k}{\partial F_k(\cdot)/\partial r_{m,\underline{n}}^k} = \frac{\tau_{m,n}}{\tau_{m,\underline{n}}} = \frac{\partial F_{\underline{k}}(\cdot)/\partial r_{m,n}^k}{\partial F_{\underline{k}}(\cdot)/\partial r_{m,\underline{n}}^k} \tag{4.11}$$

For firms k and $\underline{k}$ disposing residual n in *two* media m and $\underline{m}$ we obtain

$$\frac{\partial F_k(\cdot)/\partial r_{m,n}^k}{\partial F_k(\cdot)/\partial r_{\underline{m},n}^k} = \frac{\tau_{m,n}}{\tau_{\underline{m},n}} = \frac{\partial F_{\underline{k}}(\cdot)/\partial r_{m,n}^{\underline{k}}}{\partial F_{\underline{k}}(\cdot)/\partial r_{\underline{m},n}^{\underline{k}}} \tag{4.12}$$

The shadow prices $\tau_{m,n}$, $\tau_{m,\underline{n}}$ and $\tau_{\underline{m},n}$ must also satisfy

$$\frac{\sum_{l=1}^{L} \lambda_l \partial U_l(\cdot)/\partial R_{m,n}}{\sum_{l=1}^{L} \lambda_l \partial U_l(\cdot)/R_{m,\underline{n}}} = \frac{\tau_{m,n}}{\tau_{m,\underline{n}}} \tag{4.13}$$

and

$$\frac{\sum_{l=1}^{L} \lambda_l \partial U_l(\cdot)/\partial R_{m,n}}{\sum_{l=1}^{L} \lambda_l \partial U_l(\cdot)/\partial R_{\underline{m},n}} = \frac{\tau_{m,\underline{n}}}{\tau_{\underline{m},n}} \qquad (4.14)$$

Upon equating (4.13) with (4.11) and (4.14) with (4.12) one observes that the rate of residual transformation (RRT) must be equated to the rate of damage substitution (RDS). Residuals can be "transformed" in form (from n to $\underline{n}$) or via medium of disposal (from m to $\underline{m}$). Note that

$$\tau_{m,n} = -\sum_{l=1}^{L} \lambda_l \partial U_l(\cdot)/\partial R_{m,n} \qquad (4.15)$$

is the social damage associated with the marginal unit of residual n disposed in medium m.

Equations (4.11)–(4.15) hold for $r_{m,n}^k > 0$ and thus $R_{m,n} > 0$. The case where $r_{m,n}^k = 0$ may arise if it is infeasible for the kth firm to "produce" or dispose of residual n in the mth media or if it is not socially optimal to do so. In this case

$$\left. \begin{array}{r} -\mu_k \partial F_k(\cdot)/\partial r_{m,n}^k - \tau_{m,n} \leq 0 \\ [-\mu_k \partial F_k(\cdot)/\partial r_{m,n}^k - \tau_{m,n}]r_{m,n}^k = 0 \\ r_{m,n}^k \geq 0 \end{array} \right\}$$

We may interpret $-\mu_k \partial F_k(\cdot)/\partial r_{m,n}^k$ as the marginal cost of in-plant treatment or transformation of residual n so as to avoid disposal in media m. Within a *decentralized* pollution control policy $\tau_{m,n}$ might be a tax on residual n disposed via media m. If the tax, reflecting marginal social damage, is greater than marginal treatment cost for the first unit from firm k then zero discharge is optimal ($r_{m,n}^k = 0$).

For a toxic or radioactive residual it may be socially optimal for $R_{m,n} = 0$. The Kuhn–Tucker conditions in this case require

$$\left.\begin{array}{r}
\displaystyle\sum_{l=1}^{L} \lambda_l \partial U_l(\cdot)/\partial R_{m,n} + \tau_{m,n} \leq 0 \\[2ex]
\displaystyle\left[\sum_{l=1}^{L} \lambda_l \partial U_l(\cdot)/\partial R_{m,n} + \tau_{m,n}\right] R_{m,n} = 0 \\[2ex]
R_{m,n} \geq 0
\end{array}\right\}$$

When the first condition holds as a strict inequality the marginal social damage is so large for even the first unit of n disposed via media m that $R_{m,n} = 0$. It must also be true that the first Kuhn–Tucker condition holds as a strict inequality in the previous set and $r^k_{m,n} = 0$ for all firms.

The fact that a particular $R_{m,n} = 0$ does not rule out $R_{\underline{m},n} > 0$. For example, radioactive waste disposed via concrete encasement at a land site or storage in a deep shaft salt formation may be allowed (based on expected marginal social damage) while ocean dumping may not.

Baumol and Oates (1975) show how an effluent charge (or in our model a vector of effluent charges) can be employed to restore optimality to a competitive (price-taking) economy. They view their analysis as a vindication of the Pigouvian tradition of taxing negative externalities which Coase (1960) had impugned within the context of a two-person, negotiable externality. In the two-person (or small numbers case) the imposition of an effluent charge and subsequent negotiation between affected parties will lead to a nonoptimal level of pollution whereas in the large-number, pure public (or "undepletable") externality, negotiation between polluters and "victims" is not viewed as possible because of high transactions costs. Thus a policy of effluent charges, in the large-number case would, in theory, permit the attainment of a Pareto optimal state. By duality it can be shown that the optimal vector of effluent charges would minimize the cost of treatment and environmental damage.

Aside from the political and administrative problems inherent in effluent charges, Baumol (1972), Baumol and Oates (1975), and others have noted the difficulty of estimating marginal social damage. These indirect utility losses, while real, are probably impossible to measure with any degree of accuracy. As an alternative to basing $\tau_{m,n}$ on some imperfect marginal damage assessment it has been proposed that the appropriate agency specify an ambient standard for each residual and medium. Then, via trial and error, adjust the vector $\tau_m = (\tau_{m,1}, \ldots, \tau_{m,N})$ until the ambient standards are achieved. Let $S_m = (S^*_{m,1}, \ldots, S^*_{m,N})$ be the target vector of ambient

standards for the mth disposal media. It is possible that in the enthusiasm
to clean up the environment the initial target vector S_m is infeasible under
any charge vector τ_m. Alternatively the cost of achieving a particular target
vector may not be well known at the time of initiating the standards and
charge system. The trial and error process may entail successive increases
in some of the elements of τ_m and, in the process, firms, individuals, and
their duly elected representatives may wish to reassess the desirability of
the initial standards.

The system of effluent charges is, of course, identical in spirit to the
landing tax for fish discussed in Section 2.8. Both attempt to introduce
a financial incentive for the firm or vessel owner to take into account a
"user cost." It should come as no surprise then that *transferable pollution
rights* have also been proposed (see Dales 1968). Under such a scheme the
disposal of residual n into some medium would be determined on historical
loading or on the best analysis as to the ambient quality under a reduced
loading. The aggregate allowable loading would then be divided into a
finite number of shares (or quotas) and issued gratis to current polluters
or sold at auction. If sold at auction the firm discharging residual n into
medium m would have to decide whether to pay that price for a sufficient
number of rights to cover his historical discharge or to treat the residual (or
transform it for disposal in a "less costly" medium). If the rights were issued
gratis the firm would in theory respond to the *opportunity* that their sale
might generate revenues in excess of treatment costs. Thus, as in the case
of transferable fishing quotas, transferable pollution rights are, in theory,
capable of producing the same vectors of inputs, outputs, residuals, and
media disposal as achievable with effluent charges.

Consider the problem of an electric utility using a single input (X) to
produce electricity $(Q$, in megawatts) and sulfur emissions $(S$, in tons) for
a specified time period, according to the production function:

$$F(Q; S, X) = X(Q - 100X^{0.75} - S^{0.50}) = 0$$

and the side-order constraint $100 \leq Q \leq 200$. The utility receives a per
unit price of 10 for electricity but must pay a sulfur emissions tax of 0.10
per unit of S. Suppose in the short run the input is fixed at $X = 1$. What
is the optimal mix of Q and S?

With $X = 1$ the production function becomes $F(Q; S) = Q - 100 - S^{0.50}$
$= 0$. With no variable inputs the utility would seek to maximize net revenue

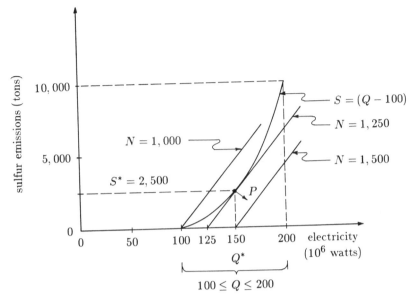

Figure 4.1   The optimal production of electricity and sulfur emissions for the utility facing an emissions tax.

which simply equals revenue from the sale of electricity less emission taxes, $N = 10Q - 0.10S$. The utility's Lagrangian may be written as

$$L = 10Q - 0.10S - \lambda(Q - 100 - S^{0.50})$$

The first order conditions are

$$\frac{\partial L}{\partial Q} = 10 - \lambda = 0$$

$$\frac{\partial L}{\partial S} = -0.10 + 0.50\lambda S^{-0.50} = 0$$

and

$$\frac{\partial L}{\partial \lambda} = -(Q - 100 - S^{0.50}) = 0$$

which may be solved straight away for $\lambda = 10$, $S = 2,500$ and $Q = 150$. Note that the side-order constraint on Q is satisfied.

     Graphically the solution is depicted in Figure 4.1. The electricity–sulfur transformation curve is the nonlinear curve running from $(100, 0)$ to $(200, 10,000)$. If the fixed input $X = 1$ is allocated so that sulfur emissions are zero, electricity output is 100 (megawatts). Diverting resources from emission control to electricity generation would allow Q to increase to 200 but sulfur emissions would increase to 10,000 (tons). The optimal mix of Q and S is at the point of tangency between the transformation curve and the "highest" net (after-tax) revenue line, where the preference direction P indicates the direction of steepest ascent. This occurs at $Q^* = 150$, $S^* = 2,500$ where $N = 1,250$. [What is the optimal solution if Q must satisfy $75 \leq Q \leq 125$? If S must satisfy $S \leq 2,000$?]

As another example, consider a small country transforming two resources X_1 and X_2 into commodities Y_1 and Y_2 which sell on the world market at constant prices P_1 and P_2, respectively. The transformation process employs labor L_1 and L_2 and also produces residuals R_1 and R_2. Let

$$Y_i/X_i = f_i(L_i) \qquad i = 1, 2$$

be the proportion of X_i transformed into Y_i, where $0 \leq f_i(L_i) \leq 1$, $f_i(0) = 0$, and $f_i(\infty) = 1$. A convenient form for $f_i(\cdot)$ is

$$f_i(L_i) = 1 - e^{-\alpha_i L_i}$$

where $\alpha_i > 0$. In this case

$$Y_i = (1 - e^{-\alpha L_i})X_i$$

and assuming that X_i, Y_i, and R_i are measured in the same units and $X_i = Y_i + R_i$ (mass balance), then

$$R_i = e^{-\alpha_i L_i} X_i$$

This specification assumes that the more labor employed in transforming X_i, the smaller will be the amount of residual waste. Food processing might be an example. By slower, more careful, processing (cutting or peeling) less of the agricultural raw material is wasted.

Whereas the finished products are sold internationally suppose that the residuals must be disposed locally. Assume that prior research has estimated *damage functions*, expressing monetary damage as a function of residual production, as

$$D_i = D_i(R_i) = \beta_i R_i^2$$

Let L denote the fixed amount of labor and assume X_1 and X_2, the amounts of the raw material inputs, are also fixed. Maximization of export revenue net of environmental damage and subject to labor availability leads to the Lagrangian

$$V = P_1\left(1 - e^{-\alpha_1 L_1}\right)X_1 + P_2\left(1 - e^{-\alpha_2 L_2}\right)X_2$$
$$- \beta_1 e^{-2\alpha_1 L_1}X_1^2 - \beta_2 e^{-2\alpha_2 L_2}X_2^2 + \lambda(L - L_1 - L_2)$$

First order necessary conditions require

$$\frac{\partial V}{\partial L_1} = \alpha_1 P_1 X_1 e^{-\alpha_1 L_1} + 2\alpha_1\beta_1 X_1^2 e^{-2\alpha_1 L_1} - \lambda = 0$$

$$\frac{\partial V}{\partial L_2} = \alpha_2 P_2 X_2 e^{-\alpha_2 L_2} + 2\alpha_2\beta_2 X_2^2 e^{-2\alpha_2 L_2} - \lambda = 0$$

$$\frac{\partial V}{\partial \lambda} = L - L_1 - L_2 = 0$$

Equating the first two equations to eliminate λ and substituting $L_2 = L - L_1$ yields a single nonlinear equation in L_1 which may be solved via Newton's method (see Problem 4.5.2).

As a final example of static externality consider the decision facing a company that owns two plants which have been disposing organic residuals into a large lake. Without treatment, and under normal operating conditions, the level of residual discharge would be $\bar{R}_1$ and $\bar{R}_2$. Because of differences in plant age, equipment, and technology, the plants face different treatment alternatives for reducing the level of residual discharge. Let

$$C_1 = a_1(\bar{R}_1 - R_1) + a_2(\bar{R}_1 - R_1)^2$$

and

$$C_2 = b_1(\bar{R}_2 - R_2) + b_2(\bar{R}_2 - R_2)^2$$

be the treatment cost functions where R_i is the level of untreated residual from the ith plant disposed in the lake.

The pollution control agency determines that the combined discharge from both plants cannot exceed Z if local water quality is to be suitable for recreation, i.e.,

$$R_1 + R_2 \leq Z$$

If the firm seeks to minimize combined treatment cost subject to just meeting the allowable discharge standard it would wish to

$$\text{minimize} \quad a_1(\bar{R}_1 - R_1) + a_2(\bar{R}_1 - R_1)^2 + b_1(\bar{R}_2 - R_2) + b_2(\bar{R}_2 - R_2)^2$$
$$\text{subject to} \quad R_1 + R_2 = Z$$

(assuming that $\bar{R}_1 + \bar{R}_2 > Z$). The Lagrangian for this problem is

$$L = a_1(\bar{R}_1 - R_1) + a_2(\bar{R}_1 - R_1)^2 + b_1(\bar{R}_2 - R_2) + b_2(\bar{R}_2 - R_2)^2 \\ - \lambda(Z - R_1 - R_2)$$

with first order conditions requiring

$$\frac{\partial L}{\partial R_1} = -a_1 - 2a_2(\bar{R}_1 - R_1) + \lambda = 0$$

$$\frac{\partial L}{\partial R_2} = -b_1 - 2b_2(\bar{R}_2 - R_2) + \lambda = 0$$

$$\frac{\partial L}{\partial \lambda} = -(Z - R_1 - R_2) = 0$$

As in the previous problem we may equate the first two equations and substitute $R_2 = Z - R_1$ into the resulting expression. In this problem it is possible to solve for the optimal level of R_1 as an explicit function of the parameters yielding

$$R_1 = \frac{a_1 - b_1 + 2a_2\bar{R}_1 - 2b_2(\bar{R}_2 - Z)}{2(a_2 + b_2)}$$

Depending on the parameter values it is possible to obtain corner solutions where, for example $R_2 = 0$ and $R_1 = Z$ (see Problem 4.5.3).

4.3 Dynamic externality

A dynamic analysis of residual generation must take into account the nature of the residual and the biological, chemical, and physical processes which may degrade, transform, or diffuse the residual after discharge into the natural environment. In this section we will consider several simple models that examine the problems of optimal consumption and residual accumulation, optimal treatment and discharge, and the optimal depletion of an exhaustible resource when processing results in residual generation and (local) environmental damage. Additional models may be found in Keeler, Spence, and Zeckhauser (1972), d'Arge and Kogiku (1973), and Spence and Starrett (1975).

4.3.1 Optimal consumption and residual generation:
the case of fixed proportions

Consider a simple economy whose welfare depends on the consumption of a single commodity $q(t)$ and a jointly generated residual whose accumulated mass is denoted $X(t)$. In particular suppose the net benefits (or welfare) at instant t are given by

$$W(t) = B(q(t)) - D(X(t)) \qquad (4.16)$$

where $B(\cdot)$ is a strictly concave benefit function and $D(\cdot)$ is a strictly convex damage function.

The residual is assumed to accumulate according to

$$\dot{X} = -\beta X(t) + \alpha q(t) \qquad (4.17)$$

Implicit in Equation (4.17) is a process of decomposition or biodegradation at the rate β and a process of residual generation at rate αq: Residuals are generated in fixed proportion to the rate of consumption $q(t)$. Also implicit is the assumption that the raw material or resource used in making $q(t)$ is freely available in unlimited amounts and is transformed into $q(t)$ at zero cost.

The problem confronting our simple economy is to

$$\text{maximize} \int_0^\infty [B(q(t)) - D(X(t))]e^{-\delta t}\, dt$$
$$\text{subject to} \quad \dot{X} = -\beta X(t) + \alpha q(t) \qquad (4.18)$$
$$X(0) \quad \text{given}$$

The current-value Hamiltonian is

$$\tilde{\mathcal{H}} = B(q(t)) - D(X(t)) + \mu(t)[-\beta X(t) + \alpha q(t)] \qquad (4.19)$$

with first order necessary conditions that include

$$\frac{\partial \tilde{\mathcal{H}}}{\partial q(t)} = B'(\cdot) + \alpha\mu(t) = 0 \qquad (4.20)$$

and

$$\dot{\mu} - \delta\mu(t) = -\frac{\partial \tilde{\mathcal{H}}}{\partial X(t)} = D'(\cdot) + \beta\mu(t) \qquad (4.21)$$

Following the usual procedure, (4.20) implies $\mu(t) = -B'(\cdot)/\alpha$ and

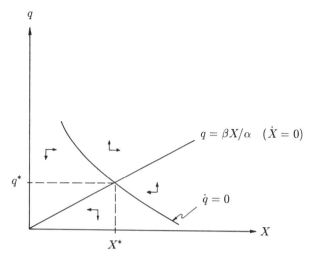

Figure 4.2   Phase plane diagram for equations (4.17) and (4.22) when $B(\cdot)$ is strictly concave, $D(\cdot)$ strictly convex, and α, β, and δ positive.

$\dot{\mu} = -B''(\cdot)\dot{q}/\alpha$. Substituting these expressions into (4.21) and solving for $\dot{q}$ yields

$$\dot{q} = [(\delta + \beta)B'(\cdot) - \alpha D'(\cdot)]/B''(\cdot) \qquad (4.22)$$

which along with equation (4.17) forms a nonlinear plane-autonomous system. The isoclines are defined by $(\delta + \beta)B'(\cdot) = \alpha D'(\cdot)$ when $\dot{q} = 0$ and $q = \beta X/\alpha$ when $\dot{X} = 0$. The slope of the $\dot{q} = 0$ isocline is determined according to

$$dq/dX = \alpha D''(\cdot)/[(\delta + \beta)B''(\cdot)] \qquad (4.23)$$

For $D(\cdot)$ strictly convex, $B(\cdot)$ strictly concave and α, β, and δ positive, we have $dq/dX < 0$ The phase plane diagram might look similar to Figure 4.2. The steady state equilibrium (X^*, q^*) is a saddle point, and the optimal approach follows the convergent separatrix as usual. For a numerical exercise see Problem 4.5.1.

4.3.2 Optimal treatment and discharge

Suppose that a residual from a single firm is causing the pollution of a lake once valued for fishing and water-based recreation. Let $E(t)$ denote the residual flow at instant t and, as before, $X(t)$ the accumulated stock. Suppose that with *no* treatment and normal production the rate of residual flow would be K, some positive number. Let $C(t)$ denote the cost of treatment (or residual reduction) and assume that treatment costs are quadratic; specifically:

$$C(t) = \alpha(K - E(t))^2 \qquad 0 \le E(t) \le K \qquad (4.24)$$

As before we will denote the damage from the accumulated stock of residuals as $D(t)$ and specifically assume

$$D(t) = \gamma X(t)^2 \qquad (4.25)$$

The equation describing residual accumulation is similar to (4.17) but since $E(t)$ is the rate of residuals discharge the equation of motion is simply

$$\dot{X} = -\beta X(t) + E(t) \qquad X(0) \quad \text{given} \qquad (4.26)$$

The problem of minimizing the sum of treatment and damage costs subject to (4.26) has the current-value Hamiltonian

$$\tilde{\mathcal{H}} = \alpha(K - E(t))^2 + \gamma X(t)^2 + \mu(t)[-\beta X(t) + E(t)] \qquad (4.27)$$

with necessary conditions that include

$$\frac{\partial \tilde{\mathcal{H}}}{\partial E(t)} = -2\alpha(K - E(t)) + \mu(t) = 0 \qquad (4.28)$$

$$\dot{\mu} - \delta\mu(t) = -\frac{\partial(\tilde{\mathcal{H}})}{\partial X(t)} = -2\gamma X(t) + \beta\mu(t) \qquad (4.29)$$

Equation (4.28) implies $\mu(t) = 2\alpha(K - E(t))$, $\dot{\mu} = -2\alpha\dot{E}$. Substitution into (4.29) yields

$$\dot{E} = \gamma X(t)/\alpha - (\delta + \beta)(K - E(t)) \qquad (4.30)$$

Equations (4.26) and (4.30) constitute a *linear* dynamical system with a saddle point at $X^* = \alpha K(\delta + \beta)/[\alpha\beta(\delta + \beta) + \gamma]$ and $E^* = \alpha\beta K(\delta + \beta)/[\alpha\beta(\delta + \beta) + \gamma]$. The $\dot{E} = 0$ isocline is a downward sloping line with intercepts of K on the E-axis and $\alpha K(\delta + \beta)/\gamma$ on the X-axis. Depending on $X(0)$ it may be optimal to remove accumulated waste if previous discharges have resulted in $X(0) > X^*$ (see Problem 4.5.4).

4.3.3 Resource depletion and residual accumulation

We now consider a more complex model involving the depletion of an exhaustible resource which in turn is processed for export from a given region or country. The region is assumed to have a labor force $N(t)$ of fixed size, normalized so that $N(t) = 1$ for all t. The proportion of the workforce engaged in mining ore is denoted $n(t)$ where $0 \leq n(t) \leq 1$. Residual wastes result when the ore, $q(t)$, is processed into metal, $y(t)$. The rate of residual generation will depend on the proportion of the workforce devoted to processing, with larger values for $(1 - n(t))$ producing lower residuals flows from a given amount of ore. Thus the lower the value of $n(t)$ the more thorough will be the processing of the available ore $q(t)$.

If $R(t)$ indicates the remaining reserves at instant t then let

$$q(t) = F(R(t), n(t)) \tag{4.31}$$

be the production of ore where $F(\cdot)$ is a concave production function. Let

$$y(t) = G(q(t), 1 - n(t)) = G(F(\cdot), 1 - n(t)) = H(R(t), n(t)) \tag{4.32}$$

be the production of metal where the function $H(\cdot)$ explicitly relates the production of metal to the reserves of ore and proportion of the workforce *in mining*. The first order partials of $F(\cdot)$ and $H(\cdot)$ would have the following signs: $F_n > 0$, $F_R > 0$, $H_n < 0$, and $H_R > 0$.

The rate of residual generation is denoted $e(t)$ and would be determined according to

$$e(t) = q(t) - y(t) = F(\cdot) - H(\cdot) \tag{4.33}$$

The stock of the residual accumulates according to

$$\dot{X} = -\beta X(t) + e(t) = -\beta X(t) + F(\cdot) - H(\cdot) \tag{4.34}$$

where, as before $\beta \geq 0$ is the rate of biodegradation.

The stock of the residual results in a social cost (damage) to the local environment (inhabited by our fixed workforce). Let

$$D(t) = D(X(t)) \tag{4.35}$$

be a convex damage function associated with the stock of the accumulated residual.

Finally, it is assumed that the metal $y(t)$ is exported outside the region at a constant world price of p. The constant price, typical of "small country" trade models will facilitate the dynamic analysis, and the export of $y(t)$ eliminates the need to consider any residual flow from its consumption.

The structure of the problem, in particular the explicit function $H(R(t), n(t))$ results in a single control variable: $n(t)$—the proportion of the workforce devoted to mining. If an optimal time path $n^*(t)$ can be found then, given $R(0)$ and $X(0)$, all other variables can be optimally deduced. Maximization of the present value of export revenues net of local environmental damage may be represented by the problem

$$\underset{\{n(t)\}}{\text{maximize}} \int_0^T [pH(\cdot) - D(\cdot)]^{-\delta t}\, dt$$

$$\text{subject to} \quad \dot{R} = -F(\cdot)$$

$$\dot{X} = -\beta X(t) + F(\cdot) - H(\cdot) \tag{4.36}$$

$$R(0), X(0) \quad \text{given}$$

$$R(T) \geq 0 \qquad 0 \leq n(t) \leq 1$$

The current-value Hamiltonian is:

$$\tilde{\mathscr{H}} = pH(\cdot) - D(\cdot) - \mu_1(t)F(\cdot) + \mu_2(t)[-\beta X(t) + F(\cdot) - H(\cdot)] \tag{4.37}$$

where $\mu_1(t)$ and $\mu_2(t)$ are the current-value costate variables associated with remaining reserves and the stock of accumulated residuals, respectively. The first order necessary conditions include

$$\frac{\partial \tilde{\mathscr{H}}}{\partial n(t)} = pH_n - \mu_1 F_n + \mu_2[F_n - H_n] = 0 \tag{4.38}$$

$$\dot{\mu}_1 - \delta\mu_1 = -\frac{\partial \tilde{\mathscr{H}}}{\partial R(t)} = -(pH_R - \mu_1 F_R + \mu_2[F_R - H_R]) \tag{4.39}$$

and

$$\dot{\mu}_2 - \delta\mu_2 = -\frac{\partial \tilde{\mathscr{H}}}{\partial X(t)} = D'(\cdot) + \beta\mu_2 \tag{4.40}$$

Solving Equation (4.38) for μ_1 yields

$$\mu_1 = pH/F_n + \mu_2[1 - H_n/F_n] = pA + \mu_2[1 - A] \tag{4.41}$$

where $A = H_n/F_n$. Taking the time derivative of (4.41) results in

$$\dot{\mu}_1 = p\dot{A} - \mu_2\dot{A} + \dot{\mu}_2[1 - A] = [p - \mu_2]\dot{A} + \dot{\mu}_2[1 - A] \qquad (4.42)$$

where taking the time derivatives of $A = H_n(F_n)^{-1}$ and noting $\dot{R} = -F$ yields

$$\dot{A} = (H_{nn} - F_{nn}H_n/F_n)(F_n)^{-1}\dot{n} - (H_{nR} - F_{nR}H_n/F_n)^{-1}F \qquad (4.43)$$

Substituting Equations (4.41) and (4.42) into (4.39) and solving for $\dot{A}$ leads to

$$\dot{A} = (\delta + F_R)A - H_R + (\delta\mu_2 - \dot{\mu}_2[1 - A])\Big/[p - \mu_2] \qquad (4.44)$$

Equating (4.44) to (4.43) and solving for $\dot{n}$ yields

$$\dot{n} = \Big[(H_{nR} - F_{nR}H_n/F_n)F + (\delta + F_R)H_n$$

$$- H_RF_n + (\delta F_n\mu_2 - \dot{\mu}_2[F_n - H_n]/[p - \mu_2])\Big]\Big/\Big[H_{nn} - F_{nn}H_n/F_n\Big]$$

$$(4.45)$$

To proceed we must eliminate μ_2 and $\dot{\mu}_2$ from (4.45). Suppose $\dot{\mu}_2 = 0$. Then from (4.40) $\mu_2 = -D'(\cdot)/(\delta + \beta)$ and (4.45) becomes

$$\dot{n} = \Big[(H_{nR} - F_{nR}H_n/F_n)F + (\delta + F_R)H_n - H_RF_n$$

$$- \delta F_nD'(\cdot)/[p(\delta + \beta) + D'(\cdot)]\Big]\Big/\Big[H_{nn} - F_{nn}H_n/F_n\Big] \qquad (4.46)$$

It is not possible to sign $\dot{n}$, but it seems likely that $\dot{n} < 0$ and thus $\dot{R} < 0$ for $0 \le t \le T$. If $\beta = 0$ (no degradation of the residual) two possible trajectories are shown in Figure 4.3. Trajectories A and B start at the same initial point but $n(t)$ along A declines more rapidly in response to the damage from accumulated waste. Thus, along A $(1 - n(t))$ increases *more* rapidly resulting in smaller residual flows as a result of more thorough (less wasteful) processing.

Along trajectory B reserves would be depleted more rapidly and residuals flows would be larger. This is shown in Figure 4.4 where both trajectories A and B start at $R(0)$ and zero accumulated waste ($X(0) = 0$), but the more rapid (and wasteful) depletion along trajectory B leads to a larger and more rapid accumulation of waste, i.e., $X(T_B) > X(T_A)$, $T_B < T_A$.

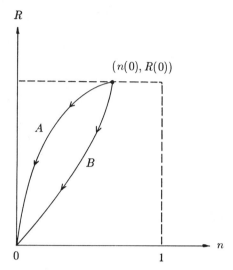

Figure 4.3   Phase plane diagram of the proportion of labor in mining and remaining reserves $(\beta = 0)$.

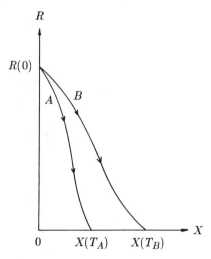

Figure 4.4   Phase plane diagram of the stock of residuals and remaining reserves $(\beta = 0)$.

With biodegradation $(\beta > 0)$ it is possible to have a more rapid depletion of the resource without as rapid a build-up of waste. In fact, it would be possible to have an interval, say $t_1 \leq t \leq t_2$, where $\dot{X} = 0$ and thus

$$F(\cdot) - H(\cdot) = \beta X(t) \tag{4.47}$$

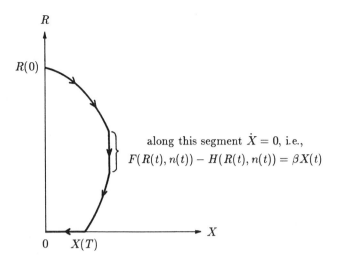

Figure 4.5   Phase plane diagram of the stock of residuals and remaining reserves with biodegradation $(\beta > 0)$. At $t = T$, $R(T) = q(T) = y(T) = 0$ and for $t \geq T$, $\dot{X} = X(T)^{-\beta t}$.

Furthermore, when the nonrenewable resource has been exhausted, say, at $t = T$, then $\dot{X} = X(T)e^{-\beta t}$ and the accumulated residual will degrade toward zero. Such a trajectory is shown in Figure 4.5.

4.4 Spatial considerations: a model of residual transport

We now consider a model with spatial dimension, specifically a model where a residual discharged at one location may be transported by physical processes (e.g., wind or ocean currents, or diffusion) to another location. In addition to physical processes, the residual may be subject to biodegradation into constituent elements or it may undergo chemical change (reaction). Various air pollutants such as NO_2 and SO_2 are examples of the latter type of chemical transformation which inflict damage in the form of smog and acid precipitation. In the following model we consider only biodegradation and transport.

Let

$X_{j,t} =$ the accumulated amount of a single residual at location j in period t, $j = 1, 2, \ldots, J$,

$R_{j,t} =$ the amount of the residual discharged at location j in period t,

$\sigma_{i,j}$ = the transport coefficient indicating the proportion of accumulated residual at location i which will move to location
j in period $t+1$,

C_j = the marginal cost of disposal at location j,

$D_j(X_{j,t})$ = the damage from the accumulated residual at location j
in period t,

$\bar{R}$ = the fixed amount of the residual which must be disposed
in each period, and

δ = the periodic discount rate.

The transport coefficients collectively define a $J \times J$ matrix

$$\sigma = \begin{pmatrix} \sigma_{1,1} & \cdots & \sigma_{1,J} \\ & \cdots & \\ \sigma_{J,1} & \cdots & \sigma_{J,J} \end{pmatrix} \tag{4.48}$$

where $\sigma_{j,j}$ is the proportion of the accumulated residual at location j which remains at location j in the next period. The rate of biodegradation at location j during the period t is thus

$$\alpha_j = \left(1 - \sum_{i=1}^{J} \sigma_{j,i}\right) \geq 0$$

The equation describing the dynamics of residual accumulation at location j is given by

$$X_{j,t+1} = R_{j,t} + \sum_{i=1}^{J} \sigma_{i,j} X_{i,t} - X_{j,t} \sum_{\substack{i=1 \\ i \neq j}}^{J} \sigma_{j,i} \tag{4.49}$$

Note the transposition of subscripts in the last term on the RHS of Equation (4.49). This equation assumes that the residual discharged at location j during period t is *not* subject to biodegradation or transport during the period. Defining $\beta_j = \sum_{\substack{i=1 \\ i \neq j}}^{J} \sigma_{j,i}$ and subtracting $X_{j,t}$ from both sides of (4.49) yields

$$X_{j,t+1} - X_{j,t} = R_{j,t} + \sum_{i=1}^{J} \sigma_{i,j} X_{i,t} - (1 + \beta_j) X_{j,t} \tag{4.50}$$

Note: β_j is interpreted as the "outflow" of accumulated residual from location j to other locations. Also note that $\alpha_j = (1 - \beta_j - \sigma_{j,j})$, i.e., outflow,is not the same thing as biodegradation.

Allocation of $\bar{R}$ across the various disposal sites is regulated by an environmental management agency. The agency is assumed to seek that pattern of disposal, $R_{j,t}$, which minimizes the present value of the sum of disposal and damage costs. This objective may be stated as

$$\underset{R_{j,t}}{\text{minimize}} \sum_{t=0}^{\infty} \rho^t \left\{ \sum_{j=1}^{J} [C_j R_{j,t} + D_j(\cdot)] \right\} \tag{4.51}$$

The constraint requiring the disposal of $\bar{R}$ in each period is simply

$$\bar{R} - \sum_{j=1}^{J} R_{j,t} = 0 \tag{4.52}$$

The current-value Hamiltonian for the environmental agency is

$$\tilde{\mathcal{H}} = \sum_{j=1}^{J} \left\{ [C_j R_{j,t} + D_j(\cdot) \right.$$

$$+ \rho \mu_{j,t+1} \left[R_{j,t} + \sum_{i=1}^{J} \sigma_{i,j} X_{i,t} - (1 + \beta_j) X_{j,t} \right] \right\} \tag{4.53}$$

$$+ \lambda_t \left[\bar{R} - \sum_{j=1}^{J} R_{j,t} \right]$$

Assuming $R_{j,t} \geq 0$ and $X_{j,t} > 0$, we have

$$\left. \begin{aligned} \frac{\partial \tilde{\mathcal{H}}}{\partial R_{j,t}} &= C_j + \rho \mu_{j,t+1} - \lambda_t \geq 0 \\ \frac{\partial \tilde{\mathcal{H}}}{\partial R_{j,t}} \cdot R_{j,t} &= [C_j + \rho \mu_{j,t+1} - \lambda_t] R_{j,t} = 0 \\ R_{j,t} &\geq 0 \end{aligned} \right\} \tag{4.54}$$

and

$$\rho \mu_{j,t+1} - \mu_{j,t} = -\frac{\partial \tilde{\mathcal{H}}}{\partial R_{j,t}} = -[D_j'(\cdot) + \rho \mu_{j,t+1}(\sigma_{j,j} - (1 + \beta_j))] \tag{4.55}$$

Condition (4.54) implies that at locations with positive disposal rates, $R_{j,t}$ > 0, the sum of marginal disposal and user cost will be the same, equaling λ_t —the marginal social cost of having to dispose of another unit of the residual during period t. At locations with no disposal, $R_{j,t} = 0$, the sum of marginal disposal costs and user costs *exceeds* the sum at other locations where disposal takes place. A zero disposal rate could result from high marginal disposal costs, C_j, or from high future environmental damage, which would be reflected in $\rho\mu_{j,t+1}$.

To further explore the short-run dynamics and steady state possibilities with our model of residual transport we will consider the case when $J = 2$; that is, there are only two locations at which to dispose of the residual. Such a situation is not far from the reality faced by New York City in negotations with the U.S. Environmental Protection Agency (EPA) over the nearshore (12-mile site) or offshore (106-mile site) for dumping of sludge generated by the treatment of municipal wastewater [see Conrad (1985)]. By virtue of its proximity, the near-shore site ($j = 1$) will have lower marginal disposal costs ($C_1 < C_2$). The long-run environmental damage from sludge accumulations at the nearshore site, however, is likely to be larger due to the diminished quality of recreational activities such as boating, swimming, and sport-fishing, as well as the possible decline in the quantity of commercially caught fish.

Several dynamic possibilities exist but we will consider only the most likely. If the municipality is starting from scratch, that is, no previous disposal, it would seem plausible that disposal would start at the nearshore site since $C_1 + \rho\mu_{1,t+1} = \lambda_t < C_2 + \rho\mu_{2,t+1}$. Thus, for some interval $0 \le t \le T_1$, $R_{1,t} = \bar{R}$ and $R_{2,t} = 0$. Marginal disposal costs will be the dominant factor in this initial stage. Depending on the proximity of the two sites and the prevailing currents, some of the residual disposed of at the nearshore site may be transported and accumulate at the offshore site.

At $t = T_1$ the environmental damage from accumulations at the nearshore site is assumed to have increased to the point where $C_1 + \rho\mu_{1,t+1} = \lambda_t = C_2 + \rho\mu_{2,t+1}$. For $t > T_1$ it may be optimal to cease disposal at site one and switch to site two (if there is no significant biodegradation or transport and if environmental damage is zero or insignificant at site two). Alternatively (and more likely) joint disposal will occur at rates designed to maintain the equality of marginal disposal and user costs.

A sequence of disposal at the nearshore site and then joint disposal

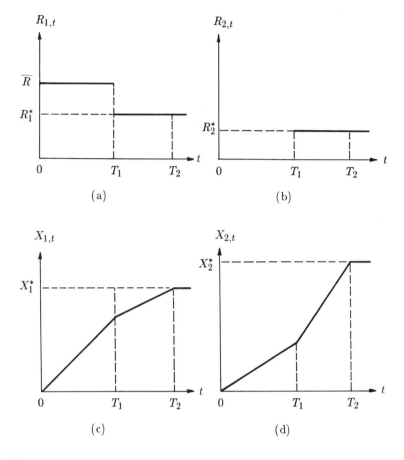

Figure 4.6   Biodegradation, dispersion, and accumulation in a two-site model of residual disposal: possible dynamics leading to a steady state with joint disposal.

is shown in Figure 4.6. Over the interval $0 \leq t \leq T_1$ all of $\bar{R}$ is disposed of at the nearshore site. With the rate of disposal greater than the rates of biodegradation and transport the residual will accumulate [panel (c)]. While not necessarily the case, panel (d) shows residual accumulation at the offshore site (site two) as a result of a transport rate in excess of biodegradation and return flows. At $t > T_1$ joint disposal commences. Panels (a) and (b) indicate that it is optimal to set $R_{1,t}$ and $R_{2,t}$ at what will ultimately be the steady state rates of disposal at sites one and two. This need not be the case and there may be an interval where $R_{2,t} > R_{1,t}$. The residual accumulates at both sites until the amount of biodegradation equals the amount of disposal and the net transport at each site. Steady state for the entire system is reached at $t = T_2$ in Figure 4.6.

In our two-location model it will be the case that $\beta_1 = \sigma_{1,2}$ and $\beta_2 = \sigma_{2,1}$. In steady state, conditions (4.55) can be shown to imply that

$$\mu_1^* = \frac{(1+\delta)D_1'(\cdot)}{(1+\sigma_{1,2}+\delta-\sigma_{1,1})} \tag{4.56}$$

and

$$\mu_2^* = \frac{(1+\delta)D_2'(\cdot)}{(1+\sigma_{2,1}+\delta-\sigma_{2,2})} \tag{4.57}$$

If the damage functions $D_1(X_1)$ and $D_2(X_2)$ have unique inverses it will be possible to solve (4.56) and (4.57) for expressions $X_1^* = \phi_1(\mu_1^*)$ and $X_2^* = \phi_2(\mu_2^*)$.

In steady state our two-location model, via Equations (4.50), also implies

$$R_1^* = (1+\sigma_{1,2}-\sigma_{1,1})X_1^* - \sigma_{2,1}X_2^* \tag{4.58}$$

and

$$R_2^* = (1+\sigma_{2,1}-\sigma_{2,2})X_2^* - \sigma_{1,2}X_1^* \tag{4.59}$$

Conditions (4.54) imply $C_1 + \rho\mu_1^* = C_2 + \rho\mu_2^*$ or

$$\mu_1^* = (1+\delta)(C_2 - C_1) + \mu_2^* \tag{4.60}$$

and of course

$$\bar{R} - R_1^* - R_2^* = 0 \tag{4.61}$$

The inverse expressions for X_1^* and X_2^* along with Equations (4.58)–(4.61) define a system of six equations in six unknowns: X_1^*, X_2^*, R_1^*, R_2^*, μ_1^*, and μ_2^*. Problem 4.5.5 asks you to devise a solution algorithm and solve for the steady state values for a two-location disposal problem.

4.5 Problems

P4.5.1. Consider a simple economy with welfare (net benefits) at instant t given by $W(t) = B(q(t)) - D(X(t)) = q(t)^{0.5} - 0.001X(t)^2$ where $q(t)$ is the level of consumption of an unlimited and zero-cost resource and $X(t)$ is the accumulated stock of the residual. The dynamics of residual accumulation are given by $\dot{X} = -0.1X(t) + 0.2q(t)$ and the discount rate is $\delta = 0.10$. Then

(a) Solve for the expression for $\dot{q}$ from the first order conditions for the problem which seeks to maximize the present value of welfare (net benefits) subject to the dynamics of residual accumulation, and

(b) draw the isoclines $\dot{X} = 0$ and $\dot{q} = 0$ and solve for the steady-state optimum.

(c) What is the effect of increasing δ from 0.1 to 0.2?

Answers

(a) $\dot{q} = 2q(t)[0.0008X(t)q(t)^{0.5} - 0.2]$

(b) $q = 62{,}500/X^2$ $(\dot{q} = 0)$ $q = 0.5X$ $(\dot{X} = 0)$ $(X^*, q^*) = (50, 25)$

(c) $(X^*, q^*) = (65.52, 32.76)$; note generally that X^* and q^* both increase with δ.

P4.5.2. A simple economy uses labor to process two distinct resources into commodities which are exported at constant prices. Let

$X_i =$ the endowment of the ith resource or raw material input, $i = 1, 2$
$Y_i =$ the commodity obtained from processing the ith resource
$L_i =$ the amount of labor used in transforming X_i into Y_i
$R_i =$ the residual (waste) from the ith process.

Suppose that the proportion of X_i transformed into Y_i is given by

$$\frac{Y_i}{X_i} = f_i(L_i) = (1 - e^{-\alpha_i L_i})$$

Thus

$$Y_i = (1 - e^{-\alpha_i L_i})X_i$$

But if $X_i = Y_i + R_i$ (according to materials balance) then

$$\frac{R_i}{X_i} = 1 - f_i(L_i) = e^{-\alpha_i L_i}$$

and

$$R_i = e^{-\alpha_i L_i} X_i$$

Suppose that the damage from R_i is given by

$$D_i(R_i) = \beta_i R_i^2$$

Finally let P_i and L denote the *fixed* values for the export prices for Y_i and the total amount of available labor. Then

(a) Write the Lagrangian corresponding to the problem of maximizing export revenues net of environmental damage and subject to resource and labor endowments.

(b) From the first order necessary conditions write an expression that might be solved for the optimal amount of labor allocated to processing resource one, and

(c) for $\alpha_1 = 0.001$, $\alpha_2 = 0.003$, $\beta_1 = 0.01$, $\beta_2 = 0.05$, $P_1 = 500$, $P_2 = 200$, $X_1 = 100$, $X_2 = 300$, and $L = 1,000$ solve for the optimal values of L_1, L_2, Y_1, Y_2, R_1, R_2, revenue, environmental damage, and net revenue.

Answers

(a) $V = P_1(1 - e^{-\alpha_1 L_1})X_1 + P_2(1 - e^{-\alpha_2 L_2})X_2 - \beta_1 e^{-2\alpha_1 L_1}X_1^2$
$- \beta_2 e^{-2\alpha_2 L_2}X_2^2 + \lambda(L - L_1 - L_2)$

(b) $\alpha_1 P_1 X_1 e^{-\alpha_1 L_1} + 2\alpha_1\beta_1 X_1^2 e^{-2\alpha_1 L_1} - \alpha_2 P_2 X_2 e^{-\alpha_2(L-L_1)}$
$- 2\alpha_2\beta_2 X_2^2 e^{-2\alpha_2(L-L_1)} = 0$

(c) $L_1 = 423.85$, $L_2 = 576.15$, $Y_1 = 34.55$, $Y_2 = 246.73$, $R_1 = 65.45$, $R_2 = 53.27$, revenue $= 66,620.33$, damage $= 184.71$, and net revenue $= 66,435.62$.

P4.5.3. A company owning two plants which discharge residuals into a lake has been told that the combined discharge must be no greater than Z units per period. With *no* treatment the discharge from each plant would be $\bar{R}_1$ for plant one and $\bar{R}_2$ for plant two. Because of age and design differences the cost of treatment (residual reduction) is different for each plant but may be approximated by

$$C_1 = a_1(\bar{R}_1 - R_1) + a_2(\bar{R}_1 - R_1)^2$$
and
$$C_2 = b_1(\bar{R}_2 - R_2) + b_2(\bar{R}_2 - R_2)^2$$

where R_i is the amount of untreated residual discharged from the ith plant and thus $(\bar{R}_i - R_i)$ is the amount treated. Then

(a) write the Lagrangian expression for the problem to minimize the joint costs of treatment subject to the combined discharge constraint $Z - R_1 - R_2 = 0$,

(b) From the first order conditions derive an expression for the optimal discharge R_1 and determine the conditions for $R_1 \geq 0$,

(c) If $a_1 = 10$, $a_2 = 0.01$, $b_1 = 5$, $b_2 = 0.001$, $\bar{R}_1 = 1{,}000$, $\bar{R}_2 = 7{,}500$, and $Z = 750$ solve for the optimal values of R_1, R_2, and λ, and

(d) Find the optimal values for R_1, R_2, and λ if $\bar{R}_2$ were changed to 5,000.

Answers

(a) $L = a_1(\bar{R}_1 - R_1) + a_2(\bar{R}_2 - R_2)^2 + b_1(\bar{R}_1 - R_1) + b_2(\bar{R}_2 - R_2)^2$
$- \lambda(Z - R_1 - R_2)$

(b) $R_1 = \dfrac{a_1 - b_1 + 2a_2\bar{R}_1 - 2b_2(\bar{R}_2 - Z)}{2(a_2 + b_2)}$

$R_1 > 0$ if $a_1 + 2a_2\bar{R}_1 > b_1 + 2b_2(\bar{R}_2 - Z)$
$R_1 = 0$ if $a_1 + 2a_2\bar{R}_1 \leq b_1 + 2b_2(\bar{R}_2 - Z)$

(c) $R_1 = 522.73$, $R_2 = 227.27$, $\lambda = 19.55$

(d) $R_1 = 750$, $R_2 = 0$, $\lambda = 15$

P4.5.4. Without any treatment a firm would normally discharge $K = 200$ tons of some residual per annum. The costs of treatment are given by

$$C(t) = 15(200 - E(t))^2 \quad (\$ \text{ per annum})$$

where $E(t)$ is the annual amount of the *un*treated residual. The stock of the accumulated residual causes damage according to

$$D(t) = 12X(t)^2 \quad (\$ \text{ per annum})$$

The residual accumulates according to

$$\dot{X} = -0.4X(t) + E(t)$$

A pollution control agency using a discount rate of $\delta = 0.10$ per annum asks you to

(a) find the steady state stock of waste (X^*) and discharge (E^*) that will minimize the discounted sum of treatment and damage costs in the long run,

(b) examine the stability of the steady state equilibrium via phase plane and characteristic root analysis,

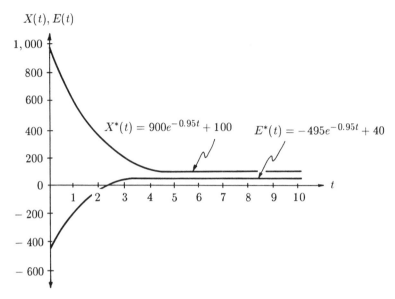

$X(t), E(t)$

$X^*(t) = 900e^{-0.95t} + 100$ $E^*(t) = -495e^{-0.95t} + 40$

Figure 4.7

(c) if $X(0) = 1,000$, derive the approach paths for $X^*(t)$ and $E^*(t)$ if the pollution control agency wishes to reach X^* at $t = 10$ while minimizing the discounted sum of treatment and damage costs, and

(d) interpret, in words, what the agency should be doing during the interval $0 \le t \le 10$.

Answers

(a) $X^* = 100$, $E^* = 40$

(b) Isoclines: $E = 200 - 1.6X$, when $\dot{E} = 0$, $E = 0.4X$, when $\dot{X} = 0$. The characteristic roots of the $\dot{X}, \dot{E}$ dynamical system are $+1.05$ and -0.95 confirming $(100, 40)$ to be a saddle point.

(c) $X^*(t) = 900e^{-0.95t} + 100$ and $E^*(t) = -495e^{-0.95t} + 40$

(d) from $0 \le t \le 2.648$ the pollution control agency actually dredges up accumulated waste [i.e., $E(t) < 0$] in order to minimize the sum of discounted treatment and damage costs. The time paths $X^*(t)$ and $E^*(t)$ are plotted in Figure 4.7.

P4.5.5. Suppose an agency regulating ocean dumping of sewage sludge is interested in finding the least cost allocation of sludge between a nearshore (site 1) and an offshore site. You are given the following information:

$$\sigma = \begin{pmatrix} \sigma_{11} & \sigma_{12} \\ \sigma_{21} & \sigma_{22} \end{pmatrix} = \begin{pmatrix} 0.60 & 0.30 \\ 0.10 & 0.50 \end{pmatrix}$$

$$C_1 = 1{,}000, \quad C_2 = 2{,}000, \quad \delta = 0.10, \quad \bar{R} = 100{,}000$$

$$D_1 = 0.005X_1^2, \quad D_2 = 0.001X_2^2$$

Using the equations defining a steady state equilibrium for the spatial model in Section 4.4

(a) write a flow chart for a solution algorithm to obtain the steady state values for X_1, X_2, R_1, R_2, μ_1, and μ_2

(b) solve for the steady state equilibrium given the above parameters.

Answers

(a)

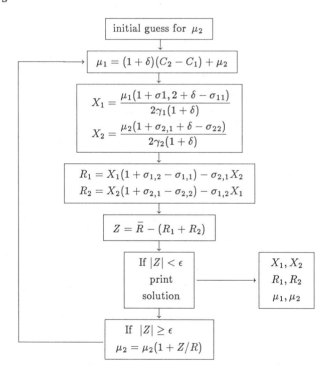

(b) $X_1 = 106{,}280$, $X_2 = 114{,}976$, $R_1 = 62{,}899$, $R_2 = 37{,}101$, $\mu_1 = 1{,}461$, $\mu_2 = 361$.

Chapter 5

Stochastic resource models

In recent years an increasing number of stochastic optimization models have appeared in the resource economics literature (see Mangel 1985 for a survey). Some of these papers employ relatively sophisticated techniques such as stochastic differential equations (the "Itô calculus"), martingale theory, and so on. In the present notes we will keep the mathematical prerequisites to a minimum, by staying mainly within a discrete-time modeling framework. Thus we employ the method of Stochastic Dynamic Programming, which is a fairly straightforward generalization of deterministic dynamic programming described in Chapter 1.

It surely goes without saying that the real world of resource and environmental economics is an uncertain one. Future prices and costs are seldom predictable with much confidence, even over the short run. Consumers' tastes and demands may change, as may government regulations. Stocks of renewable resources, such as fish and wildlife populations, and water supplies, undergo significant fluctuations. How much of a given mineral ore, or fossil fuel, may exist in the earth's crust in recoverable form is largely a matter of speculation.

One popular approach to the modeling of uncertainty is via the insertion of a stochastic component to an existing deterministic model. For example the deterministic spawner-recruit model (2.49)

$$R_{t+1} = G(S_t) \qquad (5.1)$$

might become

$$R_{t+1} = G(S_t, w_t) \qquad (5.2)$$

where w_t is a random variable with a known probability distribution. The optimization objective (2.52) now becomes

$$\text{maximize } E\{ \sum_{t=0}^{\infty} \rho^t U(R_t, S_t) \} \qquad (5.3)$$

where E denotes the expectation operator. A model of this kind will be discussed further in Section 5.2.

Numerical calculations reveal that the introduction of random "noise" in this manner often has a rather minor effect on optimal policies and on the maximum present value of the resource stock. This may seem surprising in view of the emphasis that resource management experts often place upon uncertainty. However, the apparent paradox is easily explained once it is realized that in practice uncertainty usually has a far more complex nature than can be captured by merely adding a stochastic component to a deterministic model.

For example, once we admit the possibility of natural fluctuations in resource stocks, we are unavoidably faced with the statistical problems of stock estimation. Managers may be uncertain about the present stock (let alone the future stock) of a resource. Resource exploiters may devote significant funds to exploration prior to actual exploitation.

Model parameters themselves must in practice be estimated from available, often inaccurate data. Thus the parameters are surrounded by uncertainty. Even the form of an appropriate model may be uncertain. This leads to the simultaneous problems of estimation and control. Bertsekas (1976) provides an introduction with emphasis on operations research and engineering applications while Aoki (1976), Chow (1975), and Rausser and Hochman (1979) apply linear-quadratic-Gaussian techniques to estimation and control of macroeconomic and agricultural systems.

One aspect of uncertainty of particular economic importance is learning. Uncertainty about a resource system may be reduced over time simply as a result of experience. Such learning may be called "passive," or "learning by doing." At the opposite extreme, research programs may be set up explicitly to reduce uncertainty. In the case of a fish population, for example, stock estimates may be obtained passively by analyzing catch-effort data, or alternatively derived from government stock surveys which are carried out independently from fishing operations. Such surveys can be carefully designed to eliminate bias and provide statistically valid results; unfortunately data obtained from stock surveys can be very expensive relative to data obtained from actual fishing operations.

A third possibility might be called "adaptive learning" (Walters and Hilborn 1976). In the fishery example, this would imply that fishing operations are directed not merely to maximize yield (whether biological or economic), but also to generate information useful for future management.

In the next section we extend the method of dynamic programming to stochastic problems with known distributions. In Section 5.5 a model of control with learning via Bayesian updating is presented. Other sections will apply these techniques to a spawner recruit model (5.2), optimal rotation with risk of fire (5.3), groundwater management (5.4), search and fishing (5.6), and irreversible development (5.7).

5.1 Stochastic dynamic programming

We now assume that the state variable x_t can be observed (accurately measured) *before* the selection of a value for the control variable y_t, which then results in a known net benefit (utility) $U(x_t, y_t)$. Future net benefits are uncertain because the system's dynamics are subject to a stochastic process.

$$x_{t+1} = f(x_t, y_t, w_t) \qquad (5.4)$$

where w_t is a random variable. In most cases it will be assumed that the w_t are independent and identically distributed (i.i.d.), and thus the stochastic process $\{w_t\}$ is *stationary*. We shall assume a fixed control set Y, and a finite time horizon T.

Now define the *value function* $J_k(x)$ as the maximum total expected return with k periods remaining, given $X_0 = x$:

$$J_k(x) = \max E\{\sum_{t=0}^{k} \rho^t U(x_t, y_t) | X_0 = x\} \qquad (5.5)$$

We then have[1]

$$J_0(x) = \max_{y \in Y} U(x, y) \qquad (5.6)$$

which is a straightforward deterministic (constrained) maximization problem.

Next consider $k = 1$, and suppose that some control $y \in Y$ is chosen in the first period. This will lead to

$$x_1 = f(x, y, w) \quad \text{with probability } \phi(w)$$

and will yield a second period return of

$$J_0(x_1) = J_0(f(x, y, w)) \quad \text{with probability } \phi(w) \qquad (5.7)$$

Hence we have

---

[1] Alternatively, the terminal state x_T may be specified, in which case we simply have $J_0(x) = F(x)$, the specified terminal value; no action y is chosen in the terminal period in this case.

$$J_1(x) = \max_{y \in Y}[U(x,y) + \rho E_w\{J_0(f(x,y,w))\}]$$

By the same argument,

$$J_{k+1}(x) = \max_{y \in Y}[U(x,y) + \rho E_w\{J_k(f(x,y,w))\}] \tag{5.8}$$

Equation (5.8) is the *dynamic programming equation* (DPE) for our stochastic control problem. Because one considers in turn $k = 0, 1, \ldots, T$, the number of points remaining up to some specified horizon T, the DPE is sometimes referred to as "backwards induction."

The solution of (5.5)–(5.8) by backwards induction yields a *feedback control policy* which tells us the optimal action $y^*(t)$ in each period after observing the current state x_t. A *stationary* feedback policy takes the form $y = \Phi(x)$ for all t. Under fairly general conditions it can be shown that the optimal policy converges to a stationary policy as the time horizon T approaches infinity.

For many stationary problems it will not be possible to solve for the feedback policy explicitly; that is, a closed form solution $y = \Phi(x)$ cannot be determined. In such cases it may still be possible to determine certain structural or qualitative characteristics about the optimal policy [see Ross (1983)]. In applied problems where functional forms, distributions, terminal time and initial state are given, it is frequently possible to obtain numerical solutions or approximate solutions. With the control set Y and state space X given as *finite* sets, and with w_t implying a conditional probability distribution on x_{t+1}, the problem is well defined. Problems with continuous state and control variables can be posed, and depending on the forms for $U(\cdot), f(\cdot)$ and the density or distribution of w_t it may be possible to identify a closed form control policy. Care must be taken, however, to ensure that the expectation operation is well defined (Bertsekas 1976).

To illustrate the above method we will work through two simple problems. The first deals with risky resource development and the second with determining a reservoir release policy.

Suppose the scale of a project has the potential to damage a local environment and actually reduce future net benefits to zero. Let $0 \leq Q_0 \leq 1$ indicate initial project scale and let $N_t = X_t \ln(1 + aQ_t)$ be the net benefits in period t where for simplicity $t = 0, 1$ and $Q_0 + Q_1 \leq 1$. The state variable X_t is binary, where $X_t = 1$ indicates a "healthy" local environment and $X_t = 0$ indicates a contaminated local environment. It is assumed that

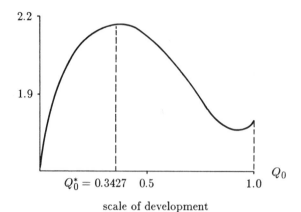

scale of development

Figure 5.1 Risky development: a plot of $N = \ln(1+5Q_0)+e^{5Q_0}\ln(1+5(1-Q_0))/(1+\delta)$, $\delta = 0.1$

$X_0 = 1$ and

$$X_1 = \begin{cases} 1 & \text{with probability } 1 - Q_0^2 \\ 0 & \text{with probability } Q_0^2 \end{cases}$$

Thus if $Q_0 = 0$ then $X_1 = 1$ with probability one (certainty) but this declines as Q_0 increases toward 1. Expected total benefits are $\overline{N} = E\{N_0 + \rho N_1\}$. What is the optimal scale of risky development?

Clearly $Q_1 = 1 - Q_0$ so that the expression for expected discounted net benefits is simply a function of Q_0 and is given by

$$\overline{N} = \ln(1 + aQ_0) + \rho(1 - Q_0^2)\ln(1 + a(1 - Q_0))$$

For $a = 5$ and $\delta = 0.1$ Newton's method yields $Q^* = 0.3427$. It turns out that N is *not* concave but a graph of N reveals Q^* to be a maximum for the domain $0 \le Q_0 \le 1$. (See Figure 5.1.) The probability of "disaster" ($X_1 = 0$) is $Q_0^2 = 0.1174$.

For our second example consider a reservoir where the state variable x_t indicates the amount of water in storage. To keep things simple let

$$x_t = \begin{cases} 0 & \text{when reservoir is empty,} \\ 1 & \text{when reservoir is half full,} \\ 2 & \text{when reservoir is full.} \end{cases}$$

The state equation takes the form

$$x_{t+1} = x_t - y_t + r_t$$

where y_t is the amount of water released during period t and r_t is a random variable representing inflow from rain or snowmelt. It is assumed that $y_t = 0, 1, 2$, $y_t \leq x_t$ and the random variable is binary such that

$$r_t = \begin{cases} 0 & \text{with probability } 1/3 \\ 1 & \text{with probability } 2/3 \end{cases}$$

The net benefits from release y_t are given by

$$N_t = \ln(1 + y_t)$$

for $t = 0, 1, 2$.

The discrete probabilities for r_t along with x_t, $y_t = 0, 1, 2$, $y_t \leq x_t$ and $x_{t+1} = x_t - y_t + r_t$ will imply the following conditional distribution for $p(x_{t+1}|x_t, y_t)$.

$x_t = 0$	$x_t = 1$	$x_t = 2$
$p(0|0,0) = 1/3$	$p(1|1,0) = 1/3$	$p(2|2,0) = 1$
$p(1|0,0) = 2/3$	$p(2|1,0) = 2/3$	$p(1|2,1) = 1/3$
	$p(0|1,1) = 1/3$	$p(2|2,1) = 2/3$
	$p(1|1,1) = 2/3$	$p(0|2,2) = 1/3$
		$p(1|2,2) = 2/3$

$p(x_{t+1}|x_t, y_t) = 0$ otherwise

The optimization problem becomes

$$\underset{\{y_t\}}{\text{maximize}} \quad E\left\{ \sum_{t=0}^{2} \rho^t \ln(1 + y_t) \right\}$$

$$\text{subject to} \quad x_{t+1} = x_t - y_t + r_t$$

$$x_t, y_t = 0, 1, 2 \qquad y_t \leq x_t$$

$$x_0 \quad \text{given}$$

With no time to go the value function is

$$J_0(x) = \max_{y \leq x} \ln(1 + y) = \ln(1 + x)$$

Thus $y_2^* = x_2$. With one period to go we have

$$J_1(x) = \max_{y \leq x}[\ln(1 + y) + \rho E\{J_0(x - y + r)\}]$$

and with two periods to go $(t = 0)$ the value function is

$$J_2(x) = \max_{y \leq x}[\ln(1 + y) + \rho E\{J_1(x - y + r)\}]$$

The optimal policy is displayed in the decision tree in Figure 5.2 for $x_0 = 1$. The three boxes at the far right in that figure contain the three possible values for J_0 when $x_2 = y_2 = 2$, $x_2 = y_2 = 1$ and $x_2 = y_2 = 0$. The state $x_2 = 2$ could be reached from x_1 in three possible ways with the numbers along each route indicating the associated probability. There are six boxes containing the calculated values of J_1. These are based on the possible values for y_1 and the discounted expected value of J_0 when $\delta = 0.1$. Examination reveals $y_1 = 1$ to be optimal when $x_1 = 2$ or $x_1 = 1$. If $x_1 = 0$ there is no choice but to set $y_1 = 0$. Finally, the values for J_2 are shown in the two large boxes on the left where in each box $\rho E(J_1)$ is based on the optimal policy after r_0 is known in $t = 1$. From $x_0 = 1$ it is initially optimal to adopt $y_0 = 1$ since $1.4950 > 1.2881$. The optimal policy, summarized by the circled values of y_t, is as follows: $y_0 = 1$, if $x_1 = 1$ then $y_1 = 1$, if $x_1 = 0$, $y_1 = 0$, and $y_2 = x_2$. In Problem 5.8.1 you are asked to reconsider the reservoir problem when $x_0 = 2$ and to determine the critical probability for recharge which leads to a switch in policy from $y_1^* = 1$ to $y_1^* = 2$.

5.2 A spawner-recruit model

We shall now consider a stochastic version of the spawner-recruit model discussed in Section 2.5; see Reed (1979). The stochastic model presumes

$$R_{t+1} = Z_t G(S_t) \tag{5.9}$$

$$S_t = R_t - Y_t \tag{5.10}$$

$$0 \leq Y_t \leq R_t \tag{5.11}$$

where R_t is the stock of recruits in period t, Y_t is harvest, and S_t is the stock level which "escapes" harvest, spawns, and subject to survival, becomes part of the next year's recruits. Z_t is a random variable with mean one (i.e., $E\{Z_t\} = 1$). Note that the random variable enters as a multiplier of the average or expected recruitment $G(S_t)$ (see Figure 5.3). Higher stock levels are associated with higher levels of variation. This seems like a reasonable assumption although it is not essential to the following discussion.

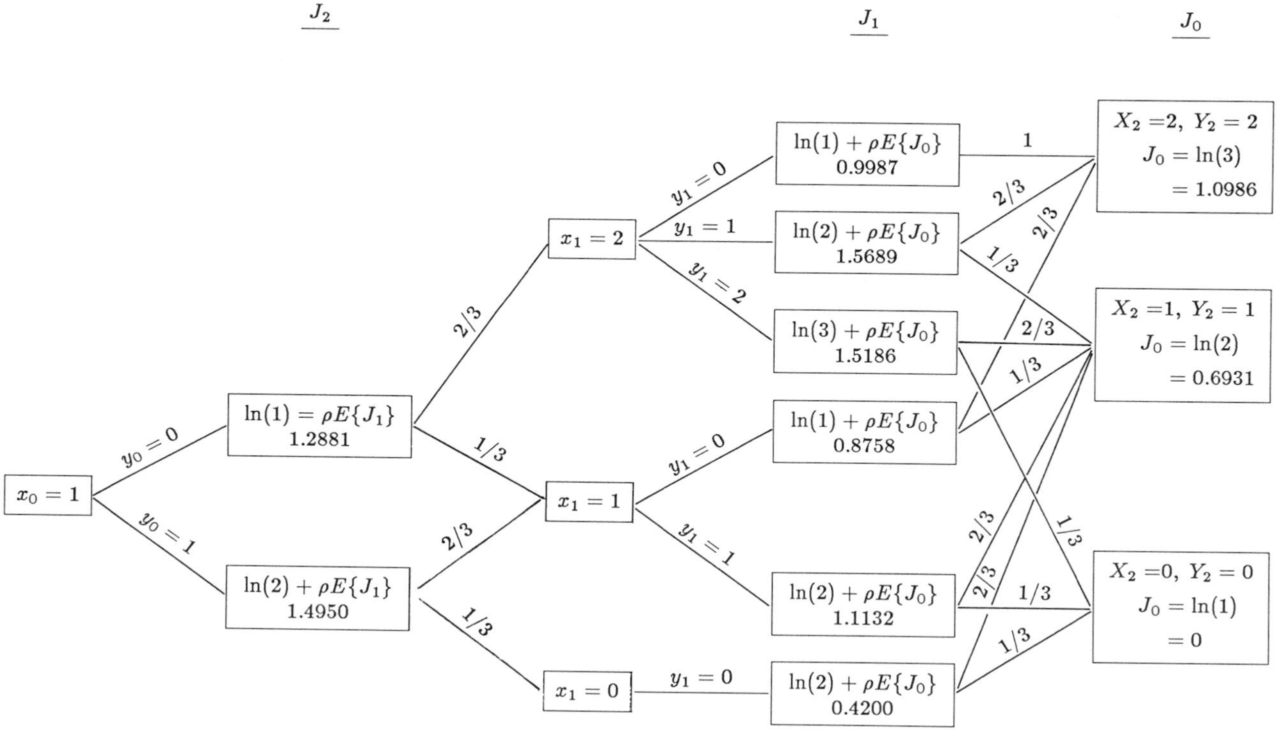

J2
J1
J0
x0 = 1
y0 = 0
y0 = 1
ln(1) = ρE{J1}
1.2881
ln(2) + ρE{J1}
1.4950
2/3
1/3
2/3
1/3
x1 = 2
x1 = 1
x1 = 0
y1 = 0
y1 = 1
y1 = 2
y1 = 0
y1 = 1
y1 = 0
ln(1) + ρE{J0}
0.9987
ln(2) + ρE{J0}
1.5689
ln(3) + ρE{J0}
1.5186
ln(1) + ρE{J0}
0.8758
ln(2) + ρE{J0}
1.1132
ln(2) + ρE{J0}
0.4200
1
2/3
2/3
1/3
2/3
1/3
2/3
2/3
1/3
1/3
1/3
X2 =2, Y2 = 2
J0 = ln(3)
= 1.0986
X2 =1, Y2 = 1
J0 = ln(2)
= 0.6931
X2 =0, Y2 = 0
J0 = ln(1)
= 0

Figure 5.2 Optimal reservoir release policy when $x_0 = 1$

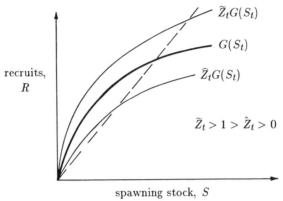

spawning stock, S

Figure 5.3   Stochastic stock-recruitment relation: $G(S)$ is average recruitment.

With R_0 given and known the initial value function may be written

$$J_T(R_0) = \max E \left\{ \sum_{t=0}^{T} \rho^t U(R_t, S_t) | R_0 \right\} \qquad (5.12)$$

The infinite horizon problem can be obtained as the limit as $T \to \infty$.

Recall that if Z is a random variable with density $\phi(z)$ then for any function $f(Z)$ the expectation of $f(Z)$ is defined by

$$E\{f(Z)\} = \int f(z)\phi(z)\,dz \qquad (5.13)$$

Alternatively, if Z has a discrete distribution with probabilities

$$p_j = \Pr(Z = z_j) \qquad j = 1, 2, \ldots, J \qquad (5.14)$$

then we have

$$E\{f(Z)\} = \sum_{j=1}^{J} p_j f(z_j) \qquad (5.15)$$

The mean and variance of Z are defined by

$$\mu_z = E\{Z\} \qquad (5.16)$$

$$\sigma_z^2 = E\{Z^2\} - \mu_z^2 \qquad (5.17)$$

and the coefficient of variation (a dimensionless parameter) is equal to σ_z/μ_z. In the stochastic spawner-recruit model we assume Z_t to be i.i.d.

The expectation in (5.13) is interpreted as a *joint* or *multiple* expectation over all the $T + 1$ random variables $Z_0, Z_1, \ldots, Z_T$.

Our stochastic optimization problem is not fully determined, because we have yet to specify how much information is available to the exploiting firms (or management agency) at the time that Y_t (and thus S_t) is chosen. It will be assumed that R_t is always known exactly at the time that a harvest decision is made. The only uncertainty in the model pertains to future recruitments. This is an unrealistic assumption for most fish stocks; an alternative assumption is discussed in Clark and Kirkwood (1986).

Let us specialize the utility function $U(\cdot)$ so that

$$U(R_t, S_t) = \psi(R_t) - \psi(S_t) = \int_{S_t}^{R_t} \psi'(x) \, dx \qquad (5.18)$$

implying that $U(\cdot)$ is *separable*. Recall in Section 2.5 that this assumption led to the optimality of the MRAP. We will show that the same result applies to the present stochastic model.

In addition, let

$$\psi'(x) = p - c(s) \qquad (5.19)$$

where, as in Section 2.4, p is the price per unit of landed fish and $c(s)$ is the unit harvest cost when the fish population is s, and recall $c'(s) < 0$.[2] Define S_∞ as the spawning escapement in open access equilibrium: $p - c(S_\infty) = 0$.

We are now ready to apply the dynamic programming algorithm to our stochastic optimization problem. With no time remaining ($t = T$)

$$
\begin{aligned}
J_0(R_T) &= \max_{0 \le S_T \le R_T} U(R_T, S_T) \\
&= \max_{0 \le S_T \le R_T} [\psi(R_T) - \psi(S_T)] \\
&= \begin{cases} 0 & \text{if } R_T \le S_\infty \\ \psi(R_T) - \psi(S_\infty) & \text{if } R_T > S_\infty \end{cases}
\end{aligned}
\qquad (5.20)
$$

This implies that the optimal escapement for $t = T$ is

$$S_T^* = \begin{cases} R_T & \text{if } R_T \le S_\infty \\ S_\infty & \text{if } R_T > S_\infty \end{cases} \qquad (5.21)$$

This result is intuitive—with no future one would harvest the stock down to the zero net-revenue level S_∞.

---

[2] In Section 2.4 $c(x) = c/(qx)$ as in the MRAP rule (2.35).

Assume in $t = T - 1$ that $R_{T-1} > S_\infty$. Then

$$J_1(R_{T-1}) = \max_{0 \le S_{T-1} \le R_{T-1}} [U(R_{T-1}, S_{T-1}) + \rho E_Z\{J_0(ZG(S_{T-1}))\}]$$

$$= \max_{0 \le S_{T-1} \le R_{T-1}} [\psi(R_{T-1}) - \psi(S_{T-1}) + \rho E_Z\{\psi(ZG(S_{T-1}))$$

$$- \psi(S_\infty)\}]$$

$$= \max_{0 \le S_{T-1} \le R_{T-1}} [\rho E_Z\{\psi(ZG(S_{T-1}))\} - \psi(S_{T-1})]$$

$$+ \psi(R_{T-1}) - \rho\psi(S_\infty) \qquad (5.22)$$

Define

$$V(S) = \rho E_Z\{\psi(ZG(S))\} - \psi(S) \qquad (5.23)$$

Then, since $\psi(R_{T-1})$ and $\rho\psi(S_\infty)$ are known constants, the maximization of (5.22) is the same as maximizing $V(S)$, where $S = S_{T-1}$. Denote S^* as the escapement value which maximizes $V(S)$ and assume it is unique. The optimal escapement policy for $t = T - 1$ becomes

$$S^*(R) = \begin{cases} S^* & \text{if } R > S^* \\ R & \text{if } R \le S^* \end{cases} \qquad (5.24)$$

It is easy to show that the same optimal escapement policy holds for all $t \le T - 1$, i.e., for all $n \ge 1$. We consider $n = 2$ with larger values of n following inductively. Assume $R > S^*$ (the case where $R \le S^*$ is easily dealt with). First we can rewrite $J_1(R)$ as

$$J_1(R) = \psi(R) + V(S_{T-1}^*) - \rho\psi(S_\infty) \qquad (5.25)$$

Then

$$J_2(R_{T-2}) = \max_{0 \le S_{T-2} \le R_{T-2}} [\psi(R_{T-2}) - \psi(S_{T-2}) + \rho E_Z\{J_1(ZG(S_{T-2}))\}]$$

$$= \max_{0 \le S_{T-2} \le R_{T-2}} [\psi(R_{T-2}) - \psi(S_{T-2}) + \rho E_Z\{ZG(S_{T-2})$$

$$+ V(S_{T-1}^*) - \rho\psi(S_\infty)\}]$$

$$= \max_{0 \le S_{T-2} \le R_{T-2}} [V(S_{T-2})] + \psi(R_{T-2}) + \rho V(S_{T-1}^*) - \rho^2\psi(S_\infty)$$

$$= \psi(R_{T-2}) + (1 + \rho)V(S^*) - \rho^2\psi(S_\infty) \qquad (5.26)$$

since, with $R_{T-2} > S^*$, the optimal escapement in $T - 2$ is $S_{T-2} = S^*$. The optimal escapement policy is again given by (5.24).

The optimal policy is nothing other than the MRAP now cast in terms of escapement, S. It says that in every year optimal escapement is S^* unless $R_t \leq S^*$ in which case the optimal escapement is R_t (and the optimal harvest is zero). The stochastic case differs from the deterministic case in that recruitment will fluctuate, possibly falling below S^* in some years. The optimal harvest policy becomes

$$Y_t = \begin{cases} R_t - S^* & \text{if } R_t > S^* \\ 0 & \text{if } R_t \leq S^* \end{cases} \tag{5.27}$$

and Y_t will fluctuate as well.

This type of management policy, with a constant target escapement level S^* is in fact commonly employed in fishery management. In practice S^* is usually determined with the objective of maximizing the long-run average yield, rather than discounted (expected) net revenue. The former is, of course, a special case (namely, when?) of the latter objective.

Assuming that the parameters of our model are specified, how would the optimal escapement level S^* actually be computed? Although maximizing $V(S)$ as given by (5.23) may at first seem formidable, notice that $V(S)$ is simply a function of S after applying the rules (5.13) or (5.15) for the expected value of an induced random variable. For example, with Z continuous and density $\phi(z)$ we obtain

$$E_z\{\psi(ZG(S))\} = \int \psi(zG(S))\phi(z)\, dz$$

which can be computed by a standard integration routine such as Simpson's method.

In practice it may be preferable to employ a finite discrete distribution for Z in which case the expectation becomes a finite sum

$$E_z\{\psi(ZG(S))\} = \sum_{j=1}^{J} p_j\psi(z_jG(S))$$

where $p_j = \Pr(Z = z_j)$.

In Problem 5.8.2 you are asked to compute S^* in an example of this kind. A simple computer search (evaluation) to determine the maximum of $V(S)$ is perhaps the easiest way to do this. When $V(S)$ is readily differentiated one may obtain the first order necessary condition

$$\rho E_z\{\psi'(ZG(S))ZG'(S)\} - \psi'(S) = \rho E_z\{Z\psi'(ZG(S))\}G'(S) - \psi'(S) = 0 \tag{5.28}$$

which could also be solved numerically. This latter equation implies

$$G'(S) \cdot \frac{E_z\{Z\psi'(ZG(S))\}}{\psi'(S)} = \frac{1}{\rho} = (1 + \delta) \tag{5.29}$$

which is a stochastic generalization of (2.62).

5.2.1 Risk aversion

We pointed out at the end of Section 2.5 that in a deterministic model the optimal approach path to equilibrium is not the MRAP unless $U(R, S)$ is separable. Recall also that a separable utility function is the discrete-time analog of a linear utility function in the continuous-time setting. Note in particular that if

$$U(R, S) = \psi(R - S) = \psi(Y)$$

then a linear ψ obviously implies a separable U.

As is well known, the case of a linear utility function $\psi(\cdot)$ corresponds to *risk neutrality*. A concave utility function ($\psi' > 0, \psi'' < 0$) is said to reflect *risk aversion*, and a convex function reflects *risk preference*. These notions are particularly relevant to the study of the economic effects of fluctuations in resource yield; the hypothesis of a concave utility function reflects the exploiting firm's (or society's) distaste for fluctuations in annual income.

Suppose, for example, that price p is exogenous and constant. Net annual revenue from harvest Y_t is

$$\pi_t = \int_{S_t}^{R_t} [p - c(x)]\, dx \qquad \text{where} \quad S_t = R_t - Y_t \tag{5.30}$$

and the resulting utility of income is then $\psi(\pi_t)$, which is not separable unless ψ is linear. In the case where price is demand-sensitive, $p = p(Y_t)$, we have

$$\pi_t = p(Y_t)Y_t - \int_{S_t}^{R_t} c(x)\, dx$$

In this case there are two sources of nonlinearity, price inelasticity and risk aversion.

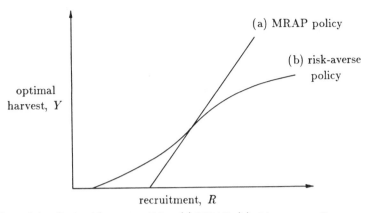

Figure 5.4   Optimal harvest policies: (a) MRAP, (b) risk-averse policy.

An obvious feature of the constant target escapement policy obtained in the stochastic spawner-recruit model is that fluctuations in recruitment result in even greater fluctuations in annual yield. Fluctuations in annual *revenue* may be *dampened* through inelastic demand (fishermen are often heard to complain that whenever they finally do get a good catch, the price always collapses!). Under risk aversion the optional exploitation policy will involve some degree of smoothing out of these fluctuations. The optimal harvest policy will be a feedback policy which is less severe than the MRAP policy (see Figure 5.4).

The risk-averse harvest policy can be computed numerically, using dynamic programming (see Problem 5.8.3).

5.2.2 Other types of fluctuations

The foregoing models treat annual fluctuations in recruitment as the only source of variation in net revenues for a renewable resource industry. But several other sources of variation may be important, including price and cost variation, and variations in the annual harvest due to luck, or to local weather conditions.

Let us first consider price variation. To begin with, imagine an individual fisherman who has to select a certain level of fishing effort E before he eventually learns what price he will receive for his catch. Catch Y is a known linear function of E, $Y = qE$. If the realized price is p then net revenue will be

$$\pi(E; p) = pqE - c(E) \tag{5.31}$$

where we assume $C', C'' > 0$.

Suppose that the fisherman is risk averse, with utility function $U(\pi)$ satisfying $U' > 0$, $U'' < 0$. Normally one would only want to apply this concept to total annual income π, so our assumption is that price p is unknown until the end of the fishing season. (This assumption may be more realistic for farmers than for fishermen; i.e., a point-output process rather than a continuous-output process.)

The fisherman's problem is then:[3]

$$\underset{E \geq 0}{\text{maximize}}\, E\{U(\pi(E; p))\} \tag{5.32}$$

A risk-neutral fisherman, on the other hand, would

$$\underset{E \geq 0}{\text{maximize}}\, E\{\pi(E; p)\} \tag{5.33}$$

Since

$$E\{\pi(E; p)\} = \bar{p}qE - c(E)$$

the risk-neutral fisherman simply employs the expected price $\bar{p}$ in his calculations; optimal risk-neutral effort E_n^* is given by

$$C'(E_n^*) = \bar{p}q$$

For the case of the risk-averse fisherman, it can be shown that

$$E^* < E_n^*$$

i.e., risk aversion results in less fishing effort than does risk neutrality (see Andersen 1982, or Clark 1985, p. 268). Whether in fact fishermen exhibit risk aversion is debatable; many commentators suggest that fishermen are risk takers.

The above model also applies to variations in the catch: simply replace the parameter q by a random variable, so that catch

$$Y = Q_t E$$

---

[3] The use of the letter E with two meanings in Equation 5.32 should cause no confusion; $E\{\ldots\}$ always refers to expectation.

now becomes a random function of effort E. We conclude that, as before, the risk-averse fisherman exerts less effort than the risk-neutral fisherman. (See Problem 5.8.4.)

5.2.3 Imperfect state information

In developing the stochastic spawner-recruit model it was assumed that R_t was observable and subject to precise measurement at the beginning of each period. It was noted that for almost all fisheries this was an implausible assumption. By imperfect state information we will mean a situation where the state of the system is no longer known to the decision maker. At each point in time the fishing firm or management agency is assumed capable of making an estimate $\hat{R}_t$ which will depend on the "true" (but unobservable) R_t, but is subject to an observation error, V_t. At each point in time the decision maker must calculate the estimate $\hat{R}_t$ and choose a control S_t. Thus the problem becomes one of both *estimation* and *control*—obviously a much more complex problem.

In the case where the objective functional is quadratic in R_t and S_t, system dynamics are linear in R_t, S_t, and Z_t, and Z_t and W_t are both Gaussian and individually i.i.d., the estimation problem can be separated from the control problem and a linear feedback control policy can be derived (see Bertsekas, 1976, Chapter 4). The LQG (linear–quadratic–Gaussian) model has been successfully applied to many problems in engineering and some problems in economics (Chow 1975; Rausser and Hochman 1979). Because the LQG approach is best suited for "tracking problems"—where nominal time paths for the state variables are presumed given and the objective is to minimize the sum of squared deviations of estimated from desired state values over time—it has not found wide application in resource economics where the objective of maximization of the present value of net benefits does not readily conform to the LQG format. For a study applying an LQG model to forest management see Dixon and Howit (1979).

A fishery model incorporating imperfect information is discussed by Clark and Kirkwood (1986).

5.3 The risk of forest fire

In this section we consider a problem of considerable importance to the forest industry, namely the risk of forest fires, and its effect on harvest policy. Surprisingly, very little work had been done on this problem until quite recently. We will follow the analysis of Reed (1984).

As in the Faustmann model discussed in Section 2.9, let $V(t)$ denote the stumpage value of a given stand of trees, as a function of age t. The (deterministic) Faustmann formula (2.95) is:

$$\frac{V'(T)}{V(T) - c} = \frac{\delta}{1 - e^{-\delta T}}$$

This formula determines the optimal age of rotation (c denotes the cost of logging and replanting the stand).

Suppose now that there exists a constant risk λ per unit time that the stand will be destroyed by fire. More specifically, we assume that forest fires are a Poisson process with rate parameter λ. This means that

$$\text{Pr (fire occurs in time period} \quad t, t + dt) = \lambda \, dt \qquad (5.34)$$

(Our simple model does not allow for λ to vary with age t.) We will prove that the optimal rotation (maximizing expected present value) now satisfies

$$\frac{V'(T)}{V(T) - c} = \frac{\delta + \lambda}{1 - e^{-(\delta + \lambda)T}} \qquad (5.35)$$

In other words, the forest-fire risk rate λ is simply added on to the discount rate δ. Thus, the appropriate discount rate for forestry includes a component for risk of fire.

It seems that zero discounting is usually the rule in forest management, at least by public management agencies. This policy can lead to very severe reductions in the economic return from forests, although there may be other valid reasons for allowing trees to grow past financial maturity (recreation and wildlife habitat, to name just two).

To derive the modified Faustmann formula, let $\tau_1, \tau_2, \ldots$ denote the times between successive destructions of the forest, whether due to fire or logging. By the same simple minded argument as in Section 2.9, we know that there will exist a single optimal age T for logging the forest. Hence the τ_n's are independent and identically distributed random variables with cumulative distribution (see Figure 5.5)

$$\Pr(\tau \leq t) = F_\tau(t) = \begin{cases} 1 - e^{-\lambda t} & (t < T) \\ 1 & (t \geq T) \end{cases} \qquad (5.36)$$

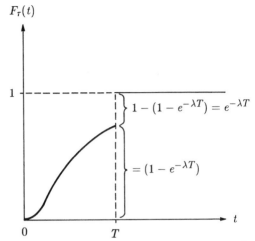

Figure 5.5   The cumulative distribution $\Pr(\tau \leq T) = F_\tau(t) = \begin{cases} 1 - e^{-\lambda t} & (t < T) \\ 1 & (t \geq T) \end{cases}$

The net economic return at each "destruction" (fire or logging) of the forest is

$$Y_n = \begin{cases} -c_2 & \text{if } \tau_n < T \\ V(T) - c_1 & \text{if } \tau_n = T \end{cases} \tag{5.37}$$

where c_2 denotes the cost of replanting a burned-over forest and $V(T) - c_1$ the net return if the forest survives to cutting. The expected net present value (depending on T) is therefore

$$J = E\left\{ \sum_{n=1}^\infty e^{-\delta(\tau_1 + \tau_2 + \cdots + \tau_n)} Y_n \right\} \tag{5.38}$$

Now use the independence of the τ_n to write

$$J = \sum_{n=1}^\infty E\left\{ e^{-\delta(\tau_1 + \tau_2 + \cdots + \tau_{n-1})} \right\} E\{ e^{-\delta \tau_n} Y_n \}$$

$$= E\{ e^{-\delta \tau_n} Y_n \} \sum_{n=1}^\infty \prod_{i=1}^{n-1} (E\{ e^{-\delta \tau_i} \})$$

$$= E\{ e^{-\delta \tau} Y \} / (1 - E\{ e^{-\delta \tau} \})$$

Also

$$E\{ e^{-\delta \tau} \} = \int_0^\infty e^{-\delta t} \, dF_\tau(t)$$

$$= \int_0^T e^{-\delta t} \lambda e^{-\lambda t} \, dt + e^{-\delta T} e^{-\lambda T}$$

$$= (\lambda + \delta e^{-(\lambda+\delta)T})/(\lambda+\delta)$$

In deriving the above expression for $E\{e^{-\delta\tau}\}$ note in Figure 5.5 that the cumulative distribution is discontinuous at $t = T$. For $t \leq T$, $dF_\tau(t) = -e^{-\lambda t}(-\lambda) = \lambda e^{-\lambda t}$ while $1 - \Pr(\tau < T) = 1 - (1 - e^{-\lambda T}) = e^{-\lambda T}$. The last expression obtains after evaluation of the definite integral, multiplying and dividing $e^{-(\lambda+\delta)T}$ by $(\lambda+\delta)$ and combining terms.

In a similar procedure we can show that

$$E\{e^{-\delta\tau}Y\} = \int_0^T (-c_2) e^{-\delta t} \lambda e^{-\lambda t} \, dt + e^{-\delta T}(V(T) - c_1)e^{-\lambda T}$$

$$= (V(T) - c_1)e^{-(\lambda+\delta)T} - \lambda c_2(1 - e^{-(\lambda+\delta)T})/(\lambda+\delta)$$

Substituting the expressions for $E\{e^{-\delta t}\}$ and $E\{e^{-\delta\tau}Y\}$ we obtain

$$J = \frac{(\lambda+\delta)(V(T) - c_1)e^{-(\lambda+\delta)T}}{\delta(1 - e^{-(\lambda+\delta)T})} - \frac{\lambda}{\delta} c_2 \qquad (5.39)$$

Differentiating with respect to T immediately yields the desired result of Equation (5.35).

Observe that the optimal rotation period does not depend on the cost c_2 of replanting a burned forest, but this cost certainly reduces the value of the forest (Equation 5.39). Also, correcting for losses due to fire can have a significant effect on the computation of long-run average yield in terms of volume of timber (see Problem 5.8.5).

5.4 Groundwater management with stochastic recharge

One of the earliest applications of stochastic dynamic programming to re-source management dealt with the optimal temporal allocation of groundwa-ter (Burt 1964, 1967). In a deterministic setting Gisser and Sanchez (1980) have examined the empirical differences between a competitive regime (where users equate price to marginal cost) and an optimal regime (where price is equated to the sum of marginal cost plus user cost). In an empirical study of the Pecos Basin in New Mexico user cost is found to be insignificant and the time-paths for withdrawals in the competitive and optimal control regimes are essentially the same. This somewhat surprising result leads

Gisser (1983) to consider the legal concepts and institutional arrangements which would encourage the optimal static allocation of water between existing and potential users. The states of New Mexico and Arizona provide an interesting comparison. We will present a model based on Burt (1967).

Let X_t represent the height of the water table in an underground aquifer. The cost of pumping water from the aquifer to the surface S is assumed to be a linear function of the lift, $(S - X_t)$; that is

$$C_t = c(S - X_t)q_t \qquad (5.40)$$

where q_t is the amount of water (measured in gallons or acre feet) withdrawn (pumped) in period t.

Assume that the inverse demand curve given by $p_t = a - bq_t$ reflects marginal benefit where p_t is the price per unit of water. Then the total benefit associated with q_t is given as

$$B_t = (a - (b/2)q_t)q_t \qquad (5.41)$$

The dynamics of the water table follow the equation

$$X_{t+1} = X_t - kq_t + R_t \qquad (5.42)$$

where k is a parameter reflecting the influence of a unit withdrawal on water table height (this parameter will depend on the size, shape, and porous medium within the aquifer) and R_t is a random variable indicating recharge (as it directly affects X_{t+1}). We assume that $E\{R_t\} = \bar{R}$ and that the objective of groundwater management is the maximization of expected net revenues over an infinite horizon. This problem may be stated as

$$\underset{\{q_t\}}{\text{maximize}}\, E \left\{ \sum_{t=0}^{\infty} \rho^t \Big[[a - (b/2)q_t]q_t - c(S - X_t)q_t \Big] \right\}$$
$$\text{subject to} \quad X_{t+1} = X_t - kq_t + R_t$$
$$X_0 \quad \text{given}$$

Note that the objective function is a concave quadratic in q_t. We thus expect a linear control policy.

Let us first consider the "certainty equivalent" problem which results when R_t is replaced by its expected value $\bar{R}$. This leads to a deterministic

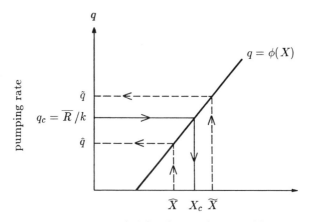

height of groundwater table

Figure 5.6   The certainty equivalence solution of the stochastic groundwater problem

problem with the current-value Hamiltonian

$$\tilde{\mathcal{H}} = [a - (b/2)q_t]q_t - c(S - X_t)q_t + \rho\lambda_{t+1}[-kq_t + \bar{R}] \qquad (5.43)$$

and first order necessary condition requiring

$$\frac{\partial \tilde{\mathcal{H}}}{\partial q_t} = a - bq_t - c(S - X_t) - k\rho\lambda_{t+1} = 0 \qquad (5.44)$$

$$\rho\lambda_{t+1} - \lambda_t = -\frac{\partial \tilde{\mathcal{H}}}{\partial X_t} = -cq_t \qquad (5.45)$$

$$X_{t+1} - X_t = \frac{\partial \tilde{\mathcal{H}}}{\partial(\rho\lambda_{t+1})} = -kq_t + \bar{R} \qquad (5.46)$$

With $\bar{R}$ replacing R_t we can solve $(5.44)-(5.46)$ for steady state equilibrium where we immediately obtain $q = \bar{R}/k$. Eliminating λ from $(5.44)-(5.45)$ yields

$$q = \phi(X) = (\delta(a - cS) + c\delta X)/(b\delta + ck) \qquad (5.47)$$

This is a linear equilibrium relationship between q and X with a positive slope and a negative intercept if $cS > a$ (see Figure 5.6).

If $\bar{R}$ is the long-run expected recharge then $q_c = \bar{R}/k$ is the long-run expected pumping rate and (5.47) can be solved for the long-run expected height X_c. (This assumes that the physical bottom of the aquifer is below X_c.) In Figure 5.6 X_c is determined by projecting q_c horizontally across to $q = \phi(X)$ and dropping a vertical from the point of intersection.

With stochastic recharge Burt (1967) suggests that (X_c, q_c) might be regarded as a "stochastic equilibrium, which is always approached but rarely experienced." The certainty equivalence policy $q = \phi(X)$ might be applied sequentially: (a) determine X_t, (b) set $q_t = \phi(X_t)$, (c) observe a particular R_t, (d) determine X_{t+1}, and so on. If X_t should fall below X_c, q_t will be below q_c and conversely. [Note $(\hat{X}, \hat{q})$ and $(\tilde{X}, \tilde{q})$ in Figure 5.6 and the direction of the arrowheads.] A sequential use of the certainty equivalence policy implies

$$X_{t+1} = X_t - k\phi(X_t) + R_t$$
$$= [1 - \delta ck/(b\delta + ck)]X_t - k\delta(a - cS)/(b\delta + ck) + R_t \quad (5.48)$$

With $0 < \delta < 1$ the coefficient of X_t is positive but less than one and the deterministic portion of (5.48) is stable.

When sequentially applied, is the certainty equivalence policy $q_t = \phi(X_t)$ optimal? Recall this policy was derived under steady state conditions and thus we would not expect it to be optimal if the height of the groundwater table were not at its stochastic equilibrium. Burt (1967, p. 55) has shown, however, that when the groundwater table is 42% above its stochastic equilibrium that the certainty equivalence rule will result in a deviation from the optimal pumping rate of only 2% and that this error further declines as $X_t \to X_c$. To solve for the optimal rate q_t one would need to solve (5.44)–(5.46) with the initial condition X_0 given and the transversality condition $\lim_{t\to\infty} \rho^t \lambda_t \to 0$.

Finally, a comparison of (5.44) with the maximizing condition for q_τ derived from the stochastic dynamic programming algorithm reveals that the values for q_t and q_τ will be identical for $t = \tau$. This is usually the case for quadratic objective functionals and linear dynamics. (An important exception is the case of irreversible development to be discussed in Section 5.7.) In problem 5.8.7 you are asked to obtain the stochastic dynamic programming condition for q_τ to verify this equivalence.

5.5 Learning, Bayesian updating, and search

The stochastic models considered so far in this chapter are devoid of any learning component. For example, in the spawner-recruit model of Section 5.2 we assumed that the probability distribution $\phi(z)$ and the mean recruitment function $G(S)$ were known, and also that annual recruitment

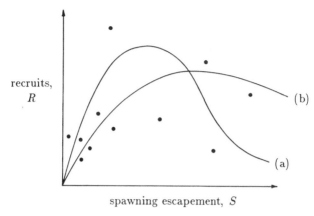

spawning escapement, S

Figure 5.7 Spawner-recruit curves: which fits the data better, (a) or (b)?

R_t becomes known precisely prior to the decision on harvesting. Even supposing that the latter assumption is valid, how could one in fact "know" $\phi(\cdot)$ and $G(\cdot)$?

In fact, these functions can only be *estimated* from the historical time series of recruitments R_t and spawning escapements S_t. Since these data are random, the estimate will inevitably involve uncertainty (see Figure 5.7), but one hopes that as experience accumulates the level of uncertainty will decrease.

Given that the spawner-recruit relationship is uncertain, what is the optimal harvest policy? This is a more complex problem than may first appear. Future uncertainty will probably be less than present uncertainty (as more sample points accumulate). Moreover, the harvest policy itself may affect the rate at which uncertainty decreases over time. In other words, the fishery manager will experience learning, which will both affect and be affected by the harvest strategy. The resulting mathematical problem, called an "adaptive control problem" in the literature, is far too difficult to be taken up here (see Ludwig and Walters 1982). We will have to be satisfied with an elementary introduction to the mathematical treatment of learning and adaptive control, recognizing that in fact almost any problem of environmental or resource economics will contain these elements to some degree.

By "learning" in the probabilistic sense we mean the improvement in the estimate of the probability distributions as the result of accumulation of information. The mathematical formulation of this concept is captured by Bayes's theorem, or the theorem of "inverse probability."

Recall first that the *conditional probability* of A, given B, is defined by

$$\Pr(A|B) = \frac{\Pr(A \text{ and } B)}{\Pr(B)} \qquad \text{for } \Pr(B) \neq 0 \qquad (5.49)$$

Bayes's theorem

(a) If $\Pr(B) \neq 0$ then

$$\Pr(A|B) = \frac{\Pr(B|A)\,\Pr(A)}{\Pr(B)} \qquad (5.50)$$

(b) If A_i are mutually disjoint and $\Sigma\,\Pr(A_i) = 1$ then

$$\Pr(A_i|B) = \frac{\Pr(B|A_i)\,\Pr(A_i)}{\Sigma_j\,\Pr(B|A_j)\,\Pr(A_j)} \qquad (5.51)$$

The proof of Bayes's theorem is very simple. From (5.49) we have

$$\Pr(A|B)\,\Pr(B) = \Pr(A \text{ and } B) = \Pr(B|A)\,\Pr(A)$$

which proves (5.50). The fact that the A_i are disjoint and $\Sigma\,\Pr(A_i) = 1$ implies that[4]

$$\Pr(B) = \Sigma j\,\Pr(B|A_j)\,\Pr(A_j) \qquad (5.52)$$

from which (5.51) follows.

A simple example will illustrate how Bayes's theorem can be used. Suppose that an object is to be searched for in a certain region of total area A. The prior probability that the object is somewhere in the region is p; the probability that it is not in the region at all is $1 - p$.

Clearly, after spending considerable effort searching for the object unsuccessfully, one tends to discount the probability that the object is really in the region. Bayes's theorem can be used to express this quantitatively. We consider two types of search:

1. *Methodical, or exhaustive search:* When a part B of A has been searched unsuccessfully, it is known for sure that the object cannot have been in B (the object does not move).
2. *Poisson search:* The probability of detecting the object (if it is actually in A) during a short search-time interval dt equals $\lambda\,dt$, where λ is a constant.

---

[4] Equation (5.52) is called the "law of total probability," and is frequently useful.

It is easy to imagine a situation where one or the other of these search models would be reasonable.

Applying Bayes's formula (5.50) to Case (1) we have

$$p' = \Pr \text{ (object in } A \mid \text{not found in } B\text{)}$$
$$= \frac{\Pr \text{ (not found in } B \mid \text{object in } A\text{)} \Pr \text{ (object in } A\text{)}}{\Pr \text{ (not found in } B\text{)}}$$

The assumption of methodical search means that

$$\Pr \text{ (not found in } B \mid \text{object in } A\text{)} = 1 - B/A$$

(so if $B = A$, then the object will be found, if it is in A). Also

$$\Pr \text{ (not found in } B\text{)} = \Pr \text{ (not found in } B \mid \text{object in } A\text{)} \cdot p$$
$$+ \Pr \text{ (not found in } B \mid \text{object } not \text{ in } A\text{)} \cdot (1 - p)$$
$$= (1 - B/A) \cdot p + (1 - p)$$

Therefore we obtain

$$p' = \frac{(1 - B/A)p}{(1 - B/A)p + (1 - p)} = \frac{p(1 - B/A)}{1 - Bp/A} \qquad (5.53)$$

The revised probability p' is called the *posterior* probability that the object is in A following the unsuccessful search of subarea $B \leq A$ (see Figure 5.8). Note that $p' = p$ when $B = 0$ and $p' = 0$ when $B = A$, as one would expect.

A similar calculation applies to the case of Poisson search (Case 2), for which

$$\Pr \text{ (object not found in time } T \mid \text{object in } A\text{)} = e^{-\lambda T}$$

Hence

$$p' = \frac{pe^{-\lambda T}}{pe^{-\lambda T} + 1 - p} = \frac{p}{p + (1 - p)e^{\lambda T}} \qquad (5.54)$$

Again we have $p' = p$ for $T = 0$, but now $p' \to 0$ asymptotically as $T \to \infty$: we can never be absolutely sure that the object is not in A (see Figure 5.8(b)).

These simple models illustrate the method of *Bayesian updating*. One begins with a *prior probability* p (or more generally a prior distribution $f(\cdot)$) which delineates the probability of a certain event. Observations or experiments, are then made, and the results are used to *update* the prior

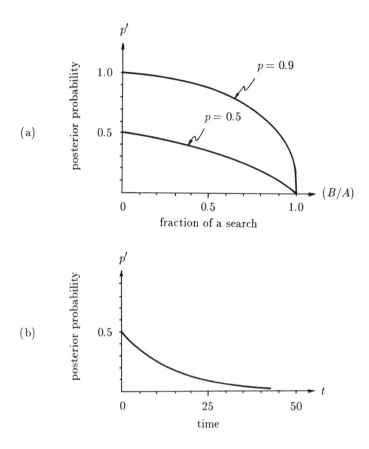

Figure 5.8 Posterior probabilities

probability [distribution] via Bayes's theorem, obtaining a new, *posterior* probability p_1 [distribution $f_1(\cdot)$]. Of course this posterior distribution may then be used as the prior distribution for a further updating. It is easy to show from Bayes's theorem that progressive updating is consistent. For example, suppose that in Case 1, area B_1 is first searched, then B_2 (separate from B_1). Then Equation (5.53) implies that

$$p' = \frac{(1 - B_1/A)p}{1 - B_1 p/A} = \frac{(A - B_1)p}{A - B_1 p}$$

$$p'' = \frac{\left[1 - \frac{B_2}{A - B_1}\right]p'}{1 - \frac{B_2 p'}{A - B_1}} = \frac{(A - B_1 - B_2)p}{A - (B_1 + B_2)p}$$

by simple algebra. Thus p'' could also be obtained from a single update. This is always the case.

5.6 Fishing as a search problem

In the preceding section we considered the problem of searching for a single object. The probability that the object is actually in the search area is updated as search proceeds. In this section we will consider the problem of searching for several objects. The information provided by searching is used to update the prior estimate of the *number* of objects in the search area.

Consider the case of a fisherman trying to decide whether to continue fishing on a certain fishing ground. He or she wishes to predict the future catch rate. If an initial sample period of t hours yields a catch of Y tons of fish, then simple projection yields an estimate of the future catch rate as Y/t tons per hour.

But locating and catching fish is a random process. In other words, the actual catch rate during the sample period is a random variable, which may differ substantially from the long-run average. An experienced fisherman may wish to combine the sample data with other prior information.

Let us assume that fishing is a Poisson process with parameter λ representing the average rate of encountering and catching schools of fish. Since the average catch rate varies from season to season in proportion to the local concentration of fish, λ itself is a random variable. The fisherman does not know the current value of λ (which we assume to remain constant for the duration of the fishing trip in question).[5] From past experience he or she does know the expected, or average value of λ, and also its variation from season to season. Using some standard form of a probability distribution, the fisherman therefore has formulated a prior density for λ:

$$\Pr(\text{average catch rate is between } \lambda, \lambda + d\lambda) = f(\lambda)\,d\lambda \qquad (5.55)$$

According to the Poisson assumption, the probability of catching n schools of fish in time t, *given* λ, equals

$$\Pr(n \text{ schools in time } t|\lambda) = \frac{(\lambda t)^n}{n!}e^{-\lambda t} \qquad (5.56)$$

Let $f(\lambda|n,t)$ denote the posterior density for λ, given that n schools of

---

[5] If λ in fact varies because of depletion of the fish population, the mathematical formulas are considerably more complex (see Mangel and Clark 1983).

fish were located in the first t hours of fishing. Bayes's formula (5.50) immediately implies that

$$f(\lambda|n,t) = \frac{\Pr(n|\lambda,t)f(\lambda)}{\int \Pr(n|\mu,t)f(\mu)\,d\mu} \qquad (5.57)$$

where $\Pr(n|\lambda,t)$ is given by equation (5.56).

In order to simplify the right side of (5.57), it is advisable to choose an appropriate functional form for the prior distribution $f(\lambda)$. A good choice, as we will see, is the gamma distribution

$$f(\lambda) = \gamma(\lambda;\nu,\alpha) = \frac{\alpha^\nu}{\Gamma(\nu)}\lambda^{\nu-1}e^{-\alpha\lambda} \qquad (\lambda > 0) \qquad (5.58)$$

(see Figure 5.9). It is easy to verify that the mean and variance of the gamma density are given by

$$\mu = \frac{\nu}{\alpha}, \qquad \sigma^2 = \frac{\nu}{\alpha^2} \qquad (5.59)$$

Thus if the mean and variance of λ are known, then the parameters ν and α can be obtained by solving equations (5.59). A useful trick can be used to derive the equation for μ and σ^2, and for other purposes. For example, we have

$$\mu = \int_0^\infty \lambda\gamma(\lambda;\nu,\alpha)\,d\lambda$$

$$= \frac{\alpha^\nu}{\Gamma(\nu)}\int_0^\infty \lambda^\nu e^{-\alpha\lambda}\,d\lambda$$

$$= \frac{\alpha^\nu}{\Gamma(\nu)}\frac{\Gamma(\nu+1)}{\alpha^{\nu+1}}\int_0^\infty \frac{\alpha^{\nu+1}}{\Gamma(\nu+1)}\lambda^\nu e^{-\alpha\lambda}\,d\lambda \qquad (5.60)$$

$$= \frac{\alpha^\nu}{\Gamma(\nu)}\frac{\Gamma(\nu+1)}{\alpha^{\nu+1}} \quad (\text{since the integral equals one})$$

$$= \frac{\nu}{\alpha} \qquad [\text{since } \Gamma(\nu+1) = \nu\Gamma(\nu)]$$

The trick was to observe that the integrand $\lambda^\nu e^{-\alpha\lambda}$ in equation (5.60) was of the same fundamental form (except for a constant) as the gamma distribution, with ν replaced by $\nu+1$. Since we know that *any* probability distribution has integral equal to one, no actual integration needs to be carried out.

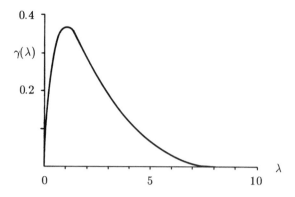

Figure 5.9 The gamma density: $\nu = 2$, $\alpha = 1$.

As an example, suppose that the average value of λ equals 0.4 schools per hour, with a standard deviation of 0.6 schools per hour. Then equations (5.59) give

$$\nu = 0.44 \qquad \alpha = 1.11$$

(when $\sigma > \mu$ we have $\nu < 1$ and the graph of the gamma density looks quite different from Figure 5.9).

We can now complete the simplification of (5.57) again without any integration. The denominator is some constant, independent of λ. Hence from (5.56) and (5.58) we have

$$f(\lambda|n,t) = \text{const} \cdot \lambda^{n+\nu-1}e^{-(\alpha+t)\lambda} \propto \gamma(\lambda; n+\nu, \alpha+t)$$

But $f(\lambda|n,t)$ is itself a probability density, with $\int_0^\infty f(\lambda|n,t)\,d\lambda = 1$. Since $\gamma(\lambda; n+\nu, \alpha+t)$ is also a density, it follows that in fact

$$f(\lambda|n,t) = \gamma(\lambda; n+\nu, \alpha+t) \tag{5.61}$$

Thus the posterior density is again a gamma density, with updated parameters

$$\nu' = n+\nu \qquad \alpha' = \alpha+t \tag{5.62}$$

and with correspondingly updated mean and variance[6]

$$\mu' = \frac{\nu'}{\alpha'} = \frac{n+\nu}{\alpha+t} \qquad \sigma'^2 = \frac{n+\nu}{(\alpha+t)^2} \tag{5.63}$$

---

[6] An alternative derivation of (5.61) is to evaluate the integral in the denominator of (5.57) by the same simple trick used following (5.60).

The coefficient of variation $CV = \sigma/\mu = 1/\sqrt{\nu}$ is therefore updated to

$$CV' = \frac{1}{\sqrt{\nu + n}}$$

Thus the coefficient of variation decreases toward zero as the size of the sample (catch) increases, indicating a progressive decrease in the degree of uncertainty regarding the current value of the uncertain parameter λ. A numerical example is covered in Problem 5.8.8. Whenever the prior and sampling distributions have the property that the posterior distribution has the same functional form as the prior distribution, as in the present example, the two original distributions are said to be *conjugate*. The use of conjugate distributions, which greatly simplify calculations, is common in Bayesian analysis and decision theory (de Groot 1970).

What is the value of search? In our fishing example it should be more than the value of catch because in the process of fishing one is learning something about the location of fish. Search provides information which in turn has value. The *expected value of information* can be defined as the difference between the expected net benefits when the information is available and when it is not. In resource industries, information can be valuable in enabling more efficient or more timely exploitation patterns. Let us use the model of the preceding section to provide an example.

Suppose that the fisherman has the option of fishing on either of two fishing grounds G_1, G_2. He or she has constructed gamma prior distributions for each ground, with parameters ν_i, α_i. For simplicity we first consider a two-period model; for example, the fisherman has a permit to fish for two weeks, and can spend one or both weeks on either ground. The information obtained from the first week's fishing may be used to decide which ground to fish the second week. Many more realistic versions of this setup could be considered, but the main features and difficulties of Bayesian decision techniques are illustrated by our simple model.

Assume that fishing costs are the same on both grounds. Then a reasonable optimization objective is simply the expected total catch. Let $J_n(\nu, \alpha)$ denote the *maximum expected total catch* when there are n weeks fishing left $(n = 1, 2, ...)$, and the current parameter estimates are $\nu = (\nu_1, \nu_2)$ and $\alpha = (\alpha_1, \alpha_2)$. This leads to a dynamic programming problem, in which the "state" variables are the vectors ν, α, representing the current state of information about the fishery.

Obviously

$$J_1(\nu, \alpha) = \max_{i=1,2} \frac{\nu_i}{\alpha_i} T \tag{5.64}$$

where T denotes the number of fishing days in one week, and where units of time are measured in days.

What is the nature of our optimization problem for $n = 2$? The fisherman is now concerned not only with his actual catch during the first week, but also with the information generated by this catch. Imagine an extreme situation, in which the average catch rate on G_1 is known exactly, say $\lambda_1 = 2.0$ tons/day while the value of λ_2 is highly uncertain, with $\mu_2 = 2.0$ tons/day and $\sigma_2 = 1.5$ tons/day. It should be clear that a risk-neutral fisherman would fish G_2 the first week. The results of the first week's fishing will then be used to update the estimate of λ_2, allowing a better decision for the second week.

If G_i is fished the first week, the expected catch for that week is $\nu_i T / \alpha_i$. Hence we have

$$J_2(\nu, \alpha) = \max_{i=1,2} \left\{ \frac{\nu_i}{\alpha_i} T + E\{J_1(\nu_i', \alpha_i')\} \right\} \tag{5.65}$$

where ν_i', α_i' denote the updated values of ν, α when G_i is sampled. If n_i units of fish are caught on G_i in the first week, these updated parameters are

$$\nu_i' = \nu_i + n_i \qquad \alpha_i' = \alpha_i + T \tag{5.66}$$

(and of course $\nu_j' = \nu_j$, $\alpha_j' = \alpha_j$ for $j \neq i$). The probability of catching n_i units of fish, *given* λ_i is

$$Pr(n_i | \lambda_i) = \frac{(\lambda_i T)^{n_i}}{n_i!} e^{-\lambda_i T}$$

Sinced λ_i has the prior distribution $\gamma(\lambda_i; \nu_i, \alpha_i)$, the prior probability of catching n_i units of fish is

$$\begin{aligned}
\Pr(n_i) &= \int_0^\infty \Pr(n_i | \lambda_i) \gamma(\lambda_i; \nu_i, \alpha_i) \, d\lambda_i \\
&= \frac{T^{n_i}}{n_i!} \frac{\alpha_i^{\nu_i}}{(\alpha_i + T)^{n_i + \nu_i}} \frac{\Gamma(n_i + \nu_i)}{\Gamma(\nu_i)}
\end{aligned} \tag{5.67}$$

by the same trick used in (5.60)—see Problem 5.8.9.

We can now write down the expectation in (5.65)

$$J_2(\nu,\alpha) = \max_{i=1,2} \left[\frac{\nu_i T}{\alpha_i} + \sum_{n_i=0}^{\infty} \Pr(n_i) J_i(\nu_i', \alpha_i') \right] \qquad (5.68)$$

where ν_i', α_i' are given by (5.66).

Perhaps you now appreciate why we made so many simplifying assumptions; you may even wish for more. For example, the infinite sum in (5.68) results from assuming no depletion of the fish stock, which is clearly unrealistic. But allowing for depletion makes the formula even *more* complicated (Mangel and Clark 1983)!

The dynamic programming equation (5.68) can immediately be extended to arbitrary $n \geq 2$, and also to the case of $m > 2$ fishing grounds. It must be noted, however, that actual numerical computation of Equation (5.68) becomes exceedingly difficult, probably even impossible, for large n. The case $n = 2$, however, can be solved analytically.

In order to compute the right side of Equation (5.68), take the case $i = 1$. From Equation (5.56) we have

$$J_1(\nu_1', \alpha_1') = J_1((\nu_1 + n_1, \nu_2), (\alpha_1 + T, \alpha_2))$$
$$= \max \left[\frac{\nu_1 + n_1}{\nu_1 + T}, \frac{\nu_2}{\alpha_2} \right] \cdot T$$

Let N_1 be the value of n_1 where this maximum switches:

$$J_1(\nu_1', \alpha_1') = \begin{cases} \frac{\nu_2}{\alpha_2} T & \text{for } n_1 < N_1 \\ \frac{\nu_1 + n_1}{\alpha_1 + T} T & \text{for } n_1 \geq N_1 \end{cases}$$

[Thus N_1 is the greatest integer $\leq (\alpha_1 + T)\nu_2/\alpha_2 - \nu_1$; if this is negative we simply take $N_1 = 0$.] We then have

$$\sum_{n_1=0}^{\infty} \Pr(n_1) J_1(\nu_1', \alpha_1')$$

$$= \sum_{n_1=0}^{N_1-1} \Pr(n_1) \frac{\nu_2}{\alpha_2} T + \sum_{n_1=N_1}^{\infty} \Pr(n_1) \frac{\nu_1 + n_1}{\alpha_1 + T} T$$

$$= T \sum_{n_1=0}^{\infty} \Pr(n_1) \frac{\nu_1 + n_1}{\alpha_1 + T} + T \sum_{n_1=0}^{N_1=1} \left[\frac{\nu_2}{\alpha_2} - \frac{\nu_1 + n_1}{\alpha_1 + T} \right] \Pr(n_1)$$

$$= \frac{\nu_1}{\alpha_1} T + T \cdot \sum_{n_1=0}^{N_1-1} \left[\frac{\nu_2}{\alpha_2} - \frac{\nu_1+n+1}{\alpha_1+T} \right] \Pr(n_1) \qquad (5.69)$$

because

$$\sum_0^\infty \Pr(n_1) = 1 \quad \text{and} \quad \sum_0^\infty n_1 \Pr(n_1) = \bar{n}_1 = \frac{\nu_1}{\alpha_1}$$

Note that we have reduced the computation of the infinite series in (5.68) to the finite sum in (5.69).

As an example, consider the following parameter values:

	G_1	G_2
ν	5.0	0.1
α	0.5	0.012
μ	10.0	8.33
CV	0.45	3.16

Assume that $T = 7$. The prior expected catch on G_1 is $\nu_1 T/\alpha_1 = 70$ tons/week, with a coefficient of variation of 45%, while G_2 yields an expected catch of 58.3 tons, with $CV = 316\%$. Which fishing ground should be fished first?

First, if the fisherman fails to use the information obtained from the first week's fishing, then clearly he should choose G_1, for both weeks. His expected catch will then be $2 \times 70 = 140$ tons. The optimal strategy, on the other hand, is to fish one ground (in fact G_2) the first week, and switch to the other ground if the updated parameters so indicate. Then the expected 2-week total catches are:

$$G_1 \text{ fished first: } 146.3 \text{ tons}$$
$$G_2 \text{ fished first: } 170.4 \text{ tons}$$

Hence G_2 is indeed the optimal choice.

These results allow us to compute the expected value of information, defined as the expected increase in (the value of) the total catch obtained by using the information from one week's fishing. The values are

$$G_1 \text{ fished first: } 6.3 \times p$$
$$G_2 \text{ fished first: } 30.4 \times p$$

where $p =$ price per ton. The optimal strategy (G_2 first) thus yields a 22% increase in expected value, relative to the nonuse of information.

Note, however, that the information obtained from week one is only used for one more week. What if in fact there are m more weeks to fish? In this case we would have to solve the dynamic programming equation for J_{m+1}, a formidable task, as we have remarked.[7] We can nevertheless easily obtain a lower estimate for the expected value of information in this case, by supposing that the fisherman only uses the first week's information to decide on the optimal G_1 for the remaining m weeks. Let $\tilde{J}_2(\nu, \alpha)$ denote the total expected catch for this "semimyopic" strategy. Then we have

$$\tilde{J}_2(\nu, \alpha) = \max_{i=1,2} \left[\frac{\nu_i T}{\alpha_i} + m E\{J_1(\nu_i', \alpha_i')\} \right]$$

which can be calculated as above. The results for $m = 10$ are:

$$G_1 \text{ fished first: } \tilde{J}_2 = 832.6 \text{ tons}$$
$$G_2 \text{ fished first: } \tilde{J}_2 = 1179.4 \text{ tons}$$

compared to the noninformation value of 770 tons. The optimal strategy thus provides an increaes of 68%, which is our estimate of the expected value of information in the case $m = 10$. This is an underestimate, but probably not a drastic one. At any rate, the result illustrates an obvious principle: the expected value of information depends on how long (or how much) it will be used.

We will not pursue this model any further, although other features can be explored (Mangel and Clark 1983, 1986).

5.7 Irreversible development

In 1964 Burton Weisbrod published an article identifying a concept he referred to as "option value." Option value was thought to arise in situations where a park or urban landmark was being evaluated for development. Weisbrod argued that the benefits of *preservation* were likely to be underestimated because potential visitors, while uncertain in their demand to visit the park or landmark, might be willing to pay some amount to preserve the option of a future visit. If the park or landmark were in some sense unique,

---

[7] Actually, since J_2 is so easy, it is quite feasible to compute J_3 (Mangel and Clark 1986); J_4 seems very hard.

development would irreversibly foreclose the option of potential visitors. At the same time the owner of the park or landmark would find it difficult to capture this option value and thus it would likely be excluded from traditional financial or cost–benefit analysis.

Since its introduction in 1964 there has been a lively debate in the economics literature as subsequent commentators have sought to clarify and quantify the concept. (See Bishop 1982 and Smith 1983 for reviews.) Two of the more interesting articles are those of Arrow and Fisher (1974) and Henry (1974). Arrow and Fisher showed that if development were irreversible and the future benefits of development uncertain, then a risk-neutral decision maker would be less likely to develop a natural environment (for example, a wilderness area) if development were irreversible. Henry showed that if development were irreversible and a risk-neutral decision maker evaluated development using both the certainty equivalence (CE) approach and stochastic dynamic programming (SDP), then development might be optimal using the CE approach while it might *not* be optimal when evaluated by SDP. This seemingly subtle point has significant policy implications because many resource management agencies are mandated to substitute expected values for random variables when performing cost–benefit analysis; thus leading to a bias for initial development.

Intuitively, the value of delaying an irreversible decision should depend on what one might expect to learn about the future net benefits from development. Conrad (1980) maintains that the "quasi-option value" identified by Arrow and Fisher is equivalent to the expected value of information (EVI) discussed in the previous section within the context of searching for the most productive fishing grounds. We will proceed with a simple two-period model of irreversible development under two information structures: no learning (fixed probabilities) and passive learning (via updated probabilities).

Consider a wilderness area being evaluated for resource development, say mining. Let

$$x_t = \begin{cases} 1 & \text{if the site is developed before or during period } t \\ 0 & \text{if site is undeveloped (wilderness) during period } t \end{cases}$$

where $t = 0, 1$. Thus, development is irreversible in the sense that if $x_t = 1$ then $x_\tau = 1$ for $\tau > t$. (In our two-period model if $x_0 = 1$ then $x_1 = 1$).

We shall ignore fixed costs and discounting and define the net benefits in period t as

$$N_t = B(1 - x_t) + Z_t D x_t \qquad (5.70)$$

where B is the net benefit from wilderness preservation, D is the net benefit from development, and Z_t is a random variable, independently distributed of all other variables.

We wish to consider the optimal initial decision x_0^* under two information structures: fixed probabilities and updated probabilities. We will refer to the first case as "no learning" and the latter case as passive learning since probability revision takes place exogenously with the passage of time.

With no learning it is assumed that

$$\Pr(Z_0 = 1) = \Pr(Z_1 = 1) = p \qquad (5.71)$$

With learning we assume

$$\Pr(Z_0 = 1) = p$$
$$\Pr(Z_1 = 1 | Z_0 = 1) = p_1 \qquad (5.72)$$
$$\Pr(Z_1 = 1 | Z_0 = 0) = p_0$$

where $1 > p_1 > p > p_0 > 0$. Then, what are the decision rules for determining x_0^* with no learning and with learning and what is the expected value of information (EVI) obtained by delaying development one period?

The case of no learning (fixed probabilities) is fairly straightforward. The expected net benefits from $x_0 = 1$ are

$$E\{N_0 + N_1 | x_0 = 1\} = pD + pD = 2pD \qquad (5.73)$$

while the expected net benefits from $x_0 = 0$ are

$$E\{N_0 + N_1 | x_0 = 0\} = B + \max[B, pD] \qquad (5.74)$$

where $\max[\cdot]$ means the largest of the elements in $[\cdot]$. Thus $x_0^* = 1$ if $pD > B$ and $x_0^* = 0$ if $pD < B$ (i.e. develop if and only if expected development benefits exceed wilderness benefits).

The case of learning is a bit more complex. Reference to the decision tree in Figure 5.10 will reveal the logic behind the expressions for expected net benefits with learning. We assume now that $pD > B$.

With learning the probability of obtaining D or zero is revised after observing Z_0. If the processes, or in our case the results, of revision are

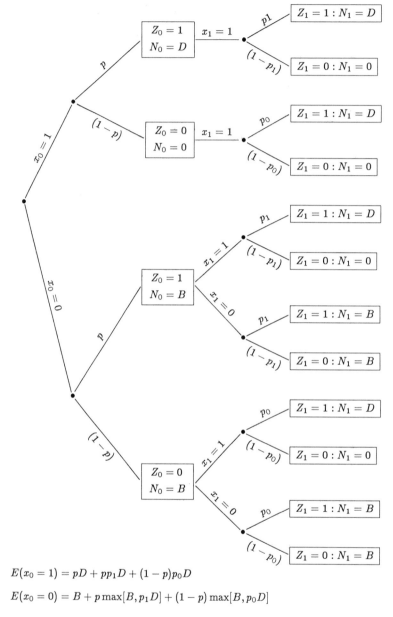

$$E(x_0 = 1) = pD + pp_1D + (1-p)p_0D$$

$$E(x_0 = 0) = B + p\max[B, p_1D] + (1-p)\max[B, p_0D]$$

Figure 5.10 The irreversible development decision with learning.

known in $t = 0$, the expected value of immediate development versus one period delay becomes

$$E\{N_0 + N_1|x_0 = 1\} = pD + pp_1D + (1 - p)p_0D \qquad (5.75)$$

versus

$$E\{N_0 + N_1|x_0 = 0\} = B + p\max[B, p_1D] + (1 - p)\max[B, p_0D] \quad (5.76)$$

Since we assume that $pD > B$, it must be the case that $p_1D > B$, since $p_1 > p$. Now suppose that $B > p_0D$. Then (5.76) becomes

$$E\{N_0 + N_1|x_0 = 1\} = B + pp_1D + (1 - p)B \qquad (5.77)$$

Subtracting (5.77) from (5.75) yields

$$E\{N_0 + N_1|x_0 = 1\} - E\{N_0 + N_1|x_0 = 0\} = (pD - B) - (1 - p)(B - p_0D) \qquad (5.78)$$

The terms $(pD - B)$ and $(B - p_0D)(1 - p)$ are both positive and therefore the sign of their difference is indeterminant. The point of the problem is to note that while $(pD - B) > 0$ implies $X_0^* = 1$ with *no* learning, if probabilities are subject to revision and $(pD - B) < (B - p_0D)(1 - p)$, then the anticipation of revision (called *preposterior analysis*) may imply $x_0^* = 0$ and thus delay (and preservation) in period $t = 0$.

By way of a numerical example suppose $B = 1.0$, $D = 1.5$, $p_1 = 0.8$, $p = 0.7$, and $p_0 = 0.2$. Then $pD - B = 0.05$ which implies $x_0^* = 1$ with no learning. With learning $(B - p_0D)(1 - p) = 0.21$ which implies $x_0^* = 0$ since $E(x_0 = 1) - E(x_0 = 0) = -0.16$. With delay $(x_0^* = 0)$ if $Z_0 = 1$, then $x_1^* = 1$, whereas if $Z_0 = 0$, $x_1^* = 0$.

By delay one is in a position to exploit new information in the form of updated probabilities. The expected value of information is

$$EVI = E(x_0^*)_{|\text{ with learning}} - E(x_0^*)_{|\text{ no learning}} \qquad (5.79)$$

For the above numerical example EVI = 0.04. Conrad (1980) notes that for information to have value there must be choice. It would be the bitterest of ironies to "learn" and yet be unable to take action which would make use of the acquired information.

Finally, the above problem assumes that information is acquired through time (perhaps by research) *independent* of x_τ. This situation is different from the active searching (fishing) required to obtain information in the previous subsection. Here we assume that information will be generated by other means and it is not necessary (nor optimal) to experiment with development to determine its value (or what one might get away with environmentally in the case of development which runs the risk of pollution).

5.8 Problems

P5.8.1. Recall the reservoir management problem where

$$\text{State of reservoir:} \quad X_t = \begin{cases} 0 & \text{empty} \\ 1 & \text{half full} \\ 2 & \text{full} \end{cases}$$

$$\text{Recharge:} \quad R_t = \begin{cases} 0 & \text{with probability } 1/3 \\ 1 & \text{with probability } 2/3 \end{cases}$$

Release: $Y_t = 0, 1, 2$ and $Y_t \le X_t$

Transition dynamics: $X_{t+1} = X_t - Y_t + R_t$

Net benefit: $N_t = \ln(1 + Y_t)$

The stochastic optimization problem was to

$$\underset{\{Y_t\}}{\text{maximize}} \, E \left\{ \sum_{t=0}^{2} \rho^t \ln(1 + Y_t) \right\}$$

$$\text{subject to} \quad X_{t+1} = X_t - Y_t + R_t \qquad Y_t \le X_t$$

$$X_0 \quad \text{given}$$

where, as before, $\rho = 1/(1 + \delta)$ and $\delta = 0.1$.

(a) Suppose now that $X_0 = 2$. Construct a decision tree to determine the optimal release policy Y_0^*, Y_1^* and Y_2^*.

(b) What value for $\Pr(R_t = 1)$ will result in $Y_1^* = 2$ when $X_1 = 2$?

Answers

(a) $Y_0^* = 1$, $Y_1^* = 1$, $Y_2^* = X_2$ (see Figure 5.11).

(b) $\Pr(R_t = 1) = 0.859$.

P5.8.2 The average spawner-recruit curve for a certain stock of Pacific salmon is given by the Ricker formula

$$\bar{R} = G(S) = S e^{a(1 - S/K)}$$

with $a = 2.0$, $K = 200{,}000$ where the units of S, K are numbers of

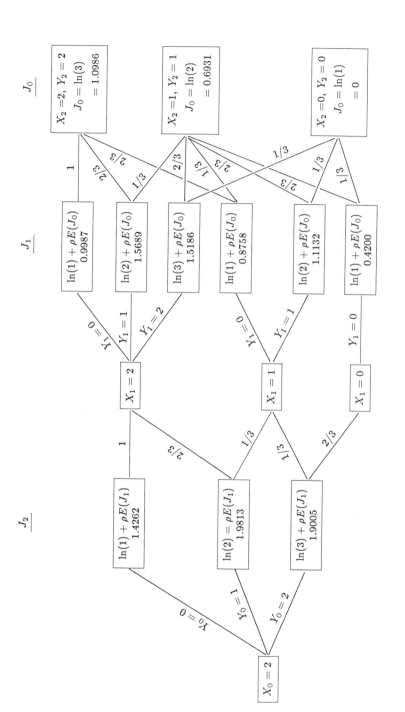

Figure 5.11

salmon. Recruitment actually fluctuates between 50% and 150% of the mean $G(S)$:

$$R_{t+1} = Z_t G(S_t)$$

Adopt the simple distribution

$$\Pr(Z = 0.5) = 0.25$$
$$\Pr(Z = 1.0) = 0.50$$
$$\Pr(Z = 1.5) = 0.25$$

Assuming a price of $p = \$2.00$ per salmon, and an annual discount rate of 10%, determine the optimal target escapement S^*:

(a) for zero costs, $c(x) \equiv 0$ [Show that this is the same as the deterministic case.]

(b) for $c(x) = c/x$ with $c = \$4000$

(c) for $c(x) = c/x$ with $c = \$4000$, but with

$$\Pr(Z = 0.2) = .33$$
$$\Pr(Z = 1.0) = .34$$
$$\Pr(Z = 1.8) = .33$$

(d) for $c(x) = c/x$ with $c = \$4000$, but with deterministic recruitment, i.e., $\Pr(Z = 1) = 1$.

Answers

(a) $S^* = 70{,}022$; in this case we have $\psi(S) = pS$, so that $V(S) = \rho E\{\psi(ZG(S))\} - \psi(S) = p[\rho G(S) - S]$ which is maximal for $G'(S) = 1/\rho = 1 + i$ as in the deterministic case.

(b) $S^* = 74{,}975$

(c) $S^* = 74{,}943$

(d) $S^* = 74{,}942$

Notice that the effect of stochastic recruitment is all but negligible. While the optimal escapement S^* is always larger with stochastic recruitment than with deterministic recruitment with the same mean (Reed 1979), the numerical difference is extremely small.

Many papers in the literature investigate stochastic versions of deterministic models in a purely theoretical fashion. It appears that in many cases, however, the actual numerical effects would be quite minor, but this is hardly ever checked. On the other hand, there certainly are situations

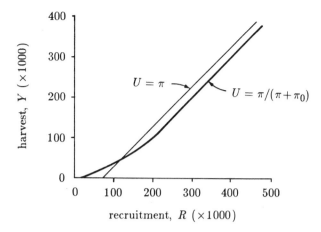

Figure 5.12   Optimal harvest, Y, as a function of recruitment R, for linear and nonlinear utility functions U.

where the predictions of a stochastic model are very different from those of a deterministic model. This is particularly true for models involving uncertain parameters; see Section 5.5.

P5.8.3. Use dynamic programming to determine the optimal escapement policy $S^* = S^*(R)$ and optimal harvest policy $Y^* = R - S^*$ for the salmon model of Problem 5.8.2 (c), with a 10-year horizon, but with a nonlinear utility of net revenue given by

$$U(\pi) = \frac{\pi}{\pi + \pi_0} \quad \text{where} \quad \pi_0 = \$5000$$

Compare your results with the linear case $U(\pi) = \pi$.

[Note: this problem involves a considerably more daunting programming chore than most other problems in this book. In setting up your dynamic programming code you must choose some mesh size ΔR; we used $\Delta R = 20,000$. (Note also that maximum possible recruitment is greater than K.) The values of $J(x,t)$ at each iteration must be stored as an array $J(x_1, \ldots, x_n)$. An interpolation routine can be used to calculate $J(x,t)$ for intermediate values of x. You must also choose some search algorithm to find the optimal escapement S^*. In the long run it will probably be more efficient to use a more flexible programming language, such as PASCAL.]

Answer. The optimal harvest policy $h^*(R)$ is shown in Figure 5.12, for both linear and nonlinear utility. The main feature of the nonlinear case is that a positive harvest occurs for all $R > x_\infty$. This is compensated by a slight reduction in harvest when R is large.

P5.8.4. A fisherman faces the net revenue fuction

$$\pi(E;p) = pqE - cE^2$$

where E denotes effort (hours fishing) over a given season. Utility is given by

$$U(\pi) = \frac{\pi}{\pi + \pi_0}$$

[thus a loss of π_0 implies "bankruptcy" since $U(\pi) \to -\infty$ as $\pi \to -\pi_0$].
(a) Suppose that $q = 5$ tons/hour, $c = \$30$ per (hour)^2, $\pi_0 = \$100,000$, and that price p is uncertain, with distribution

$$\Pr(p = \$300) = \Pr(p = \$600) = \Pr(p = \$900) = 1/3$$

Determine the levels of effort which (i) maximize expected net revenue, and (ii) maximize expected utility. [For (ii) simply compute expected utility and maximize by visual or computer search.]
(b) Same as (a), except that the catch is also uncertain, with $\Pr(q = 2) = \Pr(q = 8) = 1/2$.

Answers.
(a) (i) $E^* = 50$ hours   (ii) $E^* = 38.5$ hours
(b) (ii) $E^* = 28.5$ hours.

P5.8.5. The volume of usable wood in a hectare of B.C. spruce is given, as a function of age T, in the following table.

Age (yrs)	30	40	50	60	70	80	90	100	110	120	130
Volume (m^3)	0	3	16	51	107	167	217	252	275	289	298

In the notation of Section 5.4 assume that

$$p = \text{price of wood} = \$100/m^3$$

$$c_1 = \text{cost of logging and replanting} = \$5000 \text{ (per hectare)}$$

$$c_2 = \text{cost of replanting after fire} = \$1000 \text{ (per hectare)}$$

$$\delta = \text{annual discount rate} = .03$$

Determine the optimal rotation period T^* and maximum expected present value $J(T^*)$, for annual forest-fire risk $\lambda = 0, .01, .02$, and $.05$ respectively. Do the same for $\delta = .001$. [Suggestion: Simply calculate $J(T)$ from Equation (5.39) for $T = 30, 40, \ldots$ and find the optimum by inspection.]

Answers

λ	$\delta = .03$		$\delta = .001$	
	T^*	$J(T^*)$	T^*	$J(T^*)$
0	90 yrs	$1203	110 yrs	$193,500
.01	80	330	100	100,869
.02	-	-	90	42,409
.05	-	-	-	-

Note the strong influence of forest-fire risk on economic yield. Blanks in the above table indicate that $J(T) < 0$ for all $T > 0$. The implication of this is not that the forest is commercially worthless, but rather that replanting after fires is not economically viable [if $C_2 = 0$, then $J(T) > 0$ provided that $pV(T) > c_1$]. See Reed and Errico (1985) for further discussion.

P5.8.6. A shady character has sold you his claim to a gold mine. Before purchasing the mine, you formulated a prior distribution as to the number of kg of gold it contains:

$$\Pr(X = k) = p_k \qquad (k = 1, 2, \ldots, N)$$

(You could tell by looking that $p_0 = 0$.)

(a) Suppose that you have already dug up k_0 kg of gold, find the posterior probabilities $\Pr(X = k | X \geq k_0)$.

(b) It's a remote mine. Once a month you take all your month's gold digging, c_t, go to town and blow it, yielding utility $U(c_t)$ with $U' > 0$, $U'' < 0$. Let $J_n(\overrightarrow{p})$ denote the maximum total expected discounted utility, if the claim expires after n months, given the prior probabilities $\overrightarrow{p} = (p_k)$. Find the dynamic programming equation for $J_n(\overrightarrow{p})$. For simplicity, assume that you decide how much gold you will dig (if possible) at the beginning of each month. You *must* spend all the gold you dig, otherwise it will be stolen.

Answers

(a)
$$\Pr(X = k | X \ge k_0) = \begin{cases} 0 & \text{if } k < k_0 \\ \dfrac{p_k}{\sum_{j=k_0}^{N} P_j} & \text{if } k \ge k_0 \end{cases}$$

[Note that the conditional probabilities must always sum to 1.]

(b)
$$J_1(\overrightarrow{p}) = \sum_{k=1}^{N} p_k U(k)$$

$$J_{n+1}(\overrightarrow{p}) = \max_{0 \le c \le N} \left(\sum_{k=c}^{N} p_k \Big(U(k) + \rho J_n(\overrightarrow{p}') \Big) + \sum_{k=1}^{c-1} p_k U(k) \right)$$

where $\overrightarrow{p}'$ is the updated distribution, if you actually mine c:

$$p_k' = \Pr(X = k | X \ge c)$$

[Note: This is a thinly disguised version of the problem "How to eat a cake of unknown size" (Kemp 1976). The model has been adapted to a variety of more realistic problems of resource exhaustion under uncertainty; see Dasgupta and Heal 1979.]

P5.8.7. For the stochastic groundwater problem in Section 5.4 show that the stochastic dynamic programming algorithm will yield the same expression as the maximum condition in the certainty equivalent problem.

Answer. Consider the case where T is very large. Then for n periods-to-go and $\tau = T - (n - 1)$

$$J_n = \max_{q_\tau} [[a - (b/2)q_\tau]q_\tau - c(S - X_\tau)q_\tau + \rho E\{J_{n-1}\}]$$

$$= \max_{q_\tau} \Big[[a - (b/2)q_\tau]q_\tau - c(S - X_\tau)q_\tau + \rho E\Big\{ [a - (b/2)q_{\tau+1}]q_{\tau+1}$$
$$- c(S - X_{\tau+1})q_{\tau+1} + \rho E\{J_{n-2}\} \Big\} \Big]$$

$$= \max_{q_\tau} \Big[[a - (b/2)q_\tau]q_\tau - c(S - X_\tau)q_\tau + \rho E\Big\{ [a - (b/2)q_{\tau+1}]q_{\tau+1}$$
$$- c(S - (X_\tau - kq_\tau + R_\tau))q_{\tau+1} + \rho E\{J_{n-2}\} \Big\} \Big]$$

$$= \max_{q_\tau} \Big[[a - (b/2)q_\tau]q_\tau - c(S - X_\tau)q_\tau + \rho[[a - (b/2)q_{\tau+1}]q_{\tau+1}$$
$$- c(S - X_\tau + kq_\tau - E\{R_\tau\})q_{\tau+1} + \rho E\{J_{n-2}\} \Big]$$

Then

$$\frac{\partial(\cdot)}{\partial q_\tau} = a - bq_\tau - c(S - X_\tau) - k\rho c q_{\tau+1} = 0$$

With $\lambda_{t+1} = \frac{\partial J}{\partial X_{t+1}} = cq_{t+1}$, (5.44) and this last expression are identical.

P5.8.8. The catch-effort data for a certain local fishery over the past 8 years are given in the table.

Year	1	2	3	4	5	6	7	8
Catch (tons)	1400	2100	3800	1200	1800	1000	2000	2600
Effort (days fishing)	300	370	390	400	370	380	300	320

(a) Assume that fishing is a Poisson process with parameter λ which varies randomly from year to year. Find the mean and variance of λ. If λ has a gamma density, find the values of ν and α. [Use $\lambda_i = C_i/B_i$ as the true value of λ in year i; this ignores sampling errors.]

(b) A fisherman has just caught 8.5 tons of fish in 3 days fishing. Find his expected daily catch for the remainder of the season, using the Bayesian approach, and compare this with the naive estimate. Explain the difference.

Answers.

(a) $\mu = 5.67$ tons/day, $\sigma = 2.44$ tons/day, $\alpha = 0.95$ days/ton, $\nu = 5.40$.

(b) Naive estimate $= 8.5/3 = 2.83$ tons/day;
Bayesian estimate $= (\nu + n)/(\alpha + t) = 3.52$ tons/day.
The fisherman can figure that he has probably been rather unlucky so far. Of course if the low catch rates continue, or if other fishermen have been experiencing similar low catches, then he will lower his estimate of λ accordingly.

P5.8.9. Establish Equation (5.67). Also use the recurrence relation

$$\Gamma(\nu + 1) = \nu\Gamma(\nu)$$

to show how to calculate (5.67) without having to evaluate the gamma function.

P5.8.10

(a) Write a computer program to calculate $J_2(\nu, \alpha)$ as in Equation (5.68), using the simplification of Equation (5.69). Use your program to verify the numerical results given on pages 208-209.

(b) Given that G_2 is fished first, what is the critical number of tons of fish that must be caught the first week, so as not to switch to G_1 for week two?

Answers

(a) In calculating the sum in Equation (5.69), it greatly reduces computer time if you use a recurrence relation for $\Pr(n_i)$. You should verify that

$$\Pr(0) = \left(\frac{\alpha_i}{\alpha_i + T}\right)^{\nu_i}$$

$$\Pr(n_i + 1) = \frac{T}{\alpha_i + T} \frac{n_i + \nu_i}{n_i + 1} \Pr(n_i)$$

and use this in your program.

(b) You must catch 70 or more tons on G_2.

P5.8.11. A particular activity has the potential to alter a local environment irreversibly. Operation of the activity and the state of the environment can be represented as binary variables where

$$q_t = \begin{cases} 1 & \text{if activity is undertaken during period } t \\ 0 & \text{if activity is not undertaken during period } t \end{cases}$$

$$X_t = \begin{cases} 1 & \text{if environment is healthy} \\ 0 & \text{if environment is altered (destroyed)} \end{cases}$$

If $X_t = 0$ then $X_\tau = 0$ for $\tau > t$; also $q_t \le X_t$ for all t. Assume that the environment is currently healthy $(X_0 = 1)$ and that $t = 0, 1, 2$.

The welfare of local residents is given by the function $N_t = X_t \ln(2 + q_t)$ for $t = 0, 1, 2$. The probability distribution $f(X_{t+1}|X_t, q_t)$ is given as follows

$$f(X_{t+1}|X_t, q_t) = \begin{cases} 1 & \text{for } (1|1, 0) \\ p & \text{for } (1|1, 1) \\ (1 - p) & \text{for } (0|1, 1) \\ 1 & \text{for } (0|0, 0) \\ 0 & \text{otherwise} \end{cases}$$

The optimization problem might be written as

$$\underset{q_t=0,1}{\text{maximize}} \quad E\left\{\sum_{t=0}^{2} \rho^t X_t \ln(2+q_t)\right\}$$

$$\text{where } X_\tau = 0 \ (\tau > t) \text{ if } X_t = 0$$

$$\text{and } X_0 \text{ is given}$$

(a) Construct a decision tree and solve for the optimal q_t when $p = 0.5$ and $\delta = 0.10$.

(b) Resolve for $p = 0.6$ and $\delta = 0.10$

Answer. See Figure 5.13.

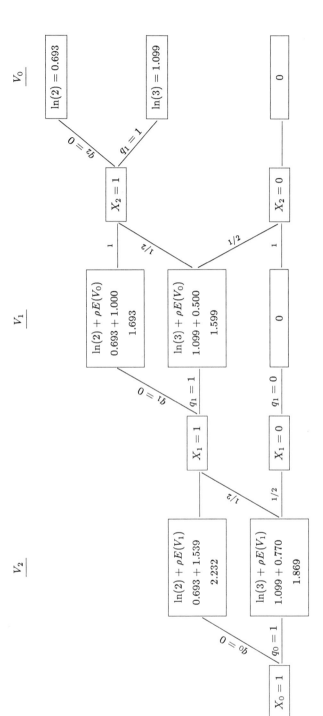

Figure 5.13 Irreversible development: $p = 1/2$, $\delta = 0.10$

References

Andersen, P. 1982. Commercial fisheries under price uncertainty. *J. Environ. Econ. Manag.* 9:11-28.

Aoki, M. 1976. *Optimal Control and System Theory in Dynamic Economic Analysis.* North Holland, New York.

Arrow, K.J. 1968. Optimal capital policy with irreversible investment, in Wolfe, J.N. (Ed.), *Value, Capital, and Growth: Papers in Honour of Sir John Hicks.* Edinburgh Univ. Press, Edinburgh, pp. 1-20.

Arrow, K.J. and A.C. Fisher. 1974. Environmental preservation, uncertainty and irreversibility. *Quart. J. Econ.* 87:312-319.

Ayres, R.U. and A.V. Kneese. 1969. Production, consumption and externalities. *Amer. Econ. Rev.* 59:282-297.

Baumol, W.J. 1972. On taxation and the control of externalities. *Amer. Econ. Rev.* 62:307-322 .

Baumol, W.J. and W.E. Oates. 1975. *The Theory of Environmental Policy.* Prentice-Hall, Englewood Cliffs, NJ.

Bellman, R. 1957. *Dynamic Programming.* Princeton Univ. Press, Princeton, NJ.

Bertsekas, D. 1976. *Dynamic Programming and Stochastic Control.* Academic Press, New York.

Birkhoff, G. and G.-C. Rota. 1969. *Ordinary Differential Equations.* Blaisdell, Waltham, MA.

Bishop, R.C. 1982. Option value: an exposition and extension. *Land Econ.* 58:1-15.

Boulding, K.E. 1966. The economics of the coming spaceship earth, in H. Jarrett (Ed.), *Environmental Quality in a Growing Economy.* Johns Hopkins Press, Baltimore.

Burt, O.R. 1964. Optimal resource use over time with an application to groundwater. *Management Sci.* 11:80-93.

Burt, O.R. 1967. Temporal allocation of groundwater. *Water Resources Res.* 3:45-56.

Cannon, M.D., C.D. Cullum, and E. Polak. 1970. *Theory of Optimal Control and Mathematical Programming.* McGraw-Hill, New York.

Chow, G.C. 1975. *Analysis and Control of Dynamic Economic Systems.* Wiley, New York.

Clark, C.W. 1976. *Mathematical Bioeconomics: The Optimal Management of Renewable Resources.* Wiley-Interscience, New York.

Clark, C.W. 1980. Restricted access to common-property fishery resources: a game-theoretic analysis, in P.T. Liu (ed.), *Dynamic Optimization and Mathematical Economics.* Plenum, New York, pp. 117-132.

Clark, C.W. 1980. Towards a predictive model for the economic regulation of commercial fisheries. *Can. J. Fish. Aquat. Sci.* 37:1111-1129.

Clark, C.W. 1985. *Bioeconomic Modelling and Fisheries Management.* Wiley-Interscience, New York.

Clark, C.W., F.H. Clarke, and G.R. Munro. 1979. The optimal exploitation of renewable resource stocks: problems of irreversible investment. *Econometrica* 47:25-49.

Clark, C.W. and Kirkwood, G.P. 1986. Optimal harvesting of an uncertain resource stock and the value of stock surveys. *J. Environ. Econ. Manag.* 13:235-244.

Clark, C.W. and R.H. Lamberson. 1982. An economic history and analysis of pelagic whaling. *Marine Policy* 6:103-120 .

Coase, R.H. 1960. On the problems of social cost. *J. Law and Econ.* 3:1-44.

Conrad, J.M. 1980. Quasi-option value and the expected value of information. *Quart. J. Econ.* 94:813-820.

Conrad, J.M. 1985. Residuals management: disposal of sewage sludge in the New York bight. *Mar. Res. Econ.* 1:321-345.

Dales, J.H. 1968. *Pollution, Property and Prices.* Univ. Toronto Press, Toronto.

d'Arge, R.C. and K.C. Kogiku. 1973. Economic growth and the environment. *Rev. Econ. Studies* 40:61-77.

Dasgupta, P.S. and G.M. Heal. 1979. *Economic Theory and Exhaustible Resources.* Cambridge Univ. Press, Cambridge.

de Groot, M.H. 1970. *Optimal Statistical Decisions.* McGraw-Hill, New York.

Dixon, B.L. and R.E. Howit. 1979. Uncertainty and intertemporal forest management of natural resources: an empirical application to the Stanislaus National Forest. Giannini Foundation Monograph No. 38, Univ. of Calif., Berkeley .

Gisser, M. 1983. Groundwater: focusing on the real issue. *J. Polit. Econ.* 91:1001-1027.

Gisser, M. and D.A. Sanchez. 1980. Competition versus optimal control in groundwater pumping. *Water Resources Res.* 16:638-642.

Gordon, H.S. 1954. The economic theory of a common-property resource: the fishery. *J. Polit. Econ.* 62:124-142.

Hasenkamp, G. 1976. *Specification and Estimation of Multiple-Output Production Functions.* Springer-Verlag, Berlin.

Henrici, P. 1982. *Essentials of Numerical Analysis with Pocket Calculator Demonstrations.* Wiley, New York.

Henry, C. 1974. Investment decisions under uncertainty: the irreversibility effect. *Amer. Econ. Rev.* 64:1006-1012.

Hotelling, H. 1931. The economics of exhaustible resources. *J. Polit. Econ.* 39:137-175.

Intriligator, M.D. 1971. *Mathematical Optimization and Economic Theory.* Prentice-Hall, Englewood Cliffs, N.J.

Kamien, M.I. and N.L. Schwartz. 1981. *Dynamic Optimization: The Calculus of Variations and Optimal Control in Economics and Management.* North Holland, New York.

Keeler, E., M. Spence, and R. Zeckhauser. 1972. The optimal control of pollution. *J. Econ. Theory* 4:19-34.

Kemp, M.C. 1976. How to eat a cake of unknown size, in M.C. Kemp (Ed.), *Three Topics in the Theory of International Trade.* North Holland, Amsterdam.

Kneese, A.V., R.U. Ayres, and R.C. d'Arge. 1970. *Economics and the Environment: A Material Balance Approach.* Johns Hopkins Press, Baltimore.

Ludwig, D.A. and C.J. Walters. 1982. Optimal harvesting with imprecise parameter estimates. *Ecol. Modelling* 14:273-292.

Mangel, M. 1985. *Decision and Control in Uncertain Resource Systems.* Academic Press, New York.

Mangel, M. and C.W. Clark. 1983. Uncertainty, search, and information in fisheries. *J. Cons. int. Explor. Mer* 41:93-103 .

Mangel, M. and C.W. Clark. 1986. Towards a unified foraging theory. *Ecology* 67:11271138.

May, R.M. 1975. Biological populations obeying difference equations: stable points, stable cycles, and chaos. *J. Theor. Biol.* 51:511-524.

Pindyck, R.S. 1978. The optimal exploration and production of nonrenewable resources. *J. Polit. Econ.* 86:841-861.

Pontryagin, L.S., V.S. Boltyanskii, R.V. Gamkrelidze, and E.F. Mishchenko. 1962. *The Mathematical Theory of Optimal Processes.* Wiley, New York.

Rausser, G.C. and E. Hochman. 1979. *Dynamic agricultural systems: economic prediction and control.* North Holland, New York.

Reed, W.J. 1979. Optimal escapement levels in stochastic and deterministic harvesting models. *J. Environ. Econ. Manag.* 6:350-363.

Reed, W.J. 1984 The effects of risk of fire on the optimal rotation of a forest. *J. Environ. Econ. and Manag.* 11:180-190.

Reed, W.J. and D. Errico. 1985. Assessing the long-run yield of a forest stand subject to the risk of fire. *Can. J. For. Res.* 15:680-697.

Ross, S. 1983. *Introduction to Stochastic Dynamic Programming.* Academic Press, New York.

Schaefer, M.B. 1954. Some aspects of the dynamics of populations important to the management of commercial marine fisheries. *Bull. Inter-Amer. Tropical Tuna Comm.* 1:25-56.

Smith, V.K. 1983. Option value: a conceptual overview. *Southern Econ. J.* 49:654-658.

Spence, M. 1974. Blue whales and applied control theory, in C.L. Zadeh et al. (Eds.), *System Approaches for Solving Mathematical Problems.* Vandenhoeck and Ruprecht, Gottingen and Zurich .

Spence, M. and D. Starrett. 1975. Most rapid approach paths in accumulation problems. *International Econ. Rev.* 16:388-403.

Stiglitz, J.E. 1976. Monopoly and the rate of extinction of exhaustible resources. *Amer. Econ. Rev.* 66:655-661.

Strang, G. 1980. *Linear Algebra and its Applications.* Academic Press, New York.

Walters, C.J. and R. Hilborn. 1976. Adaptive control of fishing systems. *J. Fish. Res. Board Canada* 33:145-159.

Index